FOUR ⌐⌐

EVALUATION   (1. testing through oral or written methods for significance or usefulness of information; 2. discovering one's own knowledge of material presented; 3. implementing ways to achieve the former two)

Compare   (seek similarities and differences among and between situations, ideas, and products usually based on external qualities)

Extrapolate   (extend given information beyond the level introduced to determine consequences, effects, implications)

Identify   (differentiate among or classify various ideas and structures selecting the meanings—definitions—which belong to each)

Judge   (test an idea or product for usability, logic, accuracy, or other internal qualities)

Restructure   (sift information, arranging it to fit a function similar to but not exactly like the original context)

APPLICATION   (implementing or applying information or knowledge recently learned, preferably in different settings through out-of-class assignments and projects)

Construct   (create models, structures, and products which do not generally lend themselves to the processes below)

Perform   (present an idea through acting, usually with audible sounds)

Solve   (decide a procedure to take; seek a solution)

Speak   (present ideas orally)

Write   (present ideas on paper)

The
English Teacher's
Activities Handbook

AN IDEABOOK FOR MIDDLE
AND SECONDARY SCHOOLS

with text and illustrations by

Floyd L. Bergman

The University of Michigan

Allyn and Bacon, Inc.
Boston • London • Sydney

To my wife,
Virginia,
and all other contributors
&
To the memory of my mother,
Anna Josephine

Copyright © 1976 by Allyn and Bacon, Inc.,
470 Atlantic Avenue, Boston, Massachusetts 02210.

Library of Congress Cataloging in Publication Data

Bergman, Floyd L   1927–
  The English teacher's activities handbook.

  Bibliography: p.
  Includes index.
  1. English language—Study and teaching (Secondary)
—Handbooks, manuals, etc. I. Title.
LB1631.B39   428'.007'12   75-19406
ISBN 0-205-05047-6

Third printing . . . September, 1976

contents

Foreword   vi

Preface   ix

How to Use This Book   xi

PART 1   COMPOSITION   1
Contents for Part 1   2

Chapter
1   Introduction   3
Argumentation 3 / Description 4 / Drama 5 /
Exposition 5 / Film Making 8 / Journalism 9 /
Narration 10 / Overview 11 / Poetry 14 /
Words 16

2   Deliberation   17
Argumentation 17 / Description 18 / Drama 23 /
Exposition 23 / Humanities 26 / Journalism 26 /
Narration 28 / Overview 32 / Poetry 34

3   Evaluation   37
Argumentation 37 / Description 37 / Exposition 39 /
Journalism 43 / Letter Writing 43 / Media 44 /
Narration 45 / Overview 46 / Poetry 58

4   Application   61
Argumentation 61 / Description 62 / Drama 63 /
Exposition 63 / Journalism 67 / Letter Writing 69 /
Media 69 / Narration 70 / Overview 74 / Poetry 78 /
Syntax 78

PART 2   GRAMMAR / LANGUAGE   79
Contents for Part 2   80

Chapter

5   **Introduction   81**
Dialect 81 / Linguistics 82 / Mechanics 85 / Overview 86 / Semantics 91 / Spelling 92 / Syntax 93 / Usage 94 / Vocabulary 96 / Words 99

6   **Deliberation   103**
Dialect 103 / Linguistics 103 / Mechanics 105 / Overview 105 / Semantics 107 / Spelling 108 / Syntax 108 / Usage 112 / Vocabulary 114 / Words 115

7   **Evaluation   119**
Dialect 119 / Mechanics 119 / Overview 120 / Semantics 123 / Spelling 123 / Syntax 126 / Usage 128 / Vocabulary 129 / Words 134

8   **Application   137**
Overview 137 / Syntax 138 / Usage 138 / Vocabulary 139 / Words 139

PART 3   LITERATURE   141
Contents for Part 3   142

Chapter

9   **Introduction   143**
Drama 143 / Humanities 146 / Media 147 / Novels 149 / Overview 153 / Poetry 158 / Short Story 163 / Vocabulary 164

10   **Deliberation   165**
Drama 165 / Humanities 166 / Novels 167 / Overview 169 / Poetry 171

11   **Evaluation   175**
Drama 175 / Humanities 175 / Nonfiction 176 / Novels 176 / Overview 184 / Poetry 191 / Short Story 192 / Vocabulary 193

12   **Application   195**
Drama 195 / Media 198 / Nonfiction 200 / Novels 201 / Overview 205 / Poetry 207 / Short Story 210

PART 4   **READING**   **213**
Contents for Part 4   *214*

Chapter
  13   **Introduction**   **215**
Journalism 215 / Media 215 / Nonfiction 216 / Novels 217 / Overview 218 / Short Story 223 / Study Skills 223 / Vocabulary 225 / Words 227

  14   **Deliberation**   **229**
Letter Writing 229 / Media 229 / Narration 230 / Novels 230 / Overview 232 / Poetry 233 / Study Skills 234 / Vocabulary 236 / Words 239

  15   **Evaluation**   **243**
Exposition 243 / Journalism 243 / Narration 244 / Novels 244 / Overview 245 / Sentences 248 / Spelling 249 / Study Skills 249 / Vocabulary 251 / Words 254

  16   **Application**   **257**
Exposition 257 / Journalism 257 / Letter Writing 258 / Media 259 / Narration 260 / Overview 261 / Poetry 262 / Short Story 263 / Study Skills 264 / Vocabulary 265

PART 5   **ROOM MANAGEMENT**   **267**
Contents for Part 5   *268*

Chapter
  17   **Introduction**   **269**
Attitudes 269 / Authorities 272 / Books 273 / Bulletin Boards 274 / Chalkboards 275 / Demonstrations 276 / Discussions 276 / Displays 277 / Games 278 / Handouts 278 / Instructions 278 / Lectures 279 / Libraries 280 / Mixed Media 280 / Newspapers 281 / Notes 282 / Periodicals 282 / Pictures 283 / Plans 283 / Projectors 286 / Slides 287 / Talk 287 / Television 288 / Transparencies 288 / Tutors 289

  18   **Deliberation**   **291**
Bulletin Boards 291 / Charts 291 / Discussions 292 /

Field Trips 293 / Games 293 / Inventories 294 / Lectures 294 / Libraries 295 / Mixed Media 295 / Plans 296 / Questions 296 / Seating 297 / Talk 297 / Tutors 298

19   Evaluation
Attitudes 299 / Charts 302 / Conferences 302 / Field Trips 303 / Forms 303 / Instructions 304 / Inventories 304 / Lectures 306 / Notes 307 / Questions 307 / Talk 310 / Tutors 311

20   Application   313
Attitudes 313 / Book Reports 314 / Bulletin Boards 314 / Demonstrations 314 / Displays 315 / Games 315 / Instructions 316 / Letters 316 / Magazines 317 / Newspapers 317 / Papers 317 / Tip 1,001 318

Appendix—Using Ideas to Frame Cognitive Objectives   319

Glossary   325

Resource Bibliography   333

Biographical Index   355

Title Index   356

Topic Index   360

foreword

A sign in a Montreal bus advertises "Canada's like this: 'Our unity is our diversity.' " And that's true of English, too.

For "What's English?" keeps coming up, year after year, when teachers stop teaching it and start talking about it—at conferences, in planning meetings, in teacher training sessions. We seem to agree about general goals although not about how to state them nor evaluate them. We are always looking for methods that work. That's what this book is about.

Admittedly a cafeteria offering, Bergman's collection—more properly his students'—reminds experienced teachers of methods that may work again and gives beginners enough ammunition for the first two years, at least.

It's a troublesome book, in a way, because it puts to rest the complaint, "I can't think of anything to do to awaken interest." And it's dangerous, too, because administrators or parents may see it and wonder why more of these ideas aren't being tried in their school.

But it's meant to be a help, a resource to keep handy, a refresher, a prod to the imagination of the English teachers. As long as that "faculty" is at work, learning's more likely.

In the end, this book is for students—to help make English lively, profound, useful, and fanciful; never dull, repetitious, or senseless.

I hope, for the student's sake, this book helps us all.

William E. Hoth
Professor of Education
Wayne State University

preface

Graduate and undergraduate teacher education students, through the years, have shared with me hundreds of practices for teaching English. In methods classes we often duplicated and distributed the ideas. These booklets became one of our most popular innovations, sought after even by others. Class members frequently suggested an expanded book of ideas which more teachers could share. This book is the result: the best of the class collections and some of my own favorites.

These ideas are not offered as unique curriculum changes but simply as succinctly phrased, proven classroom practices for the new or experienced English teacher.

Some readers might prefer more complete descriptions than this book offers: materials to use, steps to take, results of past trials, lists of resources, and the like. Such articles are found in abundance elsewhere, many listed in the comprehensive bibliography.

This book is designed to save preparation time and to encourage planned creativity. The approach here reflects several fairly safe assumptions about teachers. They do not always need detailed descriptions of techniques; they can readily expand an abbreviated idea; they prefer to innovate rather than copy.

As acknowledged above, many "co-authors" contributed to this collection—actually more than 300. I would have liked to show my appreciation by listing their names. Over the years, however, some names and ideas have become separated, and there have been many duplications. Then too, although originality was always encouraged, some suggestions probably have been passed along from various sources. Thus, all ideas, liberally edited, are published in this volume as "author unknown." Individuals whose suggestions appear here, I'm sure, will overlook the credits and understand that their contributions to the profession are appreciated.

F.L.B.

how to use this book

Those who support an English curriculum guided by cognitive—even affective—objectives will find the content and classification system of this book helpful. Those who cannot accept English structured along the performance objective route need not be turned away by the rather elaborate labeling. The ideas will still be useful and not difficult to find.

In whatever camp you find yourself, taking the time to read this short introduction will help you to get the most from this book.

All formal teaching and learning require some structure. That basic framework must be both simple and common-sensical, relying on the natural abilities of students. First, some information or concept is introduced. Then students begin to mesh new and earlier learnings, deliberating about the new until new ideas are fitted into familiar frameworks of past experience.

To prove this is not false comfort, the students need an evaluation, even if it is completed privately. The new-found information must then be applied in some lifelike, if not actual, situation. If not, the previous three steps may be wasted effort.

These steps have grown into the four-phase process which is this book's organization. And it is process rather than content which the Ideabook attempts to emphasize—process because students need to practice different methods for handling any new situations which might come along.

If we can use our best content to form long-range, useful operations which can apply to any content, education will have succeeded in one of its basic purposes, perhaps the main one.

xi

THE FIVE PARTS AND SUBDIVISIONS

To help locate ideas quickly, the Ideabook has been divided into the typical English areas: Composition, Grammar/Language, Literature, and Reading. These with an added section called Room Management form the five parts.

As a further aid for locating ideas, suggestions in each main section have also been grouped according to four generally accepted steps in the teaching-learning sequence. Here called Introduction, Deliberation, Evaluation, and Application, they are explained briefly below. Also see Glossary, page 325, and inside front cover.

Key to Steps in Teaching-Learning Sequence

Introduction—learner receives new information from various sources

Deliberation—learner derives meaning from information and fits it into familiar frameworks

Evaluation—learner or teacher discovers if the first steps have been achieved

Application—learner puts new knowledge to use, ideally outside the classroom or if relearning must take place

The above groupings also contain typical subject matter subdivisions. For example, Composition ideas are designated by Argumentation, Description, Exposition, Narration, and several other related descriptors, all arranged alphabetically for easy locating. These classifications are designed to serve the various purposes explained in the following pages.

THE IDEAS

All ideas are numbered sequentially from 1 to 1,001. Each number is followed by a code letter enabling the user to quickly locate the activity's scope. The letter "C" indicates an idea for the entire class, "G" for groups, and "I" for independent study and tutoring. All ideas coded "T"

COMPOSITION

Introduction

Narration

25-C (Read/Book) "Ncmbei ir tlicʌ ot."
mcιιy ιn lte xιnll ιι neιιιt y cyuoιt jn
An l ιv lieιι licιll tny mcʌvιrιg fcʌιιιι.
llt wh ʌll f yʌιι lh lll mev tl(velnι
Oιιn thιιιg.

are specific helps for the teacher.

Besides being located under headings for content, subdivisions, and steps in the teaching-learning sequence, each idea is further identified by an entry word in the parentheses preceding the idea. There are twenty such words representing specific processes in the teaching-learning sequence—five for each step. (See inside front cover.)

Each process word also shares parentheses with a second word which identifies the "vehicle" used to aid learning—tools such as books, bulletin boards, filmstrips, games, pictures, skits, and television. For instance, *Observe* (a process under Introduction) may be teamed with a number of different vehicles: (Observe/Filmstrips), (Observe/Movies), (Observe/Plays), (Observe/Television). The processes and vehicles can be used not only to locate ideas but also to form key words when writing objectives. (See flyleaf inside back cover.)

The following suggest ways to locate ideas dealing with composition in the Ideabook.

Locating General Ideas in a Content Area

Besides thumbing through the book until something appropriate comes along, a reader may want general ideas for *evaluating compositions.* In Part 1, the Composition section, various ideas can be found under Evaluation and then under the five processes: Compare, Extrapolate, Identify, Judge, and Restructure.

Locating Specific Processes in a Content Area

A teacher may be interested in only one approach to *evaluating compositions—through comparison.* The best way to locate suitable ideas is to check under Compare in the Index and then refer only to the Composition entries.

Locating Specific Processes in One Aspect of the Content Area

A teacher working in a composition unit, may want to locate ways to *evaluate narration by judging.* Specific ideas can be found by turning to the content area Composition (Part 1), then to Evaluation; next to Narration; finally to Judge (the specific process).

THE RATIONALE

This book has been designed to provide two types of resources: a handy reference for locating classroom activities when variety is needed and a guide for framing cognitive objectives and affective goals. All practices in the book are gathered under four basic teaching-learning steps—Introduction, Deliberation, Evaluation, and Application—and their twenty process entry words adapted from two reliable curriculum sources.

Introduction is actually the "Knowledge (1.00)" and "Comprehension (2.00)" components of Bloom's taxonomy,[1] or what Parker and Rubin[2] call "Memory and Information Input" or Step One of their suggested teaching-learning sequence.

Deliberation grows out of Bloom's categories of "Analysis (4.00)" and Parker and Rubin's "Deriving Meaning." The term *Evaluation* is listed in the Bloom taxonomy as "Evaluation (6.00)." Freely interpreted, this is the same step Parker and Rubin call "Attaching Significance" in which "testing for usability" figures prominently.

Finally, the term *Application* combines Bloom's classes of "Application (3.00)" and "Synthesis (5.00)." Parker and Rubin call this step "Action."

Perhaps the easiest way to show how the Ideabook has incorporated both the Bloom taxonomy of cognitive objectives and the Parker and Rubin Teaching-Learning Sequence is to lay out the three plans side by side and let the reader find the similarities. Since Parker and Rubin based much of their material on the Bloom taxonomy, the similarities among all three are striking. Refer to the chart on page xvi entitled Key Classifications of Cognitive Processes Compared.

Of course, liberties have been taken to establish the classifications in the Ideabook, but the original contention that there is a sequence in the teaching-learning process has been retained. The I-D-E-A organization, therefore, is more than an attempt to contrive an appropriate acronym for the Ideabook.

The notion of a teaching-learning sequence extends much further back in history than Bloom and Parker and Rubin. In the early nineteenth century, Johann F. Herbart established five inductive principles of teaching and learning: preparation, presentation, association, generalization, and application. His work and many writings earned him the title of

1. Copyright © 1956 by the David McKay Company. From the book, *Taxonomy of Educational Objectives, Handbook I: Cognitive Domain.* By B. S. Bloom. Published by the David McKay Company. Used with permission.
2. J. Cecil Parker and Louis J. Rubin, *Process as Content: Curriculum Design and the Application of Knowledge* (Chicago: Rand McNally & Co., 1966), pp. 55-6.

"father of teacher training." With a resemblance to Herbart's classic approach, the case for I-D-E-A is strengthened.

The next major contribution in sequencing curriculum and instruction came from Tyler, writing in the mid-1900's. He proposed four fundamental questions for developing any curriculum and plan of instruction:

1. What educational purposes should the school seek to attain?
2. What educational experiences can be provided that are likely to attain these purposes?
3. How can these educational experiences be effectively organized?
4. How can we determine whether these purposes are being attained?[3]

Tyler's emphasis on objectives, experiences, organization of experiences, and evaluation are seen as part of Taba's seven steps of curriculum development:

Step 1: Diagnosis of needs
Step 2: Formulation of objectives
Step 3: Selection of content
Step 4: Organization of content
Step 5: Selection of learning experiences
Step 6: Organization of learning experiences
Step 7: Determination of what to evaluate and of the ways and means of doing it[4]

Tyler also influenced Bloom and associates who, in turn, influenced Parker and Rubin, and so on.

Risking some degree of presumptuousness, then, this writer suggests that his teaching-learning sequence—Introduction, Deliberation, Evaluation, and Application—was duly influenced by the combined contributions of Herbart, Tyler, Bloom and colleagues, as well as Taba, and Parker and Rubin. In these days of accountability, performance objectives, and competency-based education, one couldn't ask for better models even without direct references to Bruner and Piaget. Both, however, are cited frequently by the authors mentioned.

The I-D-E-A format is only a portion of the needed planning for teaching, and a small portion at that. It deals with one activity at one

3. Ralph W. Tyler, *Basic Principles of Curriculum and Instruction* (Chicago: The University of Chicago Press, 1950, 1957), pp. 1-2.
4. Parker and Rubin, *ibid.*, p. 17, citing Hilda Taba, *Curriculum Development: Theory and Practice* (New York: Harcourt Brace and World, 1962), pp. 347-78.

Key Classification of Cognitive Processes Compared

Bloom[5] (summarized and re-ordered)	Parker and Rubin Model I[6]	Ideabook Teaching-Learning Steps & Processes
1.00 Knowledge Recall Understand Identify	I. Memory & Information Input Formulating questions Reading expository material Observing a phenomenon Collecting evidence	1. Introduction Discover Listen Observe Read
2.00 Comprehension Translation Interpretation Extrapolation	Listening to a presentation Discovering principles	Research
4.00 Analysis (of elements) (of relationships) (of organization)	II. Deriving Meaning Analyzing the material Experimenting with the material Reorganizing the material Consolidating the material Integrating the material	2. Deliberation Analyze Consolidate Experiment Interpret Organize

6.00 Evaluation
Judgment
Comparison
	III. Attaching Significance
	Inferring generalization
	Reconstructing the general
	  structure
	Relating the material to
	  other situations
	Testing for usability
		3. Evaluation
		Compare
		Extrapolate
		Identify
		Judge
		Restructure

5.00 Synthesis
Communication
Construction
Organization
Discovery
Solution
	IV. Action
	Using the material to
	  solve a problem
	Using the material to
	  create a problem
	Using the material to
	  clarify a problem
		4. Application
		Construct
		Perform
		Solve
		Speak
		Write

3.00 Application		

5. Bloom, *Ibid*, pp. 201–207.
6. Parker and Rubin, *Ibid.*, pp. 55, 56

stage of development as it might be introduced, deliberated, evaluated, or applied to extra-class environments. Before the Introduction phase even begins, the teacher must diagnose needs, set goals, formulate objectives upon these goals, and must select and organize content and experiences (including tools) to help achieve the goals and objectives. At this point I-D-E-A enters the picture.

The Teaching-Learning Sequence

Although an English teacher does not need explanations of the five content divisions—Composition, Grammar/Language, Literature, Reading, and Room Management—the I-D-E-A sequence and related processes warrant more definition than has been given to this point. The following explanations are summarized inside the front cover and on facing fly leaf.

Introduction, as is evident in the term, becomes the first step in the teaching-learning sequence, when students are exposed to information for improving skills and for building concepts. This is the information-intake step during which new generalizations are built upon past learning and knowledge, and it is usually the first portion of a lesson covering new material. The ideas included under Introduction suggest ways to begin teaching a concept, a lesson, or a unit.

Under this step are five main Introduction processes: *Discover*—asking questions and using other inquiry methods; *Listen, Observe*—reviewing something such as films or slides; and *Read*—translating both literal and nonliteral information, (the latter including metaphor, symbolism, irony, and exaggeration). *Research* is a fifth method which generally takes place out of class in libraries or among authorities, and it relies on its companion processes, particularly *Read*.

Admittedly, selecting only five processes (and always the same number) for each of the four phases in the teaching-learning sequence is an arbitrary decision reducing the number of processes to be kept in mind. Thus, to the Introduction phase processes described here could be added many other ways to receive the information needed for making generalizations and increasing knowledge. Material to be found inside the back cover lists some of the possibilities.

The purpose of an Introduction step is to give the learner some information and background to add to what is already known, in an effort to build generalizations about the new material. Once this is accomplished, the generalizations and associated information must be manipulated to make them more understandable and, therefore, more retainable. This becomes the function of the second step.

Deliberation suggests meditating, reflecting, considering, pondering, and reasoning. The Deliberation phase ideas collected here attempt to place recently acquired information into familiar frameworks of experience. Here the student engages in a number of different processes of which five are most frequently used.

One process in the Deliberation phase is for the student to *analyze* information—recognizing unstated assumptions and distinguishing facts from hypotheses, seeing how elements are related, and studying its structure and peculiarities. Sometimes they must *consolidate* information, selecting specific and useful new information and relating it to other previously accumulated but similar knowledge.

To understand new ideas, the learner must often practice using skills and concepts. He often *experiments* through in-class activities and practice exercises. Occasionally he needs to *interpret* the information, for example, to grasp the complete thought of a literary work to determine purpose, theme, or moral. Finally, in the Deliberation phase, the learner may have to *organize* incoming information, because classifying and ordering can make information easier to recall for later use and for conveying to others.

The third level of the teaching-learning sequence is called **Evaluation.** Here the learner performs one or more oral, written, or mental "tests" to determine if the information being learned is, for one thing, significant or even useful. Here also is a chance to discover if one's knowledge of the new material is sufficient. It also gives the teacher a chance to measure teaching effectiveness.

One way to evaluate is to *compare* or seek similarities and differences among situations, ideas, and products usually based on observable external qualities. True knowledge of material is measured by the ability to *extrapolate* beyond the given situation and data. By this process, the learner determines implications and consequences of a work and predicts what might occur when similar conditions are present in another context. Such reasoning is assisted by relating to past similar experiences.

Typical among evaluation approaches is the need to *identify* or differentiate among various ideas and structures and to select meanings and definitions which belong to particular sources. The two remaining processes in the Evaluation phase are the ability to *judge* and to *restructure.* In the former, the learner tests an idea or product for usability, accuracy, logic, or for other internal traits. "Restructure" is sifting data and arranging what is appropriate to fit a function similar to but not exactly like the original instances.

Little new information remains with a learner unless it can be applied somehow to on-going daily life. The **Application** phase, probably the most important but least understood and used, includes processes which permit knowledge and information to be implemented or applied in different settings and contexts, preferably in ways which reflect or even utilize true-to-life situations.

One way to apply learning is to *construct* something such as a model, a structure, a work of art, or a product which does not fit into any of the following Application processes. Frequently a learner uses learnings to *perform*: acting in plays or working at tasks requiring specially acquired skills. Another way to apply learning is through the need to *solve* anything from life's daily problems to completing a puzzle. Finally, a learner may put learnings into play by choosing to *write* or *speak*.

These constitute the four steps in the teaching-learning sequence along with their associated processes, twenty in number for convenience. Once again, even though more processes could have been added, those selected seem to represent the needs in the typical school. An expanded list of process words can be found inside the back cover.

In conclusion, if at least three principles of I-D-E-A are followed in each day's lessons, no pupils should be bored, at least from lack of variety. Each step in the sequence requires a switch in procedures. This book's purpose is to enhance "switching."

The Ideabook, the Methods Class, and Student Teaching

Although it is written particularly for in-service teachers, this book also has potential value in English methods classes and student teaching.

Any idea, wherever it appears in the I-D-E-A sequence, can be hypothetically traced forward or back. An idea listed in the Application phase, for instance, can be described three more times: as it might have begun in the Introduction phase, as students might work with it in the Deliberation phase, and then as some assessment might be handled in Evaluation. One idea should suggest three others at different stages with different approaches but with the same content.

Depending on its complexity, a single tip can also be expanded from one day to several days or even to several weeks. Here, then, is a resource for treating unit and daily lesson plans, developing micro- and macro-teaching demonstrations, stating objectives and competencies, developing learning modules, and many other related projects.

Even further, some ideas in this collection can be discussed orally or in writing to see how they might be improved, or, on the positive side, to determine why they are good techniques.

In the following examples, one basic idea has been described in all four phases by expanding upon an idea which could have been listed in the Evaluation phase of the Grammar/Language section.

GRAMMAR / LANGUAGE

VOCABULARY   *INTRODUCTION*

00–C   (Discover/Read) "Word Watchers"

Encourage the students to build a source of useful words by
having them keep pocket-sized spiral notebooks in which to
place new vocabulary encountered in various reading experiences. Collect the notebooks periodically to build a relevant
supply for class use. Dividing a notebook into sections will add
more interest. These are suggested: Words from Novels, Words
from Classes (textbooks), Words from the Media, Words from
Being a Good Listener.

* * * *

GRAMMAR / LANGUAGE

VOCABULARY   *DELIBERATION*

00–I   (Consolidate/Lists) "Words With Personality"

Using the new vocabulary words, students write brief definitions for the words. To help place the new word into a familiar
area, a word describing human characteristics can be paired with
fictional or actual personalities:

> garrulous: the nurse in *Romeo and Juliet*
> Philanthropist: Andrew Carnegie

By associating new vocabulary with personalities and familiar
landmarks or events, students will reinforce the retention of
word definitions.

* * * *

GRAMMAR / LANGUAGE

VOCABULARY   *EVALUATION*

00–I   (Identify/Tests) "Why Not?"

To test students' comprehension of newly introduced vocabulary, prepare a special true-false test. Give correct definitions
for some words, for others give incorrect definitions. If the
given meaning is wrong, students must also supply the correct
definition. For an extra point, they could also supply a word
which fits an incorrect definition.

* * * *

GRAMMAR / LANGUAGE

VOCABULARY   *APPLICATION*

00- C,I   (Construct/Bulletin Boards) "Who Said That?"

After they have learned a particular set of new vocabulary
words, students can locate pictures, articles, and other instances
from outside sources (magazines, newspapers, literature,
speeches) where they have seen the same words. Place a large
"graffiti board" in the room so students can share words,
contexts, and sources. If they will recognize how frequently
these words are used in everyday living, students will begin
to use this new vocabulary in their own speaking and writing.

THE REST IS UP TO YOU

If you have had time to read this introduction, you are now better informed on the rationale for the Ideabook and on ways to use it. If you
are interested in studying English methodology in teacher preparation,
you have found suggestions for expanding one idea to cover the four
phases of the teaching-learning sequence. If you want to see how classroom activities can become models for practice in writing cognitive objectives, you are invited to turn to the Appendix. There you will also discover how to develop an affective goal.

    Since this is not a methods book, the explanations are brief, perhaps
even superficial. Readers who want more depth must locate additional
readings (see Resource Bibliography).

    Those who did not read the Introduction will, through trial and error,
learn how to find specific classroom activities in the Ideabook. But they
will certainly not understand its full potential. Lack of understanding,
however, may not be a complete obstruction to either the introduction-
skippers or yourself. The more you use this book and work it into your
own teaching preferences—interweaving these ideas with your own—the
more useful the book will become. You may even want to build a file
of new ideas you encounter. On the flyleaf facing the back cover is a
suggested format such as found in the Ideabook.

    The Ideabook cannot be a panacea. It is simply a handy supply of
proven classroom activities adaptable to the unique teaching style of an

individual teacher for a specific group of students. Since no two classes are exactly the same, what works for one class may not work for another. Similarly, an idea which works for one teacher may not work for another—even with the same students. The ideas in this book worked for those who suggested them. The best way to use this handbook, therefore, is to let it jog the imagination when you believe or when your students indicate that a "shift of gears" is needed.

PART 1

composition

composition

Introduction

Chapter 1
Argumentation 3
Description 4
Drama 5
Exposition 5
Film Making 8
Journalism 9
Narration 10
Overview 11
Poetry 14
Words 16

Evaluation

Chapter 3
Argumentation 37
Description 37
Exposition 39
Journalism 43
Letter Writing 43
Media 44
Narration 45
Overview 46
Poetry 58

Deliberation

Chapter 2
Argumentation 17
Description 18
Drama 23
Exposition 23
Humanities 26
Journalism 26
Narration 28
Overview 32
Poetry 34

Application

Chapter 4
Argumentation 61
Description 62
Drama 63
Exposition 63
Journalism 67
Letter Writing 69
Media 69
Narration 70
Overview 74
Poetry 78
Syntax 78

CHAPTER
1

INTRODUCTION

ARGUMENTATION

1- C (Discover/Discussions) "Writing Relevantly"

Most problems in teaching written composition would be solved
if *all* topics were interesting to *all* students. Argumentative
compositions come closest to the life style of youth as well
as adults. Our very existence depends on good debate as it
occurs in a democracy. Composition topics which pair current
world issues with the class material heighten interest in and
awareness of history in the making and ways to communicate
the knowledge. Introduce ways to write on polarized topics
such as: "Why everyone should support (issue or idea) instead
of (opposing issue or idea)."

2- C (Observe/Magazines) "Unhidden Persuaders"

Part of a unit on argumentation should be devoted to the art
of persuasion. Clipping, collecting under types, and studying
model ads from magazines can be helpful. Add a little more
fun by deleting from the ads references to the products' names
and their manufacturers. Let the class guess the product as well
as analyzing to what basic human need the advertiser is appealing.

3- C (Observe/Periodicals) "News No-Nos"

In a unit on argumentation, have individuals bring in newspaper and magazine clippings (ads and articles) with models of fallacies underlined. Place the items attractively on a bulletin board carrying an interesting title such as "Writing Fallaciously" or "Fuzzy Thinking." Suggest the errors and prejudices which often cause reasoning to go faulty: being: (1) too humane, (2) overly selfish or egocentric, (3) strongly influenced by word and symbol, (4) swayed by formal thought (philosophy, religion, politics), (5) impressed by change for sake of change, (6) attracted to the status quo.

DESCRIPTION

4- C   (Research/Field Trips) "Something to Behold"

Writing creatively requires time to put all the senses to work as ideas are being formed. Students need to practice this "lost art." Expose the class to serious contemplation by suggestions such as these: (1) Sit in a park or anywhere slightly apart from the hustle and bustle, listening for and identifying all the sounds you hear. List them so as not to forget them. (2) Search for something unusual in nature such as a four-leaf clover or a branch covered with lichens. (3) Curl up in a comfortable chair to listen with closed eyes to a symphonic movement, i.e., the fourth movement ("storm movement") of Beethoven's *Sixth* ("Pastoral") *Symphony*. Then think deeply of what you have just experienced and consider how to describe the sensations. Such activities often become unique experiences to those who have never been that perceptive. Through close observation, students learn to recognize the experiences needed for quality creative writing.

5- C   (Research/Field Trips) "Triptoe thru the Tulips"

Obtain permission to take the class on a short excursion around the school neighborhood. Remind students to keep all senses open. Upon returning, have them jot down observations in readiness to practice organizing thoughts about an individual met along the route, a situation encountered, or simply an aesthetic description of a scene. Perhaps for the first time they will really observe the mailman's actions or the condition of the empty shopping center lot after a busy evening.

DRAMA

6- C   (Read/Plays) "Daily Forum Mirror"

To help students appreciate the difficulty and artistry involved in good writing, select a scene such as Caesar's assassination or a scene from any Elizabethan drama which has been rewritten in the style of modern journalism or in another expository form. Analyzing the original version and the rewrite will readily show the differences between the literary styles.

EXPOSITION

7- C   (Discover/Critiques) "Eye for Art"

Let students discover how a powerful writing style can influence people to accept or reject a finished product. Reviews of popular books, concerts, and films furnish examples of exposition designed to change minds. Studying the techniques of the critic helps to develop a sharper prose style as well as an analytical mind. Most important, the examples are readily available and students don't mind looking for them.

8- I   (Discover/Questions) "Shares That Gather Interest"

Everyone wants to be recognized for some skill or knowledge. Capitalize on this psychological phenomenon when helping students to choose expository topics. Ask such questions as, "What do you know that you could share with others?" "What do you really care about?" Few will say "nothing" and mean it.

9- I   (Listen/Sentences) "Least for the Most"

Explain the functions of short, choppy, sometimes incomplete sentences where extreme succinctness is required. Discuss how this style may be acceptable for telegrams and classified advertisements but not for most compositions. Prepare a set of terse telegram messages for the class to rephrase into acceptable complete sentences.

10- C   (Observe/Paragraphs) "Strip Tease"

With a paragraph board, demonstrate the principles of writing expository paragraphs. Write each sentence of the paragraph on a long strip of poster board or paper. Using a bulletin board, place the cards in the wrong order, then ask the class to tell why they are wrong. The paragraph can be corrected by changing the card positions, removing cards, or by adding new cards. For example, to teach emphasis, the main point of the paragraph could first be buried in the middle of the paragraph and then be moved to the beginning or end. Sentences can also be printed on strips of clear plastic for the overhead projector.

11-C   (Observe/Pictures) "Introduction to Introspection"

Part of being able to write a good composition is to have something to say about the immediate environment. This comes through careful observation and not superficial glances. Demonstrate by showing a picture (or project one) for a minute or less. The students write one descriptive paragraph to include everything they remember about the picture. The picture can be rich with possibilities at first to make the task easier, but after giving the students several tries, narrow the choice to very simple objects such as a paper clip or a light bulb.

12-I   (Research/Authorities) "Travel-Log"

Build a unit around the theme "Travel." Each student chooses a place he would like to visit. He must research it thoroughly to present an authoritative written paper. Related work can include such activities as business letters requesting information from the source, thank-you notes, conversations with people who have been there, or posters from travel agencies. The kinds of writing appropriate to this assignment are varied and reflect just about any writing situation one can encounter. This activity also introduces the student to the needs for and methods of research.

13-I   (Research/Authorities) "Super Snooper"

Understanding the community and its workings is important, especially at the upper levels of high school. Incorporate English

composition with problems of the city. Build on student outside interests. For one assignment, the class might spend a month
gathering information on some aspect of city organization and
then write papers on their findings. Students would speak with
persons who work in the departments they are studying. They
might also make comparisons by gathering additional information from other communities.

14- G   (Research/Books) "Telling It Like It Was"

In a unit such as "Our American Founders," students form
small groups to read numerous biographies and autobiographies.
For class presentations, each group shares its research through
any approach (individual or group): a skit, audio-visual presentation, panel discussion, and the like. Prizes might be awarded
for the best presentation.

15- I   (Research/Circulars) "Firm Footnoting"

When students are asked to document an opinion paper or research, have them go further than just providing footnotes.
Have them also make a collection of other pertinent sources
of information. For example, if a student is asked to present
and substantiate his political viewpoint, he could collect flyers,
advertising brochures, or booklets from organizations which
support his position, clip newspaper headlines and magazine
illustrations which reflect a political viewpoint he could support
or reject. Display items can then be put into a notebook along
with the composition. More creative students might prepare
collages (montages) on large sheets of tagboard to be displayed
in the room.

16- I   (Research/Letters) "Mail Order Topics"

Eventually, every student will be asked to write a term paper
about a foreign country and there will always be those who
don't know where or how to begin. In a joint effort with the
social studies department, the English class can help. Encourage
the students to write letters to the United Nations Office of
Public Information, New York City, to obtain a free list of
information, services, and foreign embassies in the U.S. Students then write letters requesting free maps, pictures, flags,
booklets, and printed material for projects.

17- T   (Research/Libraries) "Communicate to Teach"

Research techniques can be more practical than they usually
are. The teacher might open class discussion by posing a question about which he or she needs more information. For example, the problem might be deciding on the best car to buy.
The teacher must know in advance the kinds of things one
needs to know about a car before buying and can then guide
the students in finding and citing sources of information to
get the answers. By finding and documenting information usually found in the library, the students would compile their
reports, hoping the teacher would decide on their favorite car.
Not until the end of the project is it mentioned that they have
been introduced to the "research paper."

FILM MAKING

18- C   (Discover/Books) "Film-m-m-m-making"

If your school has or has access to
a motion picture camera, some
English classes might produce a
short film. Students should first
learn about the strengths and limitations of film as a communication
medium. They should also learn
some of the techniques: sequencing,
cutaway, fade, and so on. After a
theme has been proposed for a film,
a lesson on script writing is due. Scripts can be very simple or
complex depending on available equipment. For example, the
silent movie or mime script with tape-recorded narration, music,
and sound effects can be very effective when sound-film syn-
chronization is not possible. Either way everyone has a job to
do: write script, develop sound effects, choose background
music, create costumes and scenery, do makeup, operate camera,
and act. If some students still do not have jobs, become more
technical and involved. Select a producer and director. Set up
an advertising and publicity committee. At this point, funding
might be a problem. So, early in the planning, let the producer
head up a finance committee to sponsor events to raise money
for the extravaganza.

19- C   (Observe/Projectors) "Calling the Shots"

Typical projection equipment available to almost any classroom
can be used to explain the various movie camera shots. On one
side of the front wall (or screen) an overhead projector displays
a list of camera shots with brief explanations. Nearby an opaque
(or slide) projector shows appropriate pictures demonstrating
each shot. For example, an airplane view of New York City
depicts a long shot (a pan shot by moving a rectangular light
mask across the picture). A shot of a tenement house reflects
another camera angle. A close-up shot might be a child sitting
on a stairway and eating an apple. Fade-ins and fade-outs,
though tricky, can be shown by manipulating two L-shaped
pieces of cardboard to mask the light gradually. All these techniques can be used to illustrate student movie scripts or scenarios.

JOURNALISM

20- C   (Discover/Magazines) "Variety Variation"

Arrange for copies of a popular variety magazine to be sent or
brought to class once or twice a month. Point out concerns
such as format, regular features, themes, slant, advertising. Also
encourage students to read some of the new books the magazines
review. This will provide variety to the "required reading list."
Advanced classes should be able, by reading book reviews and
then the book themselves, to write book reports which resemble
magazine book reviews rather than the traditional title-author-
plot variety.

21- C   (Listen/Radio-Television) "People Baiter"

In a journalism or composition unit, include the skills of obtaining and writing interviews. Prepare students by discussing
the different interview approaches and special preparations for
conducting and writing them. Use carefully selected radio or
television interviewers as study models. Later, as a culminating
task, find someone to interview. The guest need not be famous.
All people can be interesting if the interviewer is creative and
skillful. A student, the principal, custodian, city librarian, museum
curator, or a parent can make good subjects. The finished products can be discussed, the best ones written up for the school

paper. Different interview techniques uncovered (glibness, frothiness, aggressiveness among others) can be discussed.

22- C   (Read/Newspapers) "Newsworthy Idea"

Newspapers are cheap, readily available, and offer a variety of subjects interesting to everyone. Students can also mark and cut newspapers. Besides reading and studying news articles, editorials, and features (the usual procedure), students can use them in other ways: reorganize or rewrite paragraphs of sections of articles if not the entire one, restructure sentences and strip them of excess verbiage, or write imaginative stories based on news items, even putting themselves in the story. Other activities include looking for slanted news articles and locating fallacies.

23- C   (Research/Periodicals) "Potpourri"

Encourage students to place in a notebook or journal interesting articles, cartoons, and quotations from newspapers and magazines. They can then make notes or comments beside the clippings on ways they could use the same ideas for their own papers.

NARRATION

24- C   (Listen/Anecdotes) "Anecdote-tell"

Telling short, true or fictitious stories aloud is good practice as well as fun. It prepares students for the more interesting job of writing a longer story and helps them organize thoughts. The teacher can create initial interest by telling two or three humorous anecdotes, asking students to think about what makes each story funny and where the most humorous part occurs and discussing what makes a good anecdote. Finally, set up some guidelines for choosing an incident, making it interesting, using conversation for reality, building suspense, and ending quickly with a strong line.

25- C   (Read/Books) "Anapest No Bug"

Next to nursery rhymes, perhaps the children's books by Dr. Seuss are the best known to today's youth. Even adults enjoy reading the mainly anapestic feet gamboling through his delightfully different stories. Take advantage of this natural interest and bring in some Dr. Seuss books to be read, to study for meter and for their appealing qualities.

26- C   (Read/Chalkboards) "A Bird in Hand"

Proverbs are useful for teaching literal and figurative meaning. A new proverb can be written on the chalkboard daily and then be discussed at the start of each class. This activity promotes oral discussion and suggests topics for impromptus and short compositions.

OVERVIEW

27- C   (Discover/Discussions) "What's Your Bag"

The class can brainstorm during one full class period—more if effective—to come up with topics that interest them. During some of the tangent discussion which is bound to occur, list the best ideas as a source of composition topics which will meet most interest levels.

28- I   (Discover/Handouts) "Favor or Disfavor"

At one of the early class sessions, ask each student to complete the following types of sentences: My favorite book (bird, food, hobby, pet, poem) is . . . . The thing I most fear (dislike) is . . . . I think least about . . . . This form may remain anonymous. The various replies are duplicated for the class to use as a source for writing topics and themes.

29- I   (Discover/Notes) "Recall Experiences"

When starting a composition unit, obtain a card file to use as a Topic Box. A student fills out 3 × 5 cards outlining three ideas on which he would like to write. New ideas can be added any time from discussions or reading. The teacher uses the cards to help individualize future assignments. All members use the box when they need theme topics they or others have suggested.

30- C   (Listen/Music) "Music to Write By"

Music which evokes a strong emotional response can enhance instruction or stimulate imagination. Play some unfamiliar music,
such as "Fetes" by Debussy. Class listens and tries to feel the
music. Questions to ask: "What ideas or mental pictures do you
get?" "How does the music make you feel?" After the music is
played once again, the students begin writing an appropriate
response: a personal anecdote, a poem, a descriptive scene which
can be captured in a few words, or an idea to be developed
in a longer composition. No specific length should be required.
When the exercise is used to introduce work on composition,
students should know they can write informally with incomplete
thoughts—anything to free up the thought processes.

31- C   (Listen/Music) "One More Time"

Find a disc or tape recording of a musical selection which is new
to the students—probably a portion of a symphony. Play the
record through at least three times while students write their
thoughts. Suggest questions. How does the music make you feel:
happy, sad, excited, or what? If this were background music for
a motion picture, what would you expect to see on the screen?
From this preparation, good assignments should emerge: critiques, poems, essays, and descriptions.

32- C   (Listen/Radio, Television) "On the Air"

Students listen to the radio a lot.
Various opionions have been offered
as to how well they really listen. To
emphasize the need to be more con-
sciously observant, assign a short
paper (or discussion) on the past
week's radio menu. Typical questions
may be: (1) What kinds of programs
characterize most of your listening?
(2) Why did you make the selections
you did? (3) Were the programs
mainly local or network? (4) What
were the call letters of the station you listened to more than the
rest? Then have them zero in on one favorite program: (1) Was
it sponsored or not? By whom? (2) What were the products ad-
vertised? (3) What was one "near-quote" you can remember?

(4) Who was on the program (name singers, actors, announcers)? Many other questions can be asked and could be applied to television as well as radio. If students do poorly on this assignment, it becomes a case in point that people do listen—even view—unconsciously. Or they may listen or view selectively. Discuss whether unconscious and selective viewing are good or bad.

33- C   (Observe/Bulletin Boards) "Words of Wisdom"

Create a bulletin board consisting of sayings and quotations by great people—Confucius, Kahlil Gibran, Jesus Christ, Benjamin Franklin, William Shakespeare, Winston Churchill, and others—a words-of-wisdom corner. Students may bring in their own selections or creations. This collection could serve as a source for discussions and eventually composition topics. Be sure to invite the class to contribute.

34- I   (Observe/Pictures) "Kids on Display"

On a file folder panel each student pastes a display of magazine and catalogue pictures reflecting his own personality and interests. On another face of the folder, he may attach a brief writing sample which explains his creation. When all have completed their "personality" folders, display them (names hidden) on the bulletin board under the banner *Guess Who.* When the identification game is over, folders are filed for conferences, assignment storage, and for reading and writing suggestions.

35- C   (Read/Handouts) "What's Due?"

Provide the class with a list of composition topics for the entire semester. As each of the compositions is completed and corrected, check it off. The master list then becomes a progress chart.

36- G   (Research/Authorities) "Stations, Everyone"

Reflect on a topic such as "life and death" or "war and peace." Set up several stations around the room (they may be numbered). Split the class into small groups with each starting at a different station and proceeding until all have been covered. Possible stations are: (1) chalkboard with short quotations (students add their own); (2) folder with short newspaper article(s); (3) a picture bulletin board to which students may add; (4) a participatory graffiti wall (wide wrapping paper); (5) a slide-tape show; (6) a tape-recorded radio newscast; (7) a film or field trip (if topic is war and peace) to the museum to see war relics then to the art gallery to see art depicting peace and war; (8) a wrap-up station where students can hear past comments on projects and record new comments. After they have visited all stations, have students write about their feelings, thoughts, and emotions about the topic, which have been evoked by materials at the stations. They can use whatever style they wish: essay, poetry, stream-of-consciousness, or other.

37-G   (Research/Games) "Sh-h-h!"

After studying library procedures from a book, students need to experience what was introduced by going to the library. Divide the class into teams. Give each team a list of books by author, title, subject or call number. The students must determine which books are in the card catalogue and then find them on the shelves. Articles from periodicals could also be included in the list. The team which locates all of the references first wins the competition. A natural follow-up, of course, is to research a topic for a report.

38-G   (Research/Libraries) "Class Cutter"

Besides the regular class work, individuals work on outside projects or term papers. To research the work, small groups can go to the library each day on a rotating basis. Besides decreasing daily class size by four or five students, the approach teaches students how to work without supervision. It also presents the chance to concentrate on something really interesting. This is a good opportunity to involve student teachers, teacher aides, or even student cadets.

POETRY

39-C   (Listen/Music) "Un-musical Sounds"

To help students get more use out of descriptive words, introduce onomatopoeia by using a record featuring musical instruments which imitate nonmusical sounds (*e.g.*, Prokofiev's *Peter and the Wolf*). Students can write what they hear. Later they can build their own lists of words which have built-in sounds, such as grumble, clink, lumber, plop, and splash.

40-C   (Observe/Artwork) "Poetic Bars"

In teaching poetry as an art form, explain that the first poetry was always sung. Other relationships between poetry, music, and art can be demonstrated by presenting recordings and paintings which express the same mood as a particular poem. Call attention to certain aspects of the painting which are also conveyed by the selected music and by an appropriate quotation from poetry. A good example might be a poem by Frost such as "Stopping by Woods on a Snowy Evening" or "The Runaway" juxtaposed with a winter scene by Grandma Moses, Norman Rockwell, or less contemporary painters.

As for music, select any symphonic movement which conveys the New England countryside in a muffled snowfall. Mozart and Beethoven are always reliable sources as well as Ralph Vaughn Williams or Ravel. Stress similarities in design (repeated motifs) and deliberate breaks in the design for variety. Then explore the dominant impressions created by space, form, words, or sounds. It is this dominance which creates the most distinguishable parallels. (Also see idea 531.)

41-I   (Observe/Chalkboards) "Green Poets"

To introduce the value of word associations in poetry, give the word "green." Class members call out the words or images they associate with the color. Then the class reciprocates by giving an evocative word to the teacher who lists on the board the associations, some of which are later formed into a simple word poem.

THIS LIST	AND THIS	BECOME
green	cattle	*Grass*
grass	hay	*lush-green,*
carpet	food	*carpet,*
cucumber	mow	*cool—*
cool	peas	*Spring.*
aroma	lush	*Fresh-mown*
beans	Spring	*hay.*
		Aroma.
		Cattle-food.

The "poem" in the right column is largely formed by listing all the related words from the first two columns. Next, the class is given a word, and the members list on paper all words and phrases which seem to relate. Then each creates his own poem.

42- C   (Observe/Models) "Haiku! Bless You"

A short poetic form developed in Japan centuries ago, haiku has become the achievable goal for many budding young poets. Its three unrhymed lines (with 5, 7, and 5 syllables respectively) usually reflect a season, catch a mood or an emotion, and unite for a brief moment poet and reader in a common life experience.

> *Autumn came crisply*
> *Showing its reds and yellows*
> *In each dancing leaf.*

Resembling haiku, tanka—another Japanese poetic device—uses five unrhymed lines of 5, 7, 5, 7, and 7 syllables. Before letting the class write their own, show and read some samples.

WORDS

43- C   (Listen/Lists) "Going Jotting"

Bring in a list of words (preferably adjectives). The class jots down each word as it is read. They also include the first word(s) called to mind as they hear the trigger-word. Try to make the original word list as interesting and provocative as possible. The words can be reorganized into a poem, essay, or a narration. A simple word like *blue* may evoke anything from the flashing blue light of the county sheriff's car to the sparkling water of a mountain stream.

CHAPTER
2

DELIBERATION

ARGUMENTATION

44- C   (Analyze/Models) "Fallaciously Speaking"

Students are interested in analyzing sentences for fallacies in reasoning such as these models: (1) appeal to force: "Your grandchildren will live under communism" (Khrushchev); (2) appeal to mass emotion: almost any political speech; (3) non sequitur: "Smith is a good lawyer, and he attends church." Many more models appear in any logic book. Commercial advertising fits nicely in this study, as well as comments in the Letters to the Editor newspaper columns.

45- G   (Experiment/Discussions) "Better Half"

Divide the class into two groups, A and B. Present a highly debatable thesis, assigning the affirmative position to one group and the negative to the other. Allow both groups a few minutes to discuss arguments for their side. The first person in group A makes a statement to be refuted by the first in line from Group B who then follows by giving a statement his side supports. The second A team member responds with a refutation and offers another statement from his side. The response pattern is A_1, B_1, A_2, B_2, A_3, and so on. If the class happens to agree on a particular issue, the teacher takes the opposing side and lets the students challenge one at a time. Finish the exercise by pointing out the value of convincing evidence, using examples of good and bad arguments which had been made.

46- I   (Experiment/Role Playing) "Pro in Conning"

After selecting a controversial topic which lends itself to argumentation, the student decides to be either pro or con. In a written exercise he argues his point as if he were, for example, a journalist, politician, or a philosopher, writing in the style of each. This exercise gives the student a chance to experiment with various argumentative approaches.

47- I   (Organize/Papers) "About Face"

To give practice in understanding principles of persuasion, assign a composition on any controversial topic. When each pupil has completed a paper taking, say, a supportive stand, assign another in which they must take the opposite view. Debate teams sometimes use this practice. But any English classroom could also use it because it forces students to see that there are two sides to most issues, each side making sense to the proponent.

DESCRIPTION

48- C   (Analyze/Papers) "Details, Details!"

Students can analyze the importance of detail and exactness in writing by briefly describing what they observed in the classroom during the previous five minutes. When the papers are read, the differences in the way each student perceives the same situation will be enlightening.

49- G   (Analyze/Games) "Com-pairing"

Students can be helped to write imaginative descriptions if they learn to observe familiar objects in new ways. To obtain some models as inspiration, play the comparison game. Select two familiar yet dissimilar objects. Competing groups try to list in a given time (five or ten minutes) as many ways as possible in which the two objects are alike. For example, a *chalkboard* is like a *window*: both are rectangles, both "shed light" on a subject, they are vertical, hard to the touch, and for both, sand is used in the manufacturing process. Have some of the comparisons read orally. Each participant is awarded two points for each comparison which he alone suggested, one point for a comparison which two or three have contributed.

50-I  (Consolidate/Notes) "See, Saw, Scene"

The class can go to a busy street corner somewhere in their own town and jot down notes describing everything they see and hear in the span of several minutes. Then, using the on-the-scene notes, they describe exactly what happened. A simple device is to use three columns headed "Sight," "Sound," and "Smell." Some may want to add "Touch." Surely, certain objects in the first column will be repeated in the others. Yet, others will be isolated. Upon returning, the class can share their collections. Most will produce a paper describing what was particularly evocative.

51-G   (Consolidate/Papers) "Character-eyes"

To develop a model for the processes of characterization, each class member picks a personal acquaintance to describe as it might be done in a short story or novel. Characterizations must include physical qualities, mannerisms, attitudes, actions, speech habits. The presentation should show how others view and inter-act with the character and how the character views himself.

52-C   (Experiment/Chalkboards) "Meet a Metaphor"

Students can practice writing their own metaphors for descrip-tion in the following manner. The class names five abstract qualities such as hatred, love, morality, pride, and virtue, which are listed on the chalkboard. Then they name five actions, for instance, baking, painting, talking, walking, and weaving which are listed next to the abstract qualities. Next, the class connects items in the two lists attempting to write extended metaphors such as "Hatred is like weaving a tapestry." Then they must tell why the analogy is drawn. They might say that hatred grows slowly one thread at a time, but soon the individual's personality becomes fixed as a tapestry, a way for people to picture that individual.

53-I   (Experiment/Displays) "Brilliant Idea"

Children need every opportunity to use their imaginations and

their senses. A surprising number, however, have not even
engaged in the joyful pleasures of conjuring images from cloud
formations. Similar in-class displays can evoke similar responses
through use of the overhead projector, if going outside is not
feasible. Place various opaque objects or cutout shapes on the
projector table. Encourage imaginations to wander.

In another approach, obtain two pieces of clear white acetate
(plastic sheets). Place several separated drops of colored liquids—
as from food dyes or water colors—on one sheet. Then place the
second sheet on top. Seal the edges with tape and project on
an overhead. The heat will cause the colors to rearrange themselves in different patterns. Pressing the sheets changes the
pattern. Also apply multicolors to clear 16 mm film. Show
through a projector for startling effects. Even ink blots, as in the
Rorschach test, will provide additional stimulation for descriptive
paragraphs or essays.

54-C   (Experiment/Games) "What Am I?"

Paste some magazine illustrations of common objects on file
cards, putting the name of the object below. Or make up cards
with only the name on them. Students draw cards at random
and write a description of the object pictured or labeled. Each
student has a different object to describe without naming it.
Descriptions must include ten qualities based on sight, touch,
taste, smell, and sound. Then the descriptions are read aloud
while the other students (or teams) try to guess what is being
described. The faster the object is guessed, the more credit
a student would get for his work, because he has learned to use
description so well.

55-C   (Experiment/Lists) "No Peeking"

To become aware of style in good writing, students need
practice in visualizing concrete images from words—building
visual images by expanding on details. Reading carefully selected
sentences, ask the class to close their eyes and imagine a scene
complete with sounds. Then they list all the details. They can
later expand these lists into descriptive compositions. Two good
stimulus sentences to read are: 1) A great, dead, sun-bleached
city lay waffle-like on white-hot sand. 2) There is nothing
quieter than the blackened skeleton of somebody's house the
morning after a fire.

56- C (Experiment/Pictures) "Going on Record"

The tape recorder can be used to help students realize composition is oral communication symbolized. After presenting a brief introductory lecture such as "Words—Vehicles for Feeling," show pictures (using slides, opaque, or bulletin board) to arouse emotions. Then allow time for students to record their emotions on tape. Point out that each has produced a mini-composition. Just as they have spoken to let others know how they feel, at times they must also write. To follow through, the teacher might have some taped descriptions transcribed and duplicated for the class to study and discuss.

57- I (Interpret/Biographies) "Guess Who"

To illustrate the importance of describing personalities when writing about people, have each student write a brief personality sketch of anyone. Later the teacher reads the sketches, not revealing the writer or subject. The class tries to guess the subject in each case. This procedure shows that personalities are important and quite different—as different as each person writes. To illustrate the importance of details when writing about people, have each student write a brief personality sketch of the same character just studied in a novel. These are discussed for the differing interpretations and possibly why some are better than others. Then as a follow-up practice, students write about anyone they all should know, choosing different subjects well-known in the community or the nation. Later these sketches are read without revealing the subject. The class tries to guess the subject in each case, depending on rich descriptive details.

58- I (Interpret/Demonstrations) "Nose for Writing"

Bring some object to class which has a pervasive but recognizable odor. Assign a short paper on what the odor reminds them of and why, i.e., a particular place, a season of the year, and the like. Kitchen spices and liquid flavorings are good to use because they can evoke memories of a variety of situations and settings. Read some of the results.

59- I,C   (Interpret/Games) "Where Am I?"

Each class member writes with clear, precise imagery a scene
which would be familiar to all students in the class. They relate
what they see, hear, smell, and touch when they are there
but cannot refer to the place by name. When the pieces are
read aloud, the rest of the class tries to guess the location.

60- I,G   (Interpret/Pictures) "No Foldouts"

Students each select a picture from a magazine, a calendar,
or a collection of famous prints. They can find their own or use
one from the teacher's collection. The object is to express
in writing the emotions which the illustration has created.
Then they must include why they think the picture made such
an impression. The reasons usually run the gamut from childhood memories to recollections of a particularly impressive
movie or television program. These are shared in groups to
save time. Perhaps each group chooses the best; these are
offered to the class.

61- C   (Interpret/Skits) "Caught in the Act"

To provide students with a single event about which all could
write descriptions, arrange to have some students (three is a
good number) come into the class and perform several
prearranged activities—one student could write a word on the
board and then erase it, another could say something and move
in an interesting way. They would remain in the room about a
minute, then leave. (The actors could be from another of the
teacher's classes.) The class which observed the unexpected
event would then write a brief description of what transpired,
including what each wore. Besides being interesting, this activity
also points out the need for careful attention to details. Papers
will reflect a great variety in quality and accuracy.

62- I   (Organize/Pictures) "Cutting the Family Tree"

Provide magazines so the class can cut out faces of men, women,
and children, all of varying ages, to create a hypothetical
family. They paste faces on a simple family tree drawn on
construction paper, give names to all members of the family,
and then write about each person (age, hobbies, personality,
and so on) until they have created as complete a family background as they can. A follow-up would be to locate a picture

of the type of house the main family would have, describe
it on paper, and draw simple floor plans. Display some projects
on the bulletin board.

DRAMA

63- I   (Interpret/Letters) "Man Called Wil"

After reading a Shakespearean play such as *Hamlet*, students
pretend they live in England at the time the play was written.
They have just seen a play written by the relatively unknown
playwright William Shakespeare. They then write a letter to a
friend who has not seen this play. The result is a play review.
The unified studies program would find this an excellent way
to enliven history through immersion in both time and language.
Producing an authentic letter requires some research and an
ability to draw inferences.

EXPOSITION

64- I   (Consolidate/Displays) "Grab This"

As practice in writing descriptive
exposition, each student prepares
a grab bag including a dozen or
so items such as bits of uniquely
shaped macaroni, some rubber
bands, a few tiny toys, two or
three empty spools, and some
small objects from Dad's workbench
or the kitchen junk drawer. Mix up
the brown paper bags so that each
student gets someone else's. Then
each constructs something from
the collection in his bag. The next activity is to come to class
prepared to describe step by step (oral or written) how the
creations were built. Vote on the best descriptions to be
used as models for class study.

65- C   (Analyze/Books) "Topical Topics"

After the class has considered what a topic sentence is, have
students look for the topic sentences or developing ideas in

their various textbooks as well as in periodicals. Seeing that professional writers need and use topic sentences encourages students to try for better-structured paragraphs in their own writing.

66-I   (Consolidate/Demonstrations) "Way Out Is In"

This idea helps encourage student creativity. The teacher (or a volunteer) brings in unusual objects such as a cartoon of Linus holding his blanket or brings some objects such as a burned-out electrical fuse or a piece of abstract art. Students could also taste a particularly unique spice, smell a rare perfume, or listen to a particularly evocative musical selection. Then they write a short exposition (any type) giving their reactions to any or several of the stimulus items, trying to be original. The best efforts are shared with the class.

67-I   (Consolidate/Essays) "Squeezey Writing"

Let class practice condensing a three- or four-page printed essay into 250 words, preserving meaning and as much of the style as possible. This paraphrasing assignment illustrates that omitting details from a well-written essay destroys its style and often its meaning.

68-C   (Experiment/Discussions) "Emote-shuns"

This approach helps reaffirm methods of definition and stimulates vital discussion. The teacher begins class by asking students for a paragraph defining "son" or "daughter," depending on which they are. The results are either collected or read aloud by volunteers. The ideas contained in these definitions are sources of discussion on how these common words have a wide variety of meanings to different people and can trigger a range of emotions.

69-C   (Experiment/Journals) "Random Thoughts"

For an alternate approach to the usual journal assignment, give the class a topic of current interest and ask them to list in their journals random thoughts on the topic. They need not consider mechanics or grammar. The purpose is to practice the art of thinking on paper.

70- I (Interpret/Periodicals) "Clipped Topic"

Newspapers and magazines can be used to practice creative
writing. The teacher clips from a newspaper or magazine an
article which involves many people, e.g., 900 people on strike
at X Factory; 100 families homeless following a tornado. After
reading the article to the class, the teacher directs each student
to do the following: Imagine what might happen to a person
involved in the incident, jot down the important ideas as they
occur to you, rearrange them in a sequence by preparing a
simple outline, then write a paper on this broad news event,
narrowing it to its effect on a single individual.

71- G (Organize/Games) "Go Fetch"

Provide practice in organizing vital facts and details. Divide the
class into teams (two or four). Each team member gets an
"assignment" card telling him to write directions for locating
something: an object in the room, a hidden item, a person,
book, magazine, or other. When the writer's team is up, one
member gets a copy of his directions. Scores are awarded by
the length of time it takes the member to locate the item; the
fewer the minutes, the higher the score.

72- C (Organize/Paragraphs) "Your Order, Please"

To demonstrate the importance of topic sentences, transitional signals, and logical progression, ask students to arrange in proper orde
scrambled sentences taken from their own paragraphs. Sentences
may be duplicated and cut apart, or they may be numbered and
the numbers themselves rearranged. This exercise may also provide
valuable suggestions for improving original paragraphs.

73-C (Experiment/Sentences) "Mini-Mini Comps"

Many students entering college or the business world discover
that they can't communicate their ideas to others. To help
eliminate this problem, require students to write and hand in
one sentence each day on any topic chosen by the student.
The assignment, which can later be structured to give practice
in using learned grammar rules, reduces the fear of writing
and increases the natural flow of written speech. Gradually
most students will feel the need to write an entire paragraph
to express ideas once they see that it is nothing more than a

collection of related sentences. The last step would be sentence combining. Give students suggestions for connecting thoughts through simple coordination in compound sentences or through subordination using phrases and clauses.

74- I   (Organize/Papers) "First Priority"

In learning how to write well, a student must first become fluent in his own use of language to express ideas. Before a student attempts to improve syntax and grammar, he should have something to say. The first concern, then, is a message. Encourage students to write first drafts as if explaining something aloud to a friend. A tape recorder would help. In this manner content is emphasized and all mechanical concerns which impede the flow of thought are pushed into the background until later. If students are allowed to feel they have an interesting message worth sharing, they will feel more justified going through the arduous task of rewriting and polishing.

HUMANITIES

75- I   (Interpret/Artwork) "Find Arts"

To teach creative writing and art appreciation at the same time, bring to class prints of contemporary paintings by famous artists. After several days in art appreciation discussion, each student selects one print he wishes to use for a practice project. First, he writes a description of the painting and its apparent theme. Then he develops both the scene and the theme into a creative story or poem.

JOURNALISM

76- I   (Analyze/Journals) "Cut and Paste"

The blank pages of a journal (see related ideas 69, 185, and 239) can be used for more than writing. Encourage students to paste in articles and pictures from magazines and newspapers. Suggest that they comment on these in terms of *why* they chose to include the items or *how* the items affected their thinking in some way. This activity also helps to show the importance of media in their lives.

77- C   (Analyze/Newspapers) "Press of English"

Slower students often find nothing in the English class which
interests them. Bring in something which will capitalize on
their natural concern for world conditions—the daily newspaper.
After a time of discussing interesting articles, branch out to
other aspects: analyzing news coverage and writing styles,
recognizing article types, or locating examples of doublespeak
(see idea 79). As interest grows, arrange to tour a newspaper
plant. This could be followed by publishing a class newspaper
using ideas learned in class and on the field trip.

78- C   (Analyze/Newspapers) "Publisher Psychout"

Purchase or borrow some of the nation's leading newspapers.
Read different accounts of one event in the various papers.
Note the differences in word choice, pictures, placement, and
the like. Collect some of these articles in scrapbooks or on the
bulletin board. For a related activity over a period of time, trace
one story in a single newspaper. Notice how the placement
changes, how it is sometimes featured and then played down,
depending on latest developments.

79- C   (Analyze/Newspapers) "Word Pollution"

After an introduction to doublespeak (ambiguous, sometimes
deceptive language, frequently using euphemisms, vague terms,
and abstract ideas which often confuse the public), have the
class locate samples of advertisements as well as news items
about education, politics, and the military. All are usually good
sources for doublespeak terms. Sentences like this abound: "If
prompt actions are implemented within the disinvestment
parameters, the core area's meaningful objectives may be maxi-
mized." Also see ideas 77 and 287.

80- C   (Experiment/Bulletin Boards) "Gigantic Antic"

Make a bulletin board display of a giant newspaper layout.
Draw in the columns and provide space for news items, editorials, features, and sports but leave columns empty. The
class provides accounts of school, community, and national
events by writing articles for the proper columns. Adding
machine tape can be used as paper for the typed or hand-lettered
copy. These contributions serve as models for further study.

81- I   (Experiment/Cartoons) "Captured Captions"

After an introduction to caption writing—really a lesson about inferential thought, supply a quantity of editorial or situation cartoons with captions removed. Each student randomly selects five and writes his own captions. Different ways to share these among class members can be devised, but the opaque projector is the simplest method. Perhaps a chance to compare student captions with the originals should be provided.

82- G   (Experiment/Interviews) "Journal-ease"

After presenting information on the interview technique, don't do the usual practice: pairing up and interviewing each other or interviewing parents or the teacher. Instead, bring a relatively unknown person to your class after giving some significant facts. Have the class conduct its own interview in press conference format. Have each student write up the interview as a culminating activity. Some of the best papers should be shared, with the very best sent to the school newspaper if the interview subject would interest the student body.

83- C   (Interpret/Newspapers) "Matchmakers"

Select short, interesting news items with well-worded headlines. Number the headings and corresponding articles so they can be matched later. Headlines are removed and kept at the teacher's desk. Each student reads his article and writes an original headline for it. As the teacher calls article numbers, each student reads the article and new headline. Then the teacher reads the original headline. The exercise provides good practice in getting the key idea from a piece of writing.

NARRATION

84- C   (Analyze/Models) "And Lo, There Was a Time"

As an exercise analyzing narrative style, rewrite a familiar children's story ("Goldilocks," "Little Red Riding Hood," or "The

Three Little Pigs," for instance) as Chaucer might have written them or as a popular news magazine or even the Bible might have presented the story. Papers are read to the class or displayed on the bulletin board.

85- I   (Consolidate/Models) "Grand Finale"

Combine knowledge of fiction and composition. Individuals write their own endings for a novel or short story they have recently studied, changing it in any way they wish. Activity provides opportunities to combine theme, tone, characterization, structure, and dialogue into a single project. An advanced class can try writing in the author's style.

86- G   (Consolidate/Pictures) "Captured Moments"

Prepare a bulletin board using very thought-provoking magazine pictures without captions. Divide the class into small groups. Each group chooses a picture to discuss for ten to fifteen minutes for the purpose of building a story around it—a group-written story. Split the workload so certain individuals specialize in perfecting certain aspects of the story. For example, various members would be responsible for embellishing each of these based on an agreed-upon outline: time and place (the setting); the sounds, colors, shapes; the mood; and the dialogue for the characters. Major items of plot, characterization, and theme would be handled by the group as a whole.

87- G   (Experiment/Audiotapes) "Off the Record"

Divide the class into groups of five or six. Each group is given a tape recorder and an opening sentence for a narrative (all groups can work with the same sentence or each may have a different one). One student in each group begins a story using this sentence. Each student in the group adds a sentence. The aim, of course, is to develop a story with plot, climax, and conclusion. When completed, the story is played back and perhaps edited to satisfaction. Although some stories are shared orally, others may be duplicated for more careful attention to organization, grammar, format, originality, and such specific narrative devices as subplots and foreshadowing.

88-I   (Experiment/Cartoons) "Balloon Talk"

Cut out entire sets of comic strips from Sunday papers. Remove the dialogue from the balloons. Give each student a comic for which he supplies his own dialogue which is both appropriate to the characters and to the situations and which tells the story succinctly. Print directly on the strip or on separate paper containing numbers corresponding to numbered balloons. This is an effective way to practice dialogue and conversational punctuation. Creativity should also be encouraged.

89-I   (Experiment/Cartoons) "Snoopy Says"

After a study of comics and how they contain the basics of the narrative, each student devises a cartoon character, drawing one frame of a comic strip each day. Each new frame must be related to the previous day's. The final frame at the end of the week terminates the series. Even if drawings are just stick figures, students will practice developing simple plots through dialogue, action, and setting.

90-C   (Experiment/Games) "Who Wrote It?"

After introducing variations in narrative style, have students imitate writings of well-known authors. The class tries to guess the author based on certain stylistic clues discussed earlier. Falkner, Steinbeck, and Hemingway's styles are always good for comparison of sentence lengths, modification, and attention to detail. Particularly useful would be comparisons such as people walking or the sun rising and setting. How each author handles such commonplace events is most interesting to observe.

91-G   (Experiment/Mysteries) "Who, What, When, Where, Why—and How!"

A study of mysteries can readily include the four types of discourse: (1) narration—giving basic plot; (2) description—setting the scene of the crime; (3) exposition—presenting the evidence; and (4) argumentation—hearing defense and prosecution. For practice, have students form groups to write a class mystery. The groups vote on basic plot as a start: something stolen, someone murdered, somebody blackmailed, for example. Each group then writes part of the story: characters and setting, the crime being committed, the investigation, the solution. Group chairmen and the teacher are responsible for continuity. The story can be read aloud with assigned speaking parts. Discuss strengths and weaknesses of each group's contribution.

92- I   (Experiment/Skits) "Sets of Vignettes"

Point out vignettes such as those throughout Hemingway's *The Sun Also Rises* or in a more contemporary novel. With these examples students can practice writing some of their own, representing humorous or dramatic scenes from their own experiences. Some papers should be read to the class or posted on a bulletin board.

93- I   (Interpret/Movies) "Selected Short Subjects"

To expand a study of narration, show a short narrative film in its entirety without turning on sound. Students write a short story giving it a title, character names, setting, dialogue, and plot based on what they think is happening. Show the film again, in short segments if needed. When the projects are in and some have been shared in class, show the film once more, this time with sound.

94- C, I   (Interpret/Records) "Sound Off"

Use sound effects records to create a background of sequential sounds which could evoke a story, *e. g.*, car motor, motor stops, car doors slam, footsteps, and so on. Students then build a short narrative on what they have heard. Most suppliers of recordings for schools have such records. If you can't locate some, ask the drama coach, local radio station, or community library.

95- I   (Organize/Pictures) "Get the Picture"

Bring in numerous copies of popular pictorial magazines. Students select and clip about twenty pictures on a single theme or idea. Do not break the news until they are finished collecting pictures that they must create a picture story complete with captions. This assignment is handled very simply—almost in storybook fashion. It offers practice in organizing thoughts and stimulates creativity, and it is suitable for both younger and older children.

96-I   (Organize/Short Stories) "Starting at the Start"

To practice narrative organization, students complete a short
story beginning with a line like this: Mr. Smith opened the door
and peeked out.

97-I   (Organize/Talks) "Follow the Leader"

A student starts an original narrative. After a sentence or two,
he chooses a second person (or volunteer) to continue the same
story. The second moves the story line along and then designates
a third. Students continue until a completion point is reached.
To promote originality along with unity and coherence, do not
allow anyone to repeat or contradict what has been said. Anyone doing so must take notes, writing down the story for later
discussion. The entire approach—even the punitive measure—is
excellent practice for organizing thoughts, a skill which will
carry over to longer papers.

OVERVIEW

98-I   (Analyze/Models) "Copy Break"

After a composition assignment is turned in by the students,
do more than simply evaluate. To get more mileage from the
compositions, take at least one full class period integrating the
assignment with grammar study. This provides variety and makes
grammar more relevant. Students also benefit from analyzing
their own writing models rather than using someone else's.

99-C   (Analyze/Models) "Generically Speaking"

Bring in different generic examples on the same theme—prose
passage, poem, or dialogue from a play on death, love, fear,
nature, social criticism, and the like. Probe the question of form,
its limitations and assets for conveying the same message.

100-T   (Analyze/Models) "Join 'Em"

To be able to teach writing well, an English teacher must participate in some class assignments. At times prepare a written
paper before assigning it to the class. Not only will it provide
a model for class analysis, but it will also alert you to problems
the students may have. Occasionally insert errors to provoke
discussion. Some assignments can be completed as the students

do theirs. Then discuss how some common problems were or were not solved. This practice reflects a "we're all in this together" feeling.

101- C   (Analyze-Organize/Audiotapes) "Musical Shares"

To illustrate the need for continuity in compositions, show the same need in music. The sonata form is easy to analyze because its exposition, development, and recapitulation are so clearly evident. Careful listening to edited tapes will demonstrate the main theme of the sonata form and variations on that theme. Someone with a little musical ability (or get help from the music teacher) can trace many similarities between organization in music and in written composition.

102- G   (Experiment/Games) "Sack It to 'em"

 After introducing just about any type of written composition, have students practice by bringing an object in a paper sack. Each must introduce the object orally, involving the item as part of an anecdote, a joke, mini-mystery, series of questions, and so forth. Class is to guess from the involvement what the object is.

103- C   (Consolidate/Field Trips) "Going Around in Circles"

Since ecology is a subject becoming important to most students, use the outdoors to stimulate their thoughts and interests and to gather ideas. Invite each class member to place five yards of grocery string in a circle on the ground. Then he either lists or brings back actual samples of the living things or objects in that circle. The natural follow-up is to let them plan on paper a possible composition by consolidating the information on objects gathered. Writing can be the next step.

104- C   (Experiment/Paragraphs) "Day to Day"

An exercise which helps promote spontaneous written expression is a daily paragraph on whatever subject the student desires. This practice is an excellent extension of the daily sentence practice (idea 73). Improving sentences tends to improve paragraphs. Thus, improving paragraphs should improve a total composition. Writing without much attention to the grammar of the sentence serves to reduce the inhibitions of confronting a blank piece of paper. But it is only a first step toward improving composition and toward getting students to use what they already know about language.

105- C   (Organize/Paragraphs) "Short But Neat"

To give frequent practice in succinct writing, place a single word—a verb, noun, or an adjective—on a 3 X 5 or 5 X 7 card and distribute one card to each person. The student writes a short paragraph using the assigned word as the focal point. Cards are exchanged mainly to check on organization. Used once or twice weekly, this activity promotes growth in writing.

106- C   (Organize/Plans) "Just a Grocery List"

Some teachers err by forcing young writers to prepare a topic or sentence outline (from roman numerals to sub-subtopics) before putting pen to paper in a composition assignment. Complete outlining is excellent for getting the "meat" out of something already written—the reason most students do their outlines *after* they write—but outlining must be simple and quick or it alienates and makes writing an even more onerous task than it often is. Just a few key words and phrases—grocery list style— along the margin of the first page will usually give the needed organization.

107- I   (Interpret/Mixed Media) "Media at the Corner"

To help students understand that knowledge in one communication area relates to other areas, have them write first on a given or self-selected situation or topic. Then they convey the same information through another medium of their choice: painting, song, dance, dramatic interpretation, picture essay, or film, for instance.

POETRY

108- C   (Analyze/Models) "Compare the Pair"

Open a discussion on how carefully a poet or author selects his words. Prepare two copies of a short selection and place them side by side. One is the original; the other a copy with key words changed to synonyms or words with other connotations. The problem is to decide which copy is the original and which is a poor substitute and to tell why.

109- I   (Compare/Models) "A Whataphor?"

To evaluate the use of metaphor, students examine a poem such as Walt Whitman's "The Noiseless Patient Spider," in which a natural object and an incident become metaphors. They then write a short free-verse poem employing the same method. Before beginning, the students should state the objects and ideas being compared and tell how they are similar. For his poem, Whitman might have approached this assignment this way:

Things compared: Spider in a web and the isolation of man's soul.

Similarities: The spider throws out physical lines to make contact with outside elements in an effort to build a home and a supportive environment. Man "throws out" emotional attachments to build his life.

110- G   (Consolidate/Collections) "If, What Then?"

As an introduction to writing poetry, challenge students with this group activity. The first student in each row writes something like this in iambic tetrameter: "My room is not the best to see." The second student (without being too concerned about a perfect sequences of ideas) extends the action in the same meter. The third student adds to the thought, and so on, until all in the row have contributed to the original idea. When each row's efforts are completed, the class will have developed several poems in the designated meter.

111-C,G (Experiment/Lists) "Poets Know It"

After a study of poetry techniques, suggest that each class write a poem together. Begin by asking for natural, spontaneous responses to a word which will serve as the theme, for example, "darkness," "Mother," or "sorrow." The class members then write phrases, clauses, or sentences growing out of their reaction to the theme word. Collect and arrange these thoughts into a master list, possibly grouping similar ideas. Have the master list reproduced and distributed. Finally announce to the class that they are to rework the list into a poem. If desirable, the students can work in groups. The entire project takes only three days at the minimum. The results are so amazing that awards might well be given for the best efforts.

112- C   (Experiment/Models) "Best Foot Forward"

To help themselves learn and identify meter, advance their listening skills, and increase awareness of different verse patterns, students write couplets to be read aloud. Each couplet should cover current subjects, be written in popular language and syntax, and should also employ a particular metrical foot (iambic, dactylic, trochaic, or anapestic). Samples from a class might look like these:

Iambic:	*If we must save dear nature's sources,*
	Then why not save us from these courses?
Dactylic:	*Graduates, graduates, all in a row,*
	Happy and sad and not wanting to go.
Trochaic:	*Machines that vend and take our doughs,*
	Will you just give me back my nose?
Anapestic:	*On a beach, on a date, he is tops in his class.*
	In a course, with a book, he can barely just pass.

113- I   (Experiment/Senses) "Poetricks"

Invite students to react in writing to the following stimuli: the aroma of gasoline, freshly mown hay, rain-wet fur, or the feel of skin, hair, or walking barefoot in warm mud. The only rules are that their reactions cannot be sentences. They must use three-, four-, or five-word phrases. When these reactions are listed together—*Poetry*! Well, it's a start anyway.

CHAPTER
3

EVALUATION

ARGUMENTATION

114- G   (Compare/Discussions) "What Would You Do?"

Using a popular, debatable issue, have students choose the pro
or con side and write a composition stating their position. After
sufficient writing time (one class period to several days), papers
are handed in but not graded. Instead, the teacher reads them
quickly to find two well-written papers—one each for pro and
con. These are duplicated in quantities so each student gets a
set. The class is then divided into groups. Each group discusses
the compositional merits of each paper as well as the argumentative qualities. In a summation later, a representative gives the
consensus of his group.

DESCRIPTION

115- C   (Compare/Essays) "Casting a Look"

After reading a play, students write a description of one character, giving physical and behavioral characteristics. Afterward,
show a movie version of the play (e.g., James Mason in *Julius
Caesar*). Such full-length films are available to schools for economical rental. The English department might sponsor an all-
school showing or contact a local theater for a special matinee.
Students then write an essay illustrating how their version of
the play character (based on their reading of the play) differs
from the movie interpretation.

116- I   (Extrapolate/Games) "What's It?"

To evaluate ability to do descriptive writing with sharpened perception, bring to class a What's-It Box. Put an unknown object into a covered box. Shake and tilt the box for the class. Let them ask only questions about the identity of the object which can be answered with a Yes or No. Then each student writes a brief paper telling what the object might be based on clues received. Discuss some of the finished papers as models.

117- I   (Extrapolate/Senses) "Sense-ative Descriptions"

Students write a short paragraph employing one of the five senses, which would not ordinarily be used to describe a topic. For example, a description of a ball game would normally tell the action of the game and the kinds of people seen. Instead, the topic could be described through smells only—the food, the crowd, the perfume of a girl nearby, the varnished floor, or new-mown grass. This activity tests ability to manipulate sensory experiences effectively.

118- C   (Judge/Games) "Monkeying Around"

A switch in the usual personality sketch is to have a student write a description of another student (omitting the name or pronouns *he* or *she* and using *the subject* or *this person*). The character clues are stated in terms of an animal most representative of that student. The accuracy of the description is then tested by how quickly the class guesses the person being described.

119- G   (Restructure/Audiotapes) "Speaking Pen"

Some students, though very articulate, are still unable to write well. For them, the teacher can emphasize the concept of "verbalizing on paper." Students in small groups tape a discussion wherein they describe an object which the teacher has provided. They then listen to the tape and note the essential discussion points. Afterward, each student writes a short description, based on these ideas and emphasizing clarity and organization. Time permitting, compositions can be read orally in groups for criticism. Finally revisions are handed to the teacher for final evaluation and comments.

120- G   (Restructure/Games) "Show and Tell"

The Show and Tell approach is a popular way to promote interest in elementary schools, yet this same method can also be used at higher levels. One way is to pair students so each can bring in some curious object for the partner to describe on paper. This usually leads to a competition for bringing in the most indescribable object and for determining who can describe it better. To promote clarity and conciseness, limit the number of pages or words. If the objects can be displayed, students can read their short papers while the class tries to pick the object being described. This method increases powers of description and reveals how well the student has learned the techniques.

EXPOSITION

121- I   (Extrapolate/Artwork) "Print Out"

Obtain prints of the work of several famous artists. Pass them around the class, allowing each student to select the one which to him appears most interesting. Students then test their abilities to write an exposition from visual data. Something like Breughel's *School Children* could produce an exposition on poverty or on school life as the artist seemed to reflect these aspects. Papers could also contrast the artist's point of view with the student's.

122- I   (Extrapolate/Books) "Get to a Ghetto"

Choose a current novel or nonfiction book which deals with life in a culture different from that of most students in your school. For example, a teacher in a middle or upper class school might choose Huey P. Newton's *Revolutionary Suicide* or George Mitchell's *I'm Somebody Important: Young Black Voices from Rural Georgia.* An inner city teacher could choose a book about people in more affluent surroundings: *The Son of Someone Famous* by M. E. Kerr or *The Gift* by Pete Hamill. Other books might describe Mexican Americans, Chinese Americans, or Indians. After the reading, students may describe in a piece of expository writing how the reality described in the

book has affected their view of another culture. This activity
tests ability to apply one set of data against another.

123- T   (Extrapolate/Essays) "Great Leveler"

Students often complain that they could write better if they
had good topics. Part way into the semester, suggest they write
about their teacher—you! They write what they like or dislike
about your teaching, or they just describe you. To prevent
stilted compositions, announce they will be graded not on
what is said but *how* it is said. The problem of anonymity can
be settled by class vote.

124- I   (Extrapolate/Essays) "Who Wrote Me?"

To heighten awareness that an author's own character and
personality can be revealed in his writing, each student writes
a personal essay reacting to something he recently observed,
read, heard, or felt. The papers are not signed, just a code or
pseudonym is used. During the next class period the essays are
shuffled so each student gets that of someone else. The task is
to read an essay and try to identify the writer. If the reader
guesses the author, (s)he must tell what traits revealed the
writer.

125- I, C (Extrapolate/Games) "Survival Game"

Here is a well-known activity which
is still good for evaluating ability to
extrapolate data. Explain that nine
people are stranded on an island because of some situation which the
students can suggest. Have each
write on the subject—if they could
save only five people, who would
they be and why? Choices might be
a navy lieutenant, thirteen-year-old
girl or boy, famous doctor, writer's
fiancee, governor of a state, movie
star, pastor (rabbi or priest), or presi-
dent of a large motor company. The situation, of course, can
be changed from an island to anywhere—even the last space-
ship from a ravaged earth to a new planet. The variations are
enormous and the discussions exciting.

126- C   (Judge/Authorities) "Crit-ticks"

Students always show interest in evaluating what they have
seen or heard. Test their ability to be critical. Take students
to (or encourage them to attend) movies, plays, and lectures;
bring in guest speakers; let students evaluate their student
teachers. The papers will be better since the subjects are real.

127- C   (Judge/Critiques) "Critical Critique"

After a class has attended a play or seen a movie, let them
write a short critical review (based on learned knowledge of
the technique of writing reviews). Observations are directed
to even the smallest details of lighting or sound as well as the
acting, story, characterization, direction, and so on. Start off,
perhaps, by reading several reviews written by previous classes.

128- C   (Judge/Games) "All for One"

Give a single word to the class for a two-minute exposition
which the word suggests. When time is up, ask volunteers to
read their short papers. Class makes suggestions which, in turn,
will help improve their own papers and the one being evaluated.
The teacher's evaluation problems will thus be reduced.

129- G   (Judge/Instructions) "Homing in on Composition"

To test concise and explicit communication, have each student
write a paragraph giving directions for getting home from school
without the aid of a diagram or map. Then classmates check each
other's work by tracing the route on a city map. If they don't
get "lost," the paper must be effective, deserving a high evaluation.

130- G   (Judge/Instructions) "In a Jam"

This exercise tests ability to write logically in an expository
paragraph. All (or several students) write in correct order the
instructions for making a peanut butter and jelly sandwich.
The needed materials can be brought to class so some students
can try another's instructions. If the writer has made a mistake in logical order, sandwiches will have peanut butter on
the top or jelly dripping from the bottom or even spread on
the hand. Of course, any number of other activities can be
substituted for the sandwich idea, for example, tying shoe

laces, bending paper clips, drawing pictures, or piling blocks. But foot preparation works best since the props can be eaten.

131- I   (Judge/Movies) "Pick the Flick"

As part of a unit on film as composition, have numerous published movie reviews available for study. After discussing such facets as purpose, technique, relationship of art to theme, quality of acting, and sensationalism, student will be able to see how different critics' opinions seem to vary on the same point. Soon students will be ready to make their own judgments and movie reviews. Continue interest by reserving bulletin board section for reviews of films being shown in your town.

132- C   (Judge/Role Playing) "If I Could Be"

Too often students write just because they have to. Without real meaning, topics are not written well, resulting in failing marks. Change the pace by suggesting they put themselves in the place of a famous person and write about a typical day. This may take some library research even if subjects are free choice. Later, papers can be read in class (or in groups) so they can be evaluated using a rating sheet as a guide.

133- I   (Judge/Role Playing) "No-Prompt Impromptu"

Ideals set forth in a creative writing unit may be in vain if students are evaluated and graded in the conventional manner. For a better way, give an impromptu writing exercise in which each student reacts to various situations written on slips of paper. No instructions are given except that the student must place himself into the role. The results are evaluated for degree of effectiveness.

134- G   (Judge/Talks) "Speak Easy"

Divide the class into four or five groups. Each person in a group speaks on a given or selected topic which must have been researched and outlined, first for an oral then for a written report. Other members of a group take turns praising, evaluating, and criticizing the speaker. This procedure encourages responses from those who are too shy to speak before a large class. It also permits more speeches in a given time.

The high noise level is not annoying within the group, just to the casual observer.

JOURNALISM

135- G   (Restructure/Newspapers) "Start the Presses"

As a follow-up and evaluation of a journalism unit—ideally including a field trip to a newspaper plant—students write a class newspaper which includes both school and community news. Divide the class into special-interest groups such as news, sports, amusements, fashions, editorials, cartoons, comics, and even advertising (if practical). Besides being good motivation, this approach really tests how well the principles of journalism have been taught and learned.

LETTER WRITING

136- I   (Compare/Letters) "Better Letter Letter Grades"

A student's composition progress can be measured less threateningly if he writes frequent letters to the teacher or to someone else (you would read these). Easier and more personal, this approach emphasizes a useful form of communication. Topics can be almost anything: reporting progress in perfecting an athletic skill, in building a model, in collecting hobby items, and others.

137- I   (Extrapolate/Newspapers) "Take a Letter"

Encourage using classified ads as the basis for an actual letter applying for a summer job, making a personal inquiry, or ordering something. Assign a letter *before* study begins to evaluate ability to use such skills and to make inferences from given data. Students must write nearly perfect letters before any can be sent.

MEDIA

138- C   (Compare-Judge/Periodicals) "Periodicalling"

To help students evaluate knowledge of media in print, have them try some of these suggestions. (1) Clip newspaper stories on current events and judge content for who, what, where, when information. (2) Compare two different accounts of the same events reported in different newspapers. (3) Judge *The New York Times* to see why it is considered one of the best daily newspapers in the nation. (4) Compare writing in different newspapers to distinguish good writing from bad. (5) Judge the content, format, and emphasis of different magazines. (6) Display favorite magazine covers on the bulletin board and give reasons for choice. (7) Introduce some unfamiliar magazines to be judged and discussed.

139- I   (Judge/Cartoons) "See You in the Funnies"

In a media or composition unit, look at the comic strip as a narrative form. Students cut out five or six newspaper comic strips, pasting each on a separate sheet of notebook paper. Then they answer questions such as these: (1) What type of strip is it (adventure, mystery, humor, satire)? (2) Are the characters true to life? (3) What quality dialogue is used (standard English, dialect, idiom, child-talk)? (4) Is the strip complete in each episode or continued? (5) Who is the artist? Questions are answered on pages bearing the strips. If the class can handle it, they might summarize a strip they have followed for about two weeks, probably a continuing story. They can follow up this activity with another short paper evaluating their favorite strip and giving reasons for the choice.

140- C   (Judge/Periodicals) "Pulling a Switch"

Often teachers duplicate copies of student writing for class criticism, because students rarely hesitate to evaluate each other's work. But given a published article, they can usually find nothing wrong. They tend to believe all printed material is "sacred." To break this misconception, the teacher implies that a duplicated article from a newspaper or magazine is a student composition and asks the class to evaluate it. Afterward, they discover the article has actually been published. Besides helping to dispel the notion that printed material is always perfect, the activity also encourages students to watch for weaknesses and strengths in everything they read.

141-C   (Judge/Television) "Check the Tube"

To determine if students understand concepts previously learned, let them write descriptions of their favorite television shows. Their papers can focus on one of several aspects: wholesomeness, character development, clarity of emotions, originality of humor, realism in plot and setting, objectivity (if a news commentator), uses of propaganda and stereotypes, or quality of advertising, depending on the type of program.

142-I   (Restructure/Radio,Television) "One-Minute Spot"

As a change of pace during a composition unit, students can check on their ability to write commercials by rewriting some from radio and television—particularly those they dislike.

NARRATION

143-I   (Extrapolate/Pictures) "Sharing a Like"

If students have time to develop only one skill, it should be the capacity to "see." To check both visual perception and written expression, have the students write dialoques among several characters found in two pictures, e.g., from photographic prints or from exhibits such as "The Family of Man." To see if they can pursue a consistent point of view, have student select things which each character might have in common and which they might discuss if brought together.

144-G   (Judge/Talks) "Pairing Up"

Students write dialogue between two characters of their own choice. The conversations are later read to the class. Subjects could range from two women (or men) having their hair styled in a salon to several citizens making their first visit to the moon when space travel is a reality. This exercise gives excellent practice in creative writing and proves whether or not the technique of dialogue writing has been learned.

145–I (Restructure/Movies) "Silents Please"

Show a silent movie (e.g., Charlie Chaplin, Buster Keaton) lasting approximately twenty minutes. Ask students to write a dialogue for the story using their knowledge of the technique. Later it could be recorded for playback with the silent film.

146–I (Restructure/Tales) "Goldie Schwartz and Her Three Mares"

A narrative demands careful structure. Students can evaluate their knowledge of this technique by updating a fairy tale, making the characters fit their own interests and times. If the ages of the new characters differ from the original, the plot should be consistent with the characters' ages, but the original fairy tale plot should be followed, including any moral. The assignment calls for imagination and compliance with a given structure.

OVERVIEW

147–T (Compare/Books) "Savings Book"

When handing back well-written assignments, mark them "Type and Save." Near the close of the term, collect all such type-and-save narratives, poetry, essays, and so on, duplicate them, and compile enough booklets so each student gets one. Current booklets can be compared to the writing in booklets from a previous class.

148–I (Compare/Charts) "Keeping Score"

Each student keeps a personal chart of composition progress by posting the points earned through accuracy in specific evaluation areas. The following chart indicates how this may be done if, for instance, twelve points represented maximum performance in each of five qualities. Areas needing extra attention are clearly delineated. Best of all, this is a way to show success concretely. Also see ideas 155 and 157.

+   Points (12 maximum)

Topic	Grammar	Usage	Mechanics	Thought	Spelling	Grade
1. Description	9	2	3	2	11	C−
2. Personal Interview	7	9	4	4	10	C
3. Book Review	8	10	5	6	10	B
4. Personal Essay	6	5	6	8	12	C+
etc.						

149- I   (Compare/Talks) "Pro-File"

Keep all written compositions in folders—along with other grades and evaluations. By comparing papers the teacher can note progress and this can serve as a talking point for individual writing conferences. The folder also helps to justify semester grades. Next year's English teacher may also welcome a file on each student to better assess needs and to plan course content.

150- I   (Extrapolate/Audiotapes) "Sounding Off on Tape"

After writing a composition, the student records it on tape. He then plays it back while following along from his paper. Lacking a tape recorder, the student might ask a friend or a parent to read the paper aloud. Even reading it to himself will often suffice. Errors will become very evident and will be corrected before the paper comes to the teacher.

151- C   (Extrapolate/Audiotapes) "Write, Record, Listen"

A tape recorder in the room is often a good way to cope with student apathy. After each student writes about something in today's society which distresses him, he records the composition for playback to the class. As each weakness in writing is noted, a class member raises his hand. The tape is stopped, criticism given, and, if necessary the portion in question is replayed. This saves having to make duplicated copies for students to evaluate.

152- T   (Extrapolate/Lists) "Starting Out Write"

The first day of class each student writes a short composition, a letter, or merely a list of all the things he has hated and/or liked about previous English classes. These responses are kept for future conferences or to plan future class work. The purpose, of course, is to make assignments more meaningful for the students.

153- G   (Extrapolate/Papers) "Seein' is Believin' "

Divide the class into groups of four or five and arrange desks accordingly. Students turn in an assigned theme and these are collected as a set from each group. Have each paper coded with a number instead of using names. Collect all sets of papers, and redistribute them, making sure none are from the group which wrote them. Each member reads all the papers given to his group. Using the code number for identification, he grades and makes comments, taking a separate sheet of paper for each composition. This procedure helps students both to see good techniques and recognize some mistakes as ones they also make. The writer also finds out what others think of his writing—not just the teacher. Usually papers receive a more thorough analysis than if the teacher does all the evaluating. Those who hesitate to employ peer evaluation might do well to read articles which extoll peer tutoring. Students learn well from each other under proper guidance.

154- T   (Extrapolate/Papers) "Yea, Team!"

Cooperative writing assignments planned by teachers in different subject fields can be very profitable for all. For example, a history instructor may not feel qualified to correct the rhetoric of assigned papers. The English teacher down the hall is always looking for suitable topics for writing practice. The two teachers should work together on an assignment: the history teacher reading for content and effectiveness of gathering information, the English teacher evaluating sentence grammar, usage, and mechanics. Since both teachers work in areas of strength, neither is subordinate to the other. They can even assign separate grades, one for content and one for structure. (See also ideas 157 and 178.)

155- T   (Identify/Charts) "G-Mut, the Writing Detective"

G	M
U	T

Show the writer exactly where improvement is needed. Form and content are subdivided into grammar, usage, mechanics (including spelling), and thought. These are evaluated separately for assigned points. Not intended to supplant teacher comments, this technique can save considerable evaluation time. It could even be enhanced by using a "G-Mut form" which the student draws at the end of a paper before handing it in or which can be imprinted with a rubber stamp.

156- T   (Extrapolate/Talks) "Conversable"

One-to-one composition conferences require a pleasant location conducive to conversation, an unthreatened student, and an understanding teacher as the needed ingredients. Conference time can be obtained by making schedule changes which provide for extra library periods, free-reading days, and off-campus projects.

157- I   ((Identify/Charts) "Watch that Profile"

When the teacher likes to note all composition errors, this idea

will help students consolidate and interpret weaknesses which
are difficult to digest when scattered throughout a paper. First,
establish a vocabulary for labeling specific weaknesses (in any
rhetoric book). To reduce written comment, devise some easily
understood abbreviations (first letters or symbols—some are
standard in the field) to mark in margins or near problems.
Then hand out a Writer's Profile Form containing an alphabetical
list of weaknesses, probably not more than twelve with easy-to-
remember abbreviations. After each weakness item (in a string of
graph-like boxes) the student fills in a section of graph, one for
each weakness or error. When the form is filled, the several areas
on which the student should concentrate for the next paper will
usually be evident. If not—which is rare—the teacher should help
decide.

THE WRITER'S PROFILE

(The Shape of Your Writing)

Symbol		*Weakness*	*Profile*
(1)	abs	abstract word	(1)
(2)	mono	monotonous sentences	(2)
(3)	ov	overloaded sentence	(3)
(4)	om	overmodification	(4)
(5)	ord	sentence order	(5)
(6)	pdec	prepositional decay	(6)
		. . . and so on	

158- C   (Identify/Lists) "Book of Note"

Too often students merely glance at composition grades but
rarely look at the evaluations, the same mistakes then appear
in the next paper. Two approaches will help to improve the
situation. First, students can keep a notebook with a section
marked "comp errors." Here they list the types and frequencies
of mechanical and grammatical errors. The object is to identify
their major problems and to see if these are being eliminated
through practice. A second approach is to write catchy, livelier
comments so students will want to read them to chuckle, satisfy
curiosity, and, yes, even to learn.

159- I   (Identify/Lists) "Way to Go"

To reduce the overwhelming comprehensive evaluation, try
focusing on one or two aspects. Each time a student begins to

write a composition, he identifies at the top of his or her page the most serious writing problem uncovered in the last paper, as indicated by the teacher. This way the student is reminded what to improve and the teacher what to check. By being able to concentrate on one problem at a time, a writer is more apt to transfer learning from one paper to the next.

160-I   (Identify/Questions) "P.S., Teacher"

After writing a paper, students often wish they could explain to the teacher where they ran into trouble, what they couldn't express as they would have liked, what they tried to research but couldn't, and many other problems. Invite students to attach an extra P.S. Sheet to their papers and to write freely about the problems they had in writing the paper. This helps the teacher understand why certain parts of the paper seem weaker and so on. Sometimes such explanations emerge as better writing than the paper itself. Thus, the P.S. Sheet gives additional writing experience painlessly.

161-I   (Judge/Audiotapes) "Speech Writing"

Student writing is often unclear, not because the writer forgot a topic sentence or a supporting element, but rather because he did not recognize the relationship between his ability to describe something orally and his ability to write effectively. The paragraph should develop like a conversation, simply and logically. The project could begin by tape recording some conversation, then transcribing it.

162-T   (Judge/Audiotapes) "Tapeographical Errors"

Teachers frequently find there is not enough time to write all the needed comments on student themes. This idea cuts down on evaluation time but not on evaluation. Correct (or denote) grammar and mechanical errors as usual, but tape record comments about content. (Usually the two aspects must be considered separately anyway.) Give each student a five-minute cartridge tape, or mark on the paper the tape counter number where his comments begin among others on a longer tape. This procedure is quicker than writing lengthy comments and encourages a more thorough evaluation. Several listening stations can be provided around the room to facilitate feedback.

163- G   (Judge/Authorities) "Commit to Committee"

Instead of each student proofreading his own composition, set up a proofreading committee or panel similar to a newspaper editing department. Sometimes the proofreaders can be subdivided into specialities such as spelling, punctuation, modification, and others. In that case, printed signs on their desks would help identify them. As usual, peer group opinion can often carry more weight than any other type.

164- T   (Judge/Charts) "What's in a Grade?"

The composition Criteria Chart (page 53) may help to place compositions into three groupings. From that point, teachers who like to assign letter grades may find the task a little easier. Teachers who like to grade by achievement within ability groups will find their task a lot easier. A chart like this may have to be modified a bit according to the type of discourse.

165–C,G   (Judge/Discussion) "Peering at Papers"

Have students correct compositions using one of the following techniques: Duplicate papers for round-robin criticism, use projector for on-the-spot checking of a paper, or have students exchange papers and write a critique.

166–C,   (Judge/Lecture, Discussion) "Composition Competition"
G,I,T

The workshop approach for improving composition writing provides a variety of techniques: lecture, individual and group projects, audio-visual demonstrations, gaming, and class participation.

Before the workshop the teacher obtains a three-or-four-page writing sample from each participant to determine writing needs and to make grouping decisions. All assignments need not be the same for all students.)

The teacher then evaluates each sample, noting weaknesses beside the words and in the margins (see idea 157), editing (revising) the first page, and specifying on each writing sample one or two sentences which the writer will later place on an overhead transparency. (These transparencies are made by writing on plastic with felt pens or grease pencils.) Students will be told that the "before" or original sentence is placed first and is followed by the rewrite or "after" sample. The teacher also plans to divide the participants into six groups with approximately five students in each. Every group is to have a resource person who will later be

Composition Criteria Chart

	LOW	MIDDLE	HIGH
Thought			
Creativity	Weak ideas	Second-hand ideas	Original
Ideas	Not planned	Erratic clarity	Thought-out
Adaptability to type	Not original	Few examples or details	Uses examples, details
Ability to follow dir.	Misses assign.	Somewhat related to topic	Related to topic
	Trite, silly	Not sincere	No padding
	Ambiguous	Often padded	Sincere
Harmony (of ideas)			
Parag. org.	Very poor start	Weak start	Good start
Emphasis	Gets nowhere	Rambles often	Doesn't ramble
Parallelism	Random thoughts	Treats triviality	Point well made
Unity	No order	Conclusion: forced, awkward, absent	Logical organization
Coherence	No effective conclusion	Barely holds together	Well-balanced
Order	No unity or coherence	Often repeats	Unified, coherent
	Repetitious		
Aesthetics			
Flavor	Uneducated statements	Impersonal	Comes from self
Style	No style	Lacks style	No airs
Attitude	Lacks suitable vocabulary	Unfairly biased	Definite style
Tone	No feeling for topic	Little feeling for topic	Takes sides fairly
Suitability of vocabulary		Broad generalities	Good feeling for topic
			Quite specific
Mechanics			
Punctuation	Many cap. and punct. errors	Many punc. errors	Observes standard forms
Capitalization	Erratic spelling	A few cap. errors	Few if any punc. or cap. errors
Spelling	Weak spelling	Some weak paragraph structure	Correct paragraphing
Paragraphing	Weak paragraph	Hard words misspelled	Accurate spelling
Format			
Expression			
Wording	Childish vocab.	Trite, hackneyed	Uses both common and uncommon words
Vocab. devel.	Substandard usage	Lifeless, simple structures	
Usage	Weak sentence structure	Some weak usage	Interesting struct.
Sent. structure	Tense switches	No experimentation	Good usage
Grammar	Poor agreement	Forced use of big words (sometimes wrong or ineffective)	Accurate grammar
	Gropes for words		Clear, attractive
	Omits words		Fluent

a judge. Usually these are the students who submitted the best writing samples in the process described above.

Each participant, meanwhile, has also prepared a brief paper from a common writing assignment and comes to the workshop with at least five copies to be distributed for discussion. When the participants report, the teacher makes an oral presentation on the common weaknesses uncovered in the original writing samples. Improvement techniques may be displayed on the chalkboard, slides, or transparencies using samples from past workshops.

Then a table competition is announced. Group members are to help each other rewrite the original sentence on the "before-after" transparencies, getting extra help from the resource person at each table.

After a sufficient time, the "before-after" transparencies are collected, their having been identified by table number and type of error (the abbreviation). A point system can be announced to award 0, 1, 2, or 3 points based on quality of the rewrite. Transparencies are projected with the rewrite masked. After the weakness is fully identified and located in the "before" version, the rewrite is displayed. The teacher may be the sole judge or may rely on the resource people (now seated as a panel) to decide the number of points to be awarded, basing their decision on the class consensus after the rewrite is discussed. When each table has had an equal number of turns (up to four or five transparencies are available for each table), the table scores are totaled and compared.

For the next activity, the students continue to work in individual groups, with each group reading and discussing the common assignment papers and basing their ideas on the first workshop activity. As papers are being circulated within the group, each student secretly rates the five papers from his group on a scale of 5 (best) to 1 (worst). The paper with the highest cumulative rating (two if tied) is turned over to the six judges who will try to determine which of the six papers turned in (one from each group) is the best and the runner-up. The teacher's rating breaks any ties. Transparencies or class copies may be made of these for class discussion.

While the judges are making their choices, the teacher is conducting individual conferences with students about their original writing samples to help them understand how to alleviate the designated weaknesses. At the same time, the rest of the class can be rewriting their writing samples using the edited first page as a guide.

The grand finale of the workshop activity occurs when the runner-up common assignment paper (10 bonus points to that table group) and the winner (15 points) are revealed and discussed in that order. Prizes can be awarded to the winning table group: pizza treat, box of candy, or money among others. The entire workshop can take several full days or two to three weeks of single class periods.

167- T   (Judge/Lists) "Logical Call"

So the students may see if a theme is well organized, have them list or underline all the key words or ideas which reflect the point of each paragraph. Usually these will be subjects, verbs, and sometimes completers (complements). If they seem logical when read in order (without the rest of the sentence), chances are good the paper follows a logical progression. This emphasis on content, in fact, should always precede structure and mechanics.

168- C   (Judge/Models) "Outreach the Teach"

Low ability students are often encouraged to work harder when they can compete against the teacher. When giving an assignment, the teacher offers as an example a paper—not his best work but one including some obvious errors—which he or she wrote on the same assignment. The class is invited to find the errors and to discuss how the paper might have been better. Students can then be challenged to write a paper "better than the teacher's." Having to write the assignment assures the teacher that it is practical and points out possible trouble areas.

169- I   (Judge/Papers) "Backward Words"

This idea cuts down on one of the nastier jobs in evaluating themes—marking misspelled words. Before students hand in their final drafts, have them read their papers backwards. This forces attention to individual words which might be misspelled or typed incorrectly. Reading in reverse, students are not likely to brush over words as in regular proof- or copyreading, since they are not caught up in the message. Armed with dictionaries, students look up words for meaning and spelling, eliminating many errors the teacher would have to catch.

170- T   (Judge/Papers) "Correctshuns"

These four suggestions are useful to keep in mind when

"correcting" themes:

Comment but do not correct.
Suggest ways to improve only one (or two) serious weakness(es).
Check introduction and conclusion for effectiveness.
Allow students to exchange papers for additional proofreading.

171- I   (Judge/Papers) "For Trying Out Loud"

Students should be encouraged to catch obvious composition
errors by reading their compositions aloud before handing them
in. Errors in agreement, sentence and paragraph order, and usage
can be found more easily when they are heard, and this clarifies
many problems of poor writing.

172- T   (Judge/Papers) "Neat Trick"

Teachers often complain about not
being able to read student writing.
And, admitted or not, neatness often
biases teacher evaluation. To encourage neatness raise composition
grades on some papers which are
especially neat. After students get
over the initial shock, tell them that
occasionally you will give this extra
credit for very neat papers.

173- T   (Judge/Papers) "Helping Hands"

Peer pressure can be more effective than teacher-nagging when
it comes to improving compositions. Also, students need to
learn the value of criticism as well as to improve their own
abilities to be critical, and with this, peer evaluation helps. In
one method, the teacher assigns a short composition. When
the papers are complete, and with the class seated in rows, each
student hands his paper to the person seated immediately behind; the student in the back seat takes his to the front. Students make all grammatical and spelling corrections directly on
the paper (perhaps with help from a guidesheet as described in
idea 164). Afterwards they write comments about content,
organization, novelty of expression, and coherence. Finally they
assign a letter grade (or two grades—one for structure and one

for content). The teacher then collects the papers and evaluates the work of both the writer and his evaluator. The papers are then returned so effectiveness can be judged. Grades are changed if necessary.

174- I   (Judge/Papers) "Pause That Refreshes"

A long-time standard, this technique is often unused or unstressed. After the student writes the first draft of a composition, he sets it aside while he does some other work such as studying some grammar in which he is weak. Later he will copyread his own paper in a new light and with greater objectivity. Mistakes will be more evident, and the student will be able to revise, using some of the new grammar he has learned.

175- T   (Judge/Papers) "Peering Around"

If time permits, experiment with this process and arrive at some eye-opening results. Locate a student paper, a fairly good one. Make three copies of it. Give them to three cooperative English teachers, asking them to evaluate each paper and assign a letter grade. Give them some criteria such as the chart for idea 164. Even with this base, evaluations may vary considerably if results are typical. Grade the paper yourself to see how you compare with the other three. Meet with the other evaluators. Try to discover reasons for discrepancies. Find out what value judgments they made. It might be the first step in improving evaluation procedures.

176- G   (Judge/Papers) "Picking Prunes"

Teachers frequently stress theme development and overlook the need to prune a paper of its superfluous elements. Students can learn to be more succinct this way. The next-to-final drafts of an assignment (writers' names removed) are exchanged, first with one student and then another. Reviewers are asked to strike out any words, phrases, or sentences which don't support the central issue. Since readers can be more objective, they will find much more padding than the writer. Twice (or more) reviewed, these copies are returned to the writer who will follow most of the acceptable suggestions when writing the final draft.

177- T   (Judge/Papers) "Seeing Red"

Heard at a departmental meeting: "Throw out or give away your

red pens. Fastened together on strings, they make good room
dividers. Using them to evaluate student themes has only fear-
ful results. Red stands for authority, blood, danger, trouble
ahead, and 'Stop!' Such a negative activity never builds rapport.
Modest, inauspicious gray lead heals the paper that 'bleeds.'
Think about it!"

178- T   (Judge/Papers) "Two For One"

Some students have never had a successful experience in writing
a composition. Teachers should try to do something about it,
such as giving two grades instead of one. Above a separating line,
place a letter grade (worth one-third the total) which reflects
the format and structure (grammar, spelling, usage, and mechanics). Beneath the line place the grade for content and appropriateness to assignment (worth two-thirds the total grade). The
content thus gets major emphasis as it should, for without anything to say the student doesn't have much to polish anyway.
More important, the slow student gets credit for his ideas even
if he can't spell or punctuate. Remind students which grade is
which by comparing the line to the deck of an ocean freighter.
The heaviest part—the cargo (the content of theme) is stored
below deck. The superstructure (form) of the ship—how well
it is decorated, painted, and polished—is above deck or above
the line when a composition is assigned a grade.

179- I   (Restructure/Paragraphs) "On the Flip Side"

In a combined literature and composition evaluation exercise,
students rewrite paragraphs, aiming for opposite or vastly
different effects by changing tragic scenes to comic, or highly
emotional writing to objective, cold descriptions. Besides assist-
ing the student in checking on various composition techniques,
this approach encourages a deeper study of both literature and
composition.

POETRY

180- C   (Judge/Models) "Saw a Flaw"

Near the end of a unit in which students have been studying
poems and learning to write them, include with some student-
written poems several from published authors—without telling

the class, of course. Then have the class spend time judging all
the poems as if they came from students. Besides seeing that
even published authors have flaws in their work, students will
discover ways to improve their own.

181- C   (Restructure/Models) "Corner on Poetry"

To see if they understand the elements of poetry, students
must try writing some. This activity may be approached either
through the idea of form (sonnet, haiku, blank verse, and so
on) or through the style of poets such as Bob Dylan or Langston
Hughes, using their kind of imagery, meter, and subject matter.
The student poetry is then read and discussed in an informal
setting, as in the teacher's living room, at the school cafeteria
with soft drinks, under the tree by the stream behind the
school, or in any relaxing place. This added effort will heighten
the feeling that poetry is something very special.

182- I   (Restructure/Music) "Lyrically Yours"

Each student copies the lyrics of several popular songs. Some
of these can be placed on overhead transparencies for study
(and singing, of course). This is a good evaluative poetry writing
exercise for slower groups. Songs are poems, yet many students
do not realize this. Perhaps if they did, poetry would be more
popular with youth than it frequently is.

CHAPTER
4

APPLICATION

ARGUMENTATION

183-G (Solve/Role Playing) "Hairy Harry"

Involvement in group dynamics is an interesting, effective way to learn communication skills. A little practice in group problem solving and role playing would be beneficial to any class. Here is one model situation: "You are a forty-year-old parent of a seventeen-year-old son who wears his hair shoulder length. You must convince Harry to cut his hair." The class functions in three or four groups. Each group is permitted only one solution.

184-G (Speak,Write/Critiques) "De Bait"

Plan a panel discussion of a literary work such as *King Lear*. Arrange a debate so students can argue pro or con on well-defined topics about the play. Mimeograph some of Samuel Johnson's adverse critical judgments. Johnson felt the play taught an immoral lesson since good people like Cordelia and King Lear suffered, and he thought that only wicked characters should be shown suffering. Students might then defend or repudiate Johnson on these points. If the school is well equipped, record or videotape the debate. Ask students to review their own discussions, preferably out of class, and to write a paper explaining who won the debate and why. The remainder of the class takes notes during the panel so they can write similar papers.

185- I   (Write/Journals) "Journalisms"

Students bring a spiral notebook to class each day. The teacher
writes a question on the board—a question which will catch
their attention. Each class member writes at least one paragraph
to answer questions like "Do students have enough freedom in
self-government at this school?" Books can be examined weekly
to check progress. One teacher started by reading every day's
assignment but later just read randomly making comments, but
not correcting usage. If a weakness persisted, he would write a
comment indicating a section in the grammar book which might
help remedy the error.

DESCRIPTION

186- I   (Write/Videotapes) "Let Imagination Rain"

Past experience conditions reactions to new stimuli more
than one realizes. To illustrate, let the class listen to some
familiar taped sound effects: a barking dog, a siren, a bell, a
small electric motor, or a squeaking sound. Students then write
paragraphs on three images they obtained from three sounds.
These can be compared to show the variations among different
students and to discuss why the differences occur.

187- C   (Write/Paragraphs) "Junkie Paragraph"

To obtain a descriptive paragraph
from an unmotivated class, try
this. Bring in a collection of
assorted objects and spread it
out on a table. Be sure you have
some thoughtful inclusions, keeping in mind the interests of
the class. Then have them write a complete and accurate description of one or more of the articles, distinguishing it from the
others by shape, size, texture, color, and so forth. Read some
of the descriptions to the class for discussion.

188- I   (Write/Paragraphs) "Martian Chronicle"

For a challenging way to apply descriptive composition skills,
students write short paragraphs to a visitor from another planet
precisely describing certain everyday objects and sensations:
taste of sugar, smell of an onion, sight of a spoon, sound of a
lowing cow, and so on.

189- I   (Write/Role Playing) "Be a Clock Watcher"

Sometimes the best compositions grow out of the most far-fetched situations. Ask students to pretend they are a clock somewhere in the school. Have them describe what they see and hear. Or they could be a street light, a light bulb (being moved from lamp to lamp), a drop of water, a brick (on a historic building), or an antique candleholder. The possibilities are endless, the results exciting.

190- I   (Write/Topics) "Solve a Weighty Problem"

Students can be motivated to write creatively by such topics as "Describe the opposite of a power pole," or "What is the heaviest object in the world and how could we weigh it?" By the perplexity of the topics, students are forced to think for themselves more than in the usual written assignments.

DRAMA

191–C   (Perform/Skits) "On the Air"

The art of story telling can be fun if the entire class participates. Students like to work on class projects such as short plays and radio skits. Some members can act out a selected story which they have rewritten as a script. With the additional required behind-the-scenes work such as selecting music, producing sound effects, costuming, and set designing, each student gets a chance for expression through interests and talents.

192- I   (Write/Role Playing) "Let's Pretend"

To encourage the use of creativity and imagination, give assignments which promote role playing through writing. Try these: (1) Pretend that you are Lady Macbeth and you keep a diary. Write the five entries just before you commit suicide. (2) A friend of yours has asked how he can better understand Edmond Rostand's *Cyrano de Bergerac.*

EXPOSITION

193- I   (Solve/Themes) "Letting Both Pen and Mind Wander"

Instead of some of the usual "explain this," "compare that," and "contrast these" compositions, suggest students write something pilosophical, to communicate abstract thoughts which they often think about but have never tried to put on paper. In this way the student reveals a lot about himself and his thoughts while he is free to let his mind wander and develop as he struggles with various philosophical inconsistencies and paradoxes.

194- I,C   (Speak/Circulars) "Futuristic Vacation"

Instead of the descriptive exposition "What I Did during My Summer Vacation," have students bring in maps, picture post cards, and brochures of places they visited during the summer. Let the students first discuss them and then write "Where I Would Like to Take My Next Vacation." Be prepared to find some students who did not do anything special. Since there probably will not be time for everyone to report, the demonstration portion of the assignment will be self-limiting.

195- I   (Speak/Library) "Kopy Kats"

Each student selects an author to research for an oral report. This gathering of information helps the student understand what incidents in the author's life affected his writing. A planning conference with each student would be helpful in developing the final report. The exercise provides a variety of experiences: researcher, reporter, critic, writer, and student.

196- I   (Write/Essays) "Gradual Take-over"

To penetrate the built-in defenses many students have against expressing their true feelings in major papers, give five-minute written assignments on simple topics: "My father always. . . ." On Mondays I. . . ." "It disgusts me to. . . ." Saturate students with these ungraded papers almost daily for several weeks; stress freedom of expression instead of form. Then gradually slide into longer, more meaningful, graded assignments. No longer will students be so "pen-tied." The teacher also gets good insights about students.

197- I   (Write/Essays) "My Ideal"

Students usually admire and try to imitate someone. Or perhaps they have read about someone with whom they would like to trade places. Suggest a short essay on the subject "If I Could Be Anybody. . . ."

198- I   (Write/Essays) "Powerful Topic"

Here is a composition topic which will always be current. "If you had the power for a day, how would you help the world?" Limits might be set on length or on ideas.

199- I   (Write/Essays) "Snow Job"

A successful essay topic must be relevant to each student's life. With this in mind, try some of the following: Wait for a blizzard— one of those days when cars and buses are stranded and when spring seems decades away—then assign a personal essay called "Snow News Is Good News" or any clever title. To stimulate the thinking process, give a few sample sentences describing how you reacted to the unscheduled vacation—or if you live south of the snow belt how a hurricane may have affected your life. Anxious moments about college admission, admission tests, term papers, athletics, girls, boys, and after-school employment can also become interesting essays. Students generally perform with extra effort if they can write about something important to themselves.

200- I   (Write/Interviews) "Friendly Compositions"

An interesting topic for the uninterested might be biographical sketches that students write about each other. Set up interviews between students, provide guidelines on types of questions to ask. Assign a short biographical sketch based on the interview. Urge that they include such items as the student's position among other siblings, a humorous childhood incident, interests, ambitions, likes and dislikes. Completed essays are read aloud so that students can guess the subject of each without being told the name. Play up interest by playing down the errors. Also consider having students write their own autobiographical sketch, exchange papers anonymously, and guess the identity of the author.

201- I   (Write/Letters) "Dear Gabby"

A student's personal problems hold the key to subjects of real interest. Concerns of any type are submitted in letter form as if to an advice-giving columnist. Everyone then draws someone else's selection and writes an answer to it in the fashion of "Dear Abby." Some of the best combinations can be duplicated for closer observation.

202- I   (Write/Movies, Television) "Way to Get a Star"

Sometimes what students watch on television or at the local theatre doesn't get enough attention at school, particularly in composition applications. Students usually do well when writing descriptions of their favorite television or film character or presenting an argument on why everyone should or should not see a particular show or film.

203- I   (Write/Television) "Humor Us"

Students are asked to watch their favorite TV comedy and to write a review giving the reasons for their choice. They can illustrate their points by describing a particularly humorous part. The papers can then be used for a discussion on humor which, in turn, leads into humor found in the literature they are studying.

204- I   (Write/Topics) "Artistrick"

Looking for a different approach for a writing assignment? Ask the students: "If you could create one of the world's great paintings, literary works, musical compositions, or scientific discoveries, which would you choose? Describe, then tell why you would like to have been the creator." One student, for example, wrote he would have liked to be talented like Rubens so he could save a fortune painting his own buxom nudes rather than buying girly magazines. Facetious or not, the paper explaining this in some detail was his best effort all year.

205- I   (Write/Topics) "Fur or Agin?"

Give theme topics which require students to qualify and substantiate opinions. Allow a choice of topics which must be either supported or refuted, topics about which students normally have strong feelings: drivers' age limits, extending the school year, integrating races and eliminating sexism in American schools and institutions, and many concerns about parental control and family responsibility. Other topics could deal with high school football games, pierced ears, pep rallies, voting and politics, student rights, and many more—just ask the class. The assignment calls forth enthusiasm but, at the same time, requires a certain objectivity not normally used in taking sides.

206- I   (Write/Topics) "Take Off"

Weekly the teacher provides a takeoff point for "thought time."

This takeoff point should be something that does not lend itself
to a preconceived idea. For example, the teacher may hold up a
battered golf shoe, or write a word on the board such as "time-
lessness." Then the students spend a half hour writing down
their thoughts on this subject. At the end of a six-week term
they hand in a composition based on *one* of the takeoff points.
The composition will be evaluated by the teacher, but it is up
to the student to ponder over each weekly paper deciding which
one to turn in.

JOURNALISM

207- C   (Construct/Magazines) "Maga-Scene"

A rather exciting way to culminate the year's work in English is
to have the class create a year-in-review classroom magazine. It
should include samples of each major activity covered during the
year, some of the samples prepared especially for this magazine.
Naturally the duties must be spread around so everyone has a
part: editor, coeditor, advertising manager, artists, layout people,
copyreaders, and proofreaders. Some students might also help
provide variety by writing horoscopes, jokes, letters to the editor,
advice columns, and by drawing cartoons and comics. The students can place their contributions on hectograph masters so the
magazine can be duplicated and copies distributed to each class
member. This activity works best if the class has completed a
study of various periodicals.

208- G   (Construct/Magazines) "Staff Competition"

As an outgrowth of a media unit, the class can publish a potpourri youth magazine. They divide into special interest groups:
literature, sports, current events, science, homemaking, puzzles,
or entertainment, for instance. If this project is introduced early
enough, students have a chance to research information in their
area, to study how to write it up effectively, and to practice by
writing several sample articles. Finally, they would meet in their
groups to choose one article from each student's collection.
This magazine differs from the typical literary magazine because
it doesn't cater to the literary "geniuses." Seeing their names in
print gives the "just average" writer the valuable encouragement
rarely found in conventional composition approaches.

209- T   (Write/Magazines) "Free-lancing Freely"

Next time you want to switch from the humdrum list of theme topics, try this: The editors of _____ magazine (whatever is popular and current) have asked you to write an article for a future issue, one featuring America's youth, their hopes, fears, interests, and attitudes toward themselves and American society. Thus, as a representative of this youth, give your views to the magazine's readers. For example, what can students do to conserve natural resources? (For an alternative assignment, one student can interview another on the same subject.)

210- I   (Write/Newspapers) "Start the Presses"

After a concentrated study of newspapers, and following some news article or feature-writing assignments, let the class produce their own newspaper—even modeled after an actual publication such as the *Chicago Sun-Times.* Depending upon finances, the publishing methods may range from a simple dittoed, Xeroxed, or mimeographed version to one produced in the school or community printshop. One class persuaded a newspaper publisher to let them put together a special insert section featuring the school. Whatever the medium, there will be much to do for everyone from the class artist to the zodiac expert. Also see idea 135.

211- G   (Write/Paragraphs) "Select Activity"

Students apply knowledge of past composition studies. They divide into groups, each to concentrate on one type of written discourse. For example, one group devises a paragraph in the form of an editorial. Another writes a humorous paragraph like those on a newspaper feature page. The best approach is to have each student submit to his group a paragraph of his best writing. These are circulated to locate the best in the group.

212- I   (Write/Pictures) "Loud Report"

Around the room place magazine illustrations which pose some form of confrontation activity. Students assume the role of reporter and write a news article as if the picture were to be used to illustrate the article.

LETTER WRITING

213- I   (Write/Letters) "Dear Napoleon"

Letter writing exercises need not be boring. In this approach, students write imaginary letters to famous people of the past, telling them about life in the present. They must keep in mind the appropriateness of the subject matter to the recipient. Students are thus challenged to use only significant details—a good concern in any type of writing.

214- I   (Write/Letters) "Dear Peer"

Junior high or middle school students find this an interesting way to begin a unit on letter writing. Each writes an informal letter telling about his interests, activities, and personality, for instance, knowing only that a student of the opposite sex in another class will receive it. Students sign their names to the letters they write. In the second phase, each student receives a reply from the person who got his letter. Then he writes a second letter including a little more about himself and a short criticism of his correspondent's letter. This procedure continues for about three rounds. The first letter is then compared with the last to see if there are any changes in the letter writing techniques.

215- I   (Write/Role Playing) "Mail Can't Fail"

A simple letter-writing assignment can be much more interesting if students write under pseudonyms, perhaps assuming roles of contemporaries of literary characters recently studied. They first write a letter and later respond to a different letter drawn at random. Or roles can be drawn for each of two correspondents. Some successful letters of the past included these pairs: Hamlet and Ann Landers, Huckleberry Finn and Holden Caulfield, Mao Tse-tung and the Maharishi Mahesh Yogi, Joe Namath and Cassius (Mohammed Ali) Clay, Eldridge Cleaver and Alice Cooper, Matt Dillon and Shane.

MEDIA

216- I   (Write/Paragraphs) "Student Bestimonials"

To add interest to what could be a rather routine media unit, suggest that each student write a short paragraph endorsing a

favorite magazine. Select the best ones and type them to be
posted with the student's picture (preferably in a hall display
case). Besides adding a little life to a usually dull display area,
the technique can be the preliminary to a magazine subscription
drive to raise money for the school. In one tenth-grade class the
best entries were actually sent to the magazine publishers, and
one student's picture and "testimonial" were published in the
magazine's house organ. Another student and her teacher were
awarded a year's subscription to the magazine. This is additional
evidence that more can be accomplished when writing for a purpose than writing for a grade.

NARRATION

217-I   (Perform/Role Playing) "On Being a Character"

This idea works particularly well in middle school or junior high
classes. Students think of a type of person—pilot, queen, con-
gressman, policewoman, and so forth—they would like to be.
Then they write and present a monologue of that person. Not
only does this approach give students a feel for the monologue
technique, but it also helps them understand the character.

218-C   (Perform/Role Playing) "Talk It Up"

To synthesize skills in writing dialogue, students use the talk-
show format and imagine conversations between strong personalities who are sometimes in conflict: the school principal and a
student, Satan and a prominent evangelist preacher, a political
conservative and a radical, a feminist and an antifeminist, or a
hawk and a dove. The best of these products could also be presented live to the class, preferably extemporaneously.

219-G,I   (Write/Books) "Book Makers"

As a culminating activity in a unit on story writing, upper classes
might write short stories for use by elementary children. This
project begins with reading and studying stories for young children. Individuals or groups would then choose plots and appropriate characters. Once written, the stories could be duplicated
and made into books with student-designed covers. This would
be a good project to provide material for tutoring slow readers
in elementary school.

220- G   (Speak/Interviews) "This Is Your Life"

Narrative writing can be both easy and difficult. Choosing the right subject will make the task easier. A particularly motivating way to locate subjects is for students to interview each other. The one interviewed relates an incident from earlier life (tragic, humorous, anything). The interviewer then converts the incident to a narrative composition. Shared with the class, these papers will be interesting because the main characters are well-known to the class.

221- G   (Write/Books) "Novel Way"

Assign a plot or have the class choose one together. Then everyone writes a chapter of the novel. Assign specific areas, or if the plot allows (as does a biography), students may write whatever they want. The latter approach sometimes results in a humorous product which can stimulate discussion on integrating plots, character development, rising and falling action, and so on. The finished manuscript could be duplicated and stapled so that each class member gets a copy.

222- C   (Write/Games) "Added Attraction"

With an especially creative class, try a progressive narrative. The teacher (or a student) starts it by writing the introductory paragraph. Each student takes a turn writing successive paragraphs directly related to the one just before. The subject must be broad enough to elicit responses from everyone. Since the finished composition will be on display, students should be specially aware of good writing skills. After several attempts, the class could select the most enjoyable or creative narrative.

223- I   (Write/Models) "Can You Top This?"

A college student shares this idea. "One of the most successful and worthwhile high school assignments ever handed me concerned the short story. Having completed a unit on Poe, we were asked to write the beginning paragraphs of a short story of our own creation. The stories were to be written in the style of Poe but were to supply only the main characters and the beginning of the plot. They were then exchanged for completion. The results were fantastic. The assignment was effective in two major ways: (1) providing an excellent, individualized culminating activity for the unit and (2) allowing the students to unconsciously express a great many personal feelings and emotions."

224- I   (Write/Movies) "To Be Continued"

Use a filmed story to stimulate writing by stopping the film at a crucial point and having students complete the story by themselves. Some short animated films such as "Moonbird" and "The Hole" lend themselves to such an assignment. Other good short films include "An Occurrence at Owl Creek Bridge" and other Ambrose Bierce short stories: "Chickamauga" and "The Mockingbird."

225- I   (Write/Movies) "Sound Off"

As a project for advanced writers, gather several short film strips or short five- or ten-minute movies, nature shorts, or cultural bits. Turn off the sound and show them to the class. Show films several times while students write their own script or narration. Then play the sound track and the film. This can be used in conjunction with narration or description as well as preparation for writing their own scripts for film, videotape, or audiotape.

226- I   (Write/Mysteries) "ABC Mystery"

Most students love good mysteries. Here is a plan to encourage them to write their own. Each student places any person's name beginning with "A" on a slip of paper, a place that starts with "B" on another, and an object starting with "C" on the third. Scramble all slips and have each child pick one slip from each set. They may come up with "Albert," "Baltimore," and "car." Now they must write a good short mystery incorporating these words as key ideas.

227- C,I   (Write/Paragraphs) "Emote Chance"

The great amount of material to be covered during a semester does not allow much time for creative writing. Paragraph assignments help take up the slack. Each student writes a narrative paragraph expressing an emotion—his reaction to some condition in his life, e.g., a catastrophe, a joy, a sadness. Later, hand out duplicated copies containing all the paragraphs. Spend at least one period discussing them. This activity can be coordinated with the study of short stories.

228- I   (Write/Paragraphs) "Words to Write By"

Write a series of words on the board such as: "boy," "crying," "train," "bridge," "water," "swim." Each student writes one or more paragraphs incorporating these words into an idea or story.

229- I   (Write/Pictures) "Cut Ups"

Mount pictures and illustrated ads from magazines (color or not) on colored construction paper, using color which reflects the mood. Give one to each student to stimulate his imagination in creating a short story. The picture can become the cover for the story.

230- I   (Write/Puzzles) "Big Finish"

Read the beginning of a short story orally in class—a detective story works well. Stop at an appropriate place so each student can write his own ending. Read some of these new endings aloud before the author's version is revealed, pointing out the need to maintain unity and credibility.

231- C   (Write/Short Stories) "Noteworthy Idea"

For the younger student, the "note in the bottle" gives rise to some very creative short stories. The teacher (or a student) brings in an interestingly shaped bottle and explains that there is a mysterious note inside and asks students to write a story on how the note got there and what it says. The next day (or several days later) after some of the stories have been read, discussed, and offered as models, the bottle is opened and the note read. It, of course, says in rhyme or some other clever way that the bottle "has a meaning which is different to everyone."

232- I,C   (Write/Short Stories) "Your Own First Person"

Each student writes a short story in which he is a character. It

could be realistic or a fantasy. The important idea is that it be
an exercise in self-awareness and an outlet for expression after a
student looks at himself seriously. The finished product would
be enhanced by a montage or visual aid presentation.

233- I   (Write/Tales) "Sister/Brother Goose"

After reading and discussing fairy (or tall) tales, students in
junior high like to write their own, illustrating them if desired.
Tales can be given a modern setting. Have the best ones duplicated, bound, and shared with children in the lower grades or
with patients at a children's hospital.

OVERVIEW

234- C   (Solve/Papers) "Communicate by Choice"

Too often English teachers stress writing as though it is the only
means of conveying a thought. Students who say they "can't
write" often feel frustrated and consider themselves academic
failures. Allow the students options in methods of communicating their term papers. Suggest alternative ways to solve the
problem—cartooning, painting or drawing, writing poetry or a
play, taking pictures, recording a tape, and other approaches.

235- I   (Write/Authorities) "Tale of Two Test Tubes"

How do you motivate a student whose interests lie in areas
completely outside of English, e.g., math and physics? Show such
a student that learning how to write can benefit him regardless
of field. When such a student must write a paper on a class novel,
let him pick his own related topic. Allow him to focus on the
social, historical, or scientific background of the novel's period,
depending on which area interests him most. It is far better to
receive a well-written paper on medicine in the late eighteenth
century than a weakly written critique of *Silas Marner*.

236- I   (Write/Bulletin Board) "Composition Competition"

Many state or national writing competitions arise during the
school year. Find out about as many of them as possible. List
them on a bulletin board. Offer extra incentive to anyone who
submits something for a contest, or give a class assignment from
which the best products can be turned in as contest entries.

237-I   (Write/Essays) "Familiar Writing"

A student should learn to write confidently about people and situations which confront him daily. Assign a brief in-class essay written either humorously, ironically, or satirically but which depicts a typical English class period. It may even be a character sketch of the teacher or another student. Read the essays in class, discussing their realistic qualities and appropriateness.

238-G   (Write/Essays) "Write Group"

Let the entire class participate in writing an essay on a popular topic. Divide the class into groups of four or five. Let them meet for two or three hours a week—possibly a half hour at a time—to decide their approach to their portion of the assigned topic. Then after the sections are completed, each group reads its contribution in the order of normal topic development. This approach can be varied by allowing each group to write the total topic and then comparing results. As a fringe benefit, working in groups helps the shy student overcome his problem.

239-I   (Write/Journals) "Getting to Know You"

The student journal remains an effective way to help remove writing inhibitions or to expand composition subjects. Sometimes a spiral notebook is used to collect a minimum number of weekly entries, as few as two or three so it won't be a chore. The journal concept encourages collecting ideas, observations, and opinions and makes students more aware of what is happening to them and to others. If students occasionally write something too personal, they should indicate this but should not use this as an excuse to avoid writing anything. Keep journals for a month or so. If the class is benefitting, continue. Naturally, the journals should not be corrected. Spot checks help evaluate the technique and assess the growth in expression and self-confidence. To increase student support, the teacher might also keep a journal to be shared.

240-I   (Write/Papers) "Eradicating the Bugs"

One way to solve the term paper problem is to urge students to write about issues which really concern them personally. Use topics such as "What's bugging you?" Urge them to write about something they think is very wrong in class, in school, or in society. They must give convincing reasons why the situation is wrong and then suggest ways to solve the problem. This should not only generate enthusiasm to write, but it should also force the students to reflect seriously on ways to improve their environment.

241- T   (Write/Papers) "Pen Names"

Invite students to use pseudonyms for their composition papers. This serves four purposes: (1) promotes impartial grading, (2) encourages creativity, (3) eliminates embarrassment, and (4) provides opportunity for fun in considering some particularly unusual names, e.g., Wilamina Shapespeer.

242- C   (Write/Papers) "Wet Composition"

Devote a class period to a surprise writing assignment to stimulate creativity. Bring in an object such as a half-filled glass of water. The class writes about it in any form, poetic to scientific. This results in a variety of themes ranging from the chemical aspects of water to space-age fiction.

243- I   (Write/Paragraphs) "On the Head of a Pin"

One student reported that the greatest composition exercise ever assigned her was when, as a seventh grader, she was asked to write one short paragraph on a single and very limited subject such as: "My Mother's Hair," "My Father's Nose," "The Color Red," "A Cow's Horn." A classmate, she recalled, produced a brilliant piece entitled "The Varied Virtues of an Ordinary Straight Pin."

244- I,G   (Write/Pictures) "Captured Captions"

The bulletin board can help students locate good topics. Pictures of varied subjects are posted minus captions. Students, either individually or as a group project, write their own captions which can be humorous or serious and should lend themselves to much broader themes. Try these:

> *Picture:* Cartoon of Snoopy hopping over croquet wickets.
> *Caption:* "That reminds me. I did a *wicked* thing today."
> *Theme idea:* Personal experience; world problem.

Picture: Full-color illustration of small forest.
Caption: "I think that I shall never see...."
Theme idea: Description of trees in various seasons: exposition
on conserving natural resources; discussion of how trees help man.

245- G   (Write/Talks) "Quality, Not Quantity"

For most people, it is easier to communicate a thought or an
emotion by speaking than by writing. The teacher, therefore,
should encourage frequent short summary-type paragraphs
emanating from short talks. What one student has to say orally
is copied (or recorded and then copied) by another student,
then read and analyzed—changed if necessary. How it is said is
more important than how much is said. Once students have
mastered the paragraph technique, they will be better equipped
to write papers of any length. Some students would probably
rather write diaries which are not read by others but which also
help reduce writing inhibitions. See also idea 239.

246- I   (Write/Topics) "Pull, Not Push"

Some students should not be pushed into class writing assignments but rather be given an independent project. They are
more likely to motivate themselves under such conditions. They
may write poetry, short stories, novels, skits, plays, or simply
copy articles from books or magazines. Writing in a journal may
also help. Most, even the very slow students, would prefer to
rely on their own ingenuity and, thereby, find writing worthwhile, even fun.

247- I   (Write/Topics) "Way-out Topics"

To stimulate more imaginative writing, get away from stereo-
typed topics such as "My Favorite Pet," "What I Saw on the
Way to School," "My Favorite Relative," ad nauseum. Offer
these titles instead: "Green," "Black," "Square," "780," "Yes,"
"No," "Cube," "665-2698," "Time," "Friday," or "Can't."
The list is endless. After the grumbling has subsided, ask students
to sit quietly and think for five or ten minutes before writing.
After several therapeutic sessions like this, imagination and
creativity begin to emerge. Some students never get beyond the
"green is the color of the grass" stage, but most results are excellent.

POETRY

248- I   (Write/Games) "Ballad-Ears"

After a unit on the *Odyssey* or another epic, students convert
the idea to a short ballad, applying their knowledge of that technique. Conduct a contest for the best ballad. Duplicate the
entire set so each student receives the collection.

SYNTAX

249- C   (Write/Sentences) "Pass Keys"

Do you start simply enough when you assign compositions?
Sentences are also miniature compositions. Give two key words
such as *soldier moaned* or *brakes screeched.* Have students write
sentences telling where, how, and why the soldier moaned or the
brakes screeched.

250- C   (Write/Sentences) "Sentence Sense"

Try this as an early composition approach: tell students to write
a sentence which will make a reader feel cold, hot, dirty, even
nauseated. Or tell them to write a noisy sentence, or a sweet
sentence, or a slimy sentence. Of course, in all instances, they
cannot use the words "cold," "hot," "dirty," "noisy," "sweet,"
or "slimy." This activity allows free-rein outlets for previously
studied writing concepts.

PART 2

grammar/language

grammar/language

INTRODUCTION

Chapter 5
Dialect 81
Linguistics 82
Mechanics 85
Overview 86
Semantics 91
Spelling 92
Syntax 93
Usage 94
Vocabulary 96
Words 99

EVALUATION

Chapter 7
Dialect 119
Mechanics 119
Overview 120
Semantics 123
Spelling 123
Syntax 126
Usage 128
Vocabulary 129
Words 134

DELIBERATION

Chapter 6
Dialect 103
Linguistics 103
Mechanics 105
Overview 105
Semantics 107
Spelling 108
Syntax 108
Usage 112
Vocabulary 114
Words 115

APPLICATION

Chapter 8
Overview 137
Syntax 138
Usage 138
Vocabulary 139
Words 139

CHAPTER
5

INTRODUCTION

DIALECT

251-C   (Discover/Lists) "Linguistic Insecurity"

Distribute a list of familiar words which may be pronounced correctly at least two different ways. Alongside each word are the numbers 1 and 2. Inform the class that you will give two pronunciations of the listed word. Instruct students to circle the number of the pronunciation they believe is correct and then to check the one they would actually use. Words such as "tomato," "aunt," "either," "vase," "root," and "route" are used. Then ask the class to count the number of discrepancies between the pronunciation they thought was correct and that which they like to use. Now tell the class that both pronunciations are correct. This exercise reveals the variety and flexibility of American regional and social dialects as well as the "prestige" often associated with certain pronunciations.

252-C   (Listen/Audiotapes) "Where Y'all From?"

With the assistance of other teachers and selected students who come from various parts of the nation or the world, tape record some passages being read in natural dialects. Such activity provides motivation for introducing ethnic and regional dialects. It also encourages acceptance of those who speak differently. If funds are available, purchase dialect records which the school librarian can locate.

253-T   (Listen/Talk) "Add a Second Language"

In a class where many students speak ethnic or regional dialects not accepted by society in general, the teacher's attitude and approaches toward acceptable spoken English are keys to one's teaching success or failure. Convincing students that learning to speak conventional English will help them in future job interviews and employment is not simple and sometimes not sufficient. Try to instill the idea that a nonstandard dialect is perfectly acceptable among family, friends, and in most informal occasions. At the same time suggest that standard English is a "second language"—the way to write and speak when formality is required or when there must be no chance for misinterpretation. Ask them to listen for language differences when popular radio and television announcers and even teachers are not on the job. Foreign language teachers could suggest ways to teach standard English as a second language.

254-C   (Observe/Demonstrations) "Why Can't I Be Sayin' Like How I Think?"

Introduce language differences through copies of various dialects found in print. Include geographical, ethnic, professional, and popular vocabulary in your examples. Point out similarities and differences between the dialects and standard English. Let the students do a unit on dialects or present a skit to illustrate dialectical concerns.

LINGUISTICS

255-T   (Discover/Definitions) "A Noun is a Noun is a . . ."

Instead of identifying nouns as "a word naming a person, place, thing, or idea," try this: Any word to which either *s* or *'s* can be added is a noun. Develop similar linguistic definitions for other parts of speech, particularly those which take various inflected endings. If you can't think of any, consult any modern grammar book.

256- C (Discover/Instructions) "Classy Words"

Grouping parts of speech could be the first step in learning them. Call nouns, verbs, adjectives, and adverbs "form class words" (words which carry meaning by themselves). Sometimes they are identified by the less technical term "full words," i.e., full of meaning. Then call pronouns, auxiliaries, prepositions, adjective and adverb qualifiers, conjunctions, and determiners (a, an, the, each, some, this, that) "structure words," sometimes called "empty words" because they do not carry meaning. Students will arrive at parts of speech less traumatically if two types are stressed instead of the usual eight or nine.

257- C (Discover/Mixed Media) "Great Grammarian Guru"

Grammar often becomes boring if confined to a set of pre-scribed textbook rules and exercises. To help solve this problem, teach grammar in much the same way as chemistry. Let the students discover the rules themselves, pragmatically, by listening to the speech of their parents, friends, and teachers, and by ex-amining the grammar used in newspapers and books. With proper direction, the students can uncover and eventually phrase all those rules from the text. Moreover, they will be much more likely to use rules they make for themselves than those of the Great Mystery Grammarian.

258- T (Discover/Self) "Built-in Grammar Systems"

Here are several reminders that experienced teachers generally suggest to those preparing to teach grammar: (1) Most essentials of a linguistic system are learned by native speakers before ado-lescence; (2) except for certain structures more common to writing than to speech, the average teen-ager uses all the major grammatical resources in day-to-day conversation; (3) most grammar vocabulary is a convenience enabling people to talk about and improve oral and written speech.

259- C (Discover/Sentences) "Quin Ud Fungle Srip?"

To introduce structure, make up nonsense sentences such as, "Ni twindle punged frackly." Ask basic questions about the sentence such as: What is the subject? What is the verb? How can you tell? Have students suggest word substitutions to make a meaningful sentence. This illustrates that in every sentence the same elements are relatively constant both in position and in-flected endings.

260- C   (Listen/Paragraphs) "Whatzit Say?"

Introduce punctuation by dictating a mispunctuated or un-
punctuated paragraph. Many will be unable to take the dicta-
tion because of the inherent problem of incorrect or no voice
modulation. Finally, hand out a duplicated copy of what was
read. Discuss its punctuation with the class; compare with
their own.

261- C   (Listen/Talk) "Pause That Inflexes"

Instead of memorizing myriads of
rules, students learn punctuation
by intonation patterns. In speech,
a pause may denote the need for a
comma in writing. Raising the voice
at sentence endings signals a question mark; lowering, a period; and
extra force, the exclamation mark.
By this method students soon understand the "why" of punctuation.

262- C   (Listen/Talk) "Po-unctuation"

When the class is listening to poetry being read aloud, suggest
they note places where punctuation is needed, particularly as
based on voice inflection. Later, then, they will be able to
choose a poem, record it, and determine what kind of punctuation is needed where, and why.

263- C   (Observe/Models) "Patterns for Saying"

If students can learn five simple basic sentence patterns, they
can easily move to transformations of them. They do so whenever they speak. The following skeletons can be repatterned
and fleshed out through the various forms of modification.
(Different linguists will have varying labels for these patterns.)

    I.   Subject / Verb (S / V)
   II.   Subject / Verb + Direct Object (S / V + DO)
  III.   Subject / Verb + Indirect Object + Direct Object
        (S / V + IO + DO)
  IV.   Subject / Verb + Predicate Nominative (S / V + PN)
   V.   Subject / Verb + Predicate Adjective (S / V + PA)

Provide a chart with these formulas pictured. Add some illustrative sentences as reference when students write. Refer to the chart when similar sentences occur in the literature.

264- C   (Observe/Television) "TV Test Pattern"

Except for face-to-face communication, television is the most abundant source of linguistic experiences for today's student. For an introduction to the social and economic values of standard English, students can observe the differences between the speech patterns of various television characters and, simultaneously, note corresponding differences in their professions, status, and dress.

265- C   (Read/Books) "Sensible Nonsense"

Use Lewis Carroll's "Jabberwocky" to illustrate built-in language signals—a structuralist idea. Although the words are nonsensical, their positions and inflected endings indicate the part of speech and the function they serve. Students can also create their own nonsense stories in the manner of Carroll.

MECHANICS

266- T   (Observe/Cartoons) "Visual Education"

A way to vitalize grammar, especially for younger children, is to personify or animate essential elements. Bring in cartoons illustrating punctuation. The period is a "traffic cop" who makes us stop. A comma is a "snake" which causes us to pause. A question mark is a fat person whose diet we question. An exclamation point is a hypodermic syringe—ouch! These mnemonic devices usually gain the students' interests and motivate them to create their own.

267- C   (Observe/Displays) "Comma-dy of Errors"

Rules for use of the comma or any other punctuation mark can be taught in more creative ways than from a textbook. Try one or several of these approaches: posters, mobiles, slogans, graffiti, cartoons, or skits. By providing channels for creative talents, a teacher can help students teach each other.

268- C   (Read/Models) "Write or Wrong"

Dramatize the importance of punctuation for a correct interpretation of a sentence by placing on the chalkboard models
which illustrate the point. For example: "He lost his wife not
only his wealth." "He lost his wife not, only his wealth."

OVERVIEW

269- T   (Discover/Papers) "Write Start"

The best motivation to study grammar is for students to see
the need in their own writing. At the beginning of the term,
assign a simple composition. From that, inventory the kinds
of grammatical and language errors made. Stress these during
the year instead of the typical bookish approach. The study
of grammar evolves most naturally out of composition.

270- T   (Discover/Plans) "Program in a Nutshell"

In planning grammar or language lessons, select experiences
which allow students to manipulate language, to learn how and
why language affects themselves and others, and to learn how
language and words change. The emphasis must be on experiences *with* language rather than *about* language. For average
students, the vocabulary of grammar is best limited to those
aspects which help describe strengths and weaknesses in writing
and speaking. Superior students could be urged to study in more
depth, but less able students should have little grammar study
which is not thoroughly functional, certainly little, if any,
memorizing rules and technical terms.

271- I   (Discover/Tutoring) "Teach Me and I'll Teach You"

Students can learn effectively from other students. Put this
theory into practice by allowing each student to be a specialist
in one grammatical or mechanical area. When writing their
own papers, or analyzing other people's, students consult with
the "specialist" who deals in his specific problem. Learning
from peers is often more lasting than receiving information
from the teacher.

272- T   (Listen/Discussions) "Your Turn"

If you hear groans when a grammar unit or lesson is announced,

tell the students it's their turn to give you their ideas and suggestions for new and interesting ways to approach the subject.
Devote some time discussing these ideas. Encourage devising
games or adapting existing games. Some of the best classroom
approaches have come from the students themselves. Thirty-five
minds working are bound to think up more ideas than one.

273–C,G (Listen/Papers) "Play It by Ear"

Teach grammar like composition—by sound. Pair off the class.
One student reads another's paper aloud and stops when something sounds incorrect to either. If sentences sound "right," no
correction is needed. Constant stress on perfection stifles the
desire to write or speak in class. Another version of this same
idea is for the teacher to read a passage aloud. Students listen
and write what they hear, including punctuation and spelling.
As writing and speaking become more natural in the classroom
and less traumatic, students will learn "correct English" when
they are ready but only when they discover the need.

274– C (Observe/Skits) "Grammar Upstage"

For those having difficulty learning parts of speech and their
functions, diagramming sentences and memorizing rules usually
do not work. Make it fun! Devise a short skit illustrating what
can happen if certain parts of speech are omitted, overused, or
improperly used. A job interview that goes awry is a popular
choice. Each student participates by being involved with the
grammatical principle which is most difficult for him.

275– T (Read/Books) "Bridge the Gap"

Today's English teacher keeps asking what grammar to teach:
traditional, structural, transformational-generative, or no grammar. For many, the latter seems to be the way out of the confusion. Their rationale, they say, is grammar does not seem to
improve students' written or oral language. Recent research,
however, has brought forth encouragement through the transformational-generative technique of sentence combining. Too
involved for detailing here, sentence combining provides a series
of models and formulas for combining simple thoughts (kernel
sentences) into more sophisticated forms. Compound sentence
structures, modifying phrases and clauses, and other forms of
imbedding are encouraged.

    For some teachers, sentence combining is the answer; for

others, it's getting students to write simple, declarative sentences. Neither the former or latter approaches can be implemented, however, without some teacher preparation. Classroom grammar problems will be settled only by reading and selecting from among the alternatives offered. Check the bibliography in this book.

276- T   (Read/Books) "Mini-text; Maxi-use"

At the beginning of the year, create a booklet which succinctly presents the grammatical strengths and weaknesses common to students at your particular grade level. Accent the positive by including many "correct" student writing samples. If 8½ X 11 and three-hole punched, the booklets could be placed in the students' looseleaf binders. With this handy guide available, students may find it easier to catch mistakes as soon as they happen.

277- C   (Read/Books) "Program Program"

Programmed instruction has become an excellent way to individualize learning. With even the scantiest knowledge of linear or branching programs, the teacher can guide students to produce their own programmed grammar "texts." One part of speech would be sufficient for each program, produced in mimeographed booklets relying mainly on student-written sentences. Half of full pages could bear certain sentence patterns suggested by any symbol system. Students use the remaining pages to paste in examples underlined in paragraphs from advertisements and articles from various media. An occasional picture slipped in will help break up the pages interestingly. One class's booklets will become another class's "text."

278- C   (Read/Books) "The More the Better"

Instead of a single set of grammar books, provide texts from various publishers. Students will enjoy comparing notes on how different authors approach similar problems and use different models. Healthy debates will ensue at times, but grammar lessons assigned en masse out of the same book will hardly be missed.

279- T   (Read/Books) "Theory of Evolution"

In dealing with grammar, students appreciate a nonprescriptive approach. If possible, the teacher and students should do some prior reading in linguistics. Then the following ideas will seem reasonable: (1) Different grammatical structures are appropriate to different situations. (2) A particular grammatical structure is not condemned as long as it gets across the meaning. (3) Words and syntax must be considered and evaluated with a specific situation and audience in mind. (4) The effect of words upon a listener or reader is probably the most important concern in communication. (5) Language and, therefore, grammar constantly change and evolve. (6) People should not be judged negatively because their speech patterns and dialects differ from the standard. (7) Language teaching is a science, not a system of prescribed rules for memorization.

280- C   (Read/Handouts) "Ten Illustrated Tips"

One teacher submits this list of Do's and Do Not's to introduce a few grammatical principles.

1. Use commas only, when needed.
2. Don't use no double negatives.
3. Prepositions are not to end sentences with.
4. Keep your ᵂᵒʳᵏₙₑₐₜ and tidy.
5. Never abbrev.
6. Pronouns must agree with its antecedents.
7. Verbs has to agree with their subjects.
8. Use commas to separate words in a series parenthetical expressions introductory clauses and the like.
9. Examine your work carefully to make sure you have not out any words.
10. While a transcendent vocabulary is laudable, one must nonetheless maintain unceasing surveillance against such loquacious, effusive, voluble verbiage that the calculated objective of the communique emerges ensconced in nebulousness and obfuscation.

281- I   (Read/Models) "Writing Recipes"

Provide a "recipe box" showing applications of each grammatical principle to be taught. Then when students have writing problems, they can refer to the appropriate card and quickly find several easy-to-follow samples. This collection can be garnered from student writing. Whenever the teacher notes a good sample sentence, he provides an index card on which the student can print the model to be used in the file.

282- C   (Read/Paragraphs) "Real World English"

At least a few students think good English is just the teacher's infatuation and it "doesn't count" in out-of-class situations. After teaching paragraph structure, from a source the student needs or respects, duplicate four paragraphs for analysis, three with forced, obvious lapses in unity and organization, and one paragraph which, while well-structured, has glaring errors in spelling, punctuation, and grammar. Ask the students to pick out the one which is best structured. The chances are good most students will notice the obvious errors in the last paragraph and reject it for that reason, not realizing that its organization and content are best of the four. When they realize how small items like spelling, punctuation, usage, and grammar can weaken even the best presentation of ideas, they will also realize the reason for the English teacher's concern.

283- T   (Read/Poems) "Better to Be Anonymous?"

Traditionalist grammarians will enjoy seeing this old poem in print and will, perhaps, use it for teaching parts of speech. Teachers with a more linguistic bent might try to rewrite the poem to meet their labeling preferences.

Couplets on Grammar

Three little words you often see
Are articles—a, an, and the.
A noun's a name of anything,
As school, or garden, hoop, or swing.
Adjectives tell the kind of noun,
As great, small, pretty, white, or brown.
Instead of nouns the pronouns stand:
I think; she sings; you frown; my hand.
Verbs tell of something to be done:
To read, count, sing, laugh, jump, or run.
How things are done the adverbs tell,
As slowly, quickly, ill, or well.
Conjunctions join the words together,
As man and woman, wind and weather.
The preposition stands before
A noun, as in or through the door.
The interjection shows surprise,
as "Oh, how pretty! Ah, how wise!"
The whole are called nine parts of speech,
Which reading, writing, speaking teach.

284- C   (Research/Bulletin Boards) "Can Labels? Yes"

For a mass media or grammar unit bulletin board, students
bring in labels from different products found in their homes.
These are displayed to show one area of communication which
is frequently overlooked. Surprisingly, some have never read
the lists of ingredients on products they eat regularly. It is a
concern because certain products are being charged as injurious
to health.

285- G   (Research/Mixed Media) "Career Care"

Combine career development with learning grammar and language
skills. Collect a variety of published materials from all occupations. Divide class (by special interests perhaps) into groups
to study occupational vocabularies, kinds of subjects written
about, sentence structures, special formats, and so on. Include
published materials from at least five areas: commercial, gov-
ernmental, informational, recreational, and social.

SEMANTICS

286- C   (Discover/Discussion) "What's in a Word?"

A good question for class discussion: Why is it that a noun
never has exactly the same meaning any time it is repeated?
It would be wise for the teacher to ponder this one carefully
before asking the class. A clue, of course, is another question:
Who or what gives meaning to words?

287- I   (Research/Mixed Media) "Linguistic Pollution"

Through a little individual research, students can learn how
society uses language to mold thoughts and sometimes to dis-
tort information. One type of this linguistic "doublespeak"
is euphemism: uplifting certain vocations or moderating un-
pleasant topics. To introduce euphemisms and doublespeak
(doubletalk), have students search newspapers, magazines, and
other resources for words and expressions to add to this list:

Common Terms	*Euphemisms*
hairdresser	beautician
undertaker	mortician
ghetto	inner city
garbage man	sanitation engineer
guard	security officer
slum clearance	urban renewal

SPELLING

288- T   (Discover/Tests) "Spelling Out Spelling Procedures"

Give pretests before teaching any spelling words. This will help determine the words which need emphasizing and which letter combinations are most troublesome. Students who can pass a pretest should receive more challenging lists. The following steps can help anyone learn to spell better:

1. Study only a few words at a time.
2. See the word used in a sentence so the full meaning is understood.
3. Pronounce each word aloud.
4. Study each part of the word: syllables, prefixes, suffixes, and any special letter combinations.
5. Apply appropriate phonetic principles.
6. Copy the word carefully.
7. Write the word from memory.
8. Allow several days to pass; then try rewriting each word from memory.
9. Restudy any troublesome words.
10. Take a posttest on the words studied in the above manner to see which need more work. (To reinforce learning which has already taken place, the words from previous lessons should be included. Also, the words under study should be used in conversation and writing as frequently as possible.)

289- T   (Read/Sentences) "Casting a Spell"

As each word being introduced is dictated, students write it down, spelling it two or three different ways, in a free association manner. They are then permitted to circle the one spelling they consider most accurate. This way the teacher can locate problems which can be anticipated for certain words. The inherent problems can then provide the focus for future study.

290- I　(Research/Models) "Loungeray Dept"

Introduce the need for accurate spelling by asking students to search the business community for misspelled words on signs, particularly hand-lettered messages. Sources are relatively easy to find.

SYNTAX

291- C　(Discover/Sentences) "Chalk One Up"

Instead of using a prepared text, teach language skills with on-the-spot sentences which the class and teacher make up together. For example, the teacher places a sample sentence on the board illustrating an awkward dangling modifier. Example: "This is a book about a little girl whose mother died and had no relatives to stay with." Without any explanation, the class is asked why the sentence is misleading. Ask students for other examples, giving them a chance to write a few on paper. Eventually define the rule of misplaced modifiers. A class secretary records the sentences placed on the board, and at the end of the lesson they are placed on handouts for use as models. If this inductive procedure for exploring grammar were followed periodically, the class would soon compose their own grammar workbook.

292- C　(Discover/Sentences) "Compound It"

Complex and compound sentences can be introduced by using sets of three related simple sentences printed on tag board strips. Students combine them on paper, adding or subtracting words as needed, and then discuss the effect.

293- C　(Listen/Audiotapes) "Sounds of Syntax"

The class listens to a tape of the teacher (or someone else) reading a paragraph from a student's paper, as originally written. Then they hear the same paragraph, rewritten according to the rules of good grammar. Students should follow along using mimeographed copies of both versions of the paragraph. From this, the teacher launches a discussion of why the second version sounds better. This *auditory* and *visual* discrimination exercise enhances learning.

294- I   (Read/Models) "Four Ways Better'

Students reluctant to vary their sentences may not realize
the many ways to do so. Show these problem writers several
related simple sentences and models illustrating ways to
combine or change them: transformation of pattern (passive
to active, for instance); inversion (questions to statements),
expansion (modifiers); and substitution (dependent clause for
an independent then subordinated with another sentence).
Just have students remember the acronym TIES (first letter
of each variation). "This idea TIES in with better writing."

295- I   (Read/Newspapers) "Blank-it Meaning"

Newspapers are loaded with quotations or cartoon captions
which are not complete sentences. Have the students bring in
samples for a good discussion on why and how blank space
can carry meaning.

USAGE

296- C   (Discover/Books) "New and Used Slanguage"

A discussion of slang both current and historical provides
a beginning study of how language changes and how it reflects
the conditions of a society in a particular era. Novels are good
sources for slang.

297- T   (Discover/Discussions) "Errorless Ways"

Ordinarily, the teacher does not interrupt a student's discussion
contribution to point out a grammatical error since this may
destroy the activity's very purpose. If rapport is good, however,
the teacher and students could combine forces to help each
other break poor oral grammar patterns. For instance, a student
who consistently said "This here " was willing to have the class
correct him the moment he used the expression. Soon he began
correcting himself, eventually eliminating the error.

298- T   (Discover/Handouts) "What Art This?"

Pick any appropriate sentence or short passage. To show how
language changes, phrase the sample as it might have appeared
in biblical times, then in other eras of history. Tracing this

development on a handout will help students understand how language has come to us over the centuries.

299- C   (Read/Poems, Dictionaries) "Germinating Words"

Introduce students to the *Oxford English Dictionary* through poetry study. Students look up all the key words found in a short poem. Many different connotations and variations in meaning will emerge from this study.

300- C   (Research/Lists) " 'Ow's Your Hinglish?"

An interesting approach to introducing the nature of language and dialect is to point out vocabulary differences between British and American English. Give the students a list of British nouns (such as the following) and ask them to give or, if necessary, discover the American equivalents:

British	*American*
braces	suspenders
biscuit	cookie
chemist	druggist
lift	elevator
stores	groceries
treacle	molasses
draughts	checkers
bonnet	automobile hood
flickers	movies
telly	TV (television)
lorry	truck
bank raider	bank robber
parking pitch	parking place
dustman	garbage collector
post	mail
portfolio	briefcase
queue	line
tube	subway
tram	streetcar

Students will see that usage is not rigidly standardized but, rather, a matter of location and family history.

301- C   (Research/Mixed Media) "Foreign Slanguage"

Taking a tip from those who teach English as a foreign language, discuss slang as needed at times for concise expression. Explain the universality of slang. Compare slang expressions in some foreign languages to American slang. Recordings, student publications, current novels, and magazines are good sources.

302- G   (Research/Mixed Media) "It's Not Groovy Anymore"

Demonstrate the short life-span of slang and illustrate the danger of using it in formal writing. Divide the class into groups of three or four to research slang jargon from the past. Assign specific time periods for each group (five years ago, ten, fifteen). Old movie magazines, school yearbooks, and interviews with parents are good resources. After compiling a list of slang terms, each group discusses lists for sharing with the class. Be ready for some laughs.

VOCABULARY

303- C   (Discover/Dictionary) "Insight to Sight Words"

Knowing the source and original meaning of a word often helps in understanding the word's present meaning and correct use. The dictionary becomes an indispensable tool for the reading or language student once he understands the functions and uses of etymology. Demonstrate how to trace the origin and development of a word by interpreting the abbreviations and symbols used in the dictionary. Then illustrate how the meaning of a word may be revealed by noting its derivation. For example, flor- flower, floral, florid; ora- oration, oracle. Prepare several lessons exploring the etymology of words. As the dictionary becomes more meaningful and useful, reading and language skills should improve.

304- C   (Discover/Games) "Word Exchange"

Hold a "new word" exchange. Students exchange 3 × 5 cards on which they have written a vocabulary word they have recently learned. When students receive cards, they try to identify the new word and use it in a sentence without looking at the meaning on the back. Each student who does so successfully gets a point for each word. The highest total of points determines the winner.

305- I   (Discover/Sentences, Paragraphs) "Adopt-a-Word"

When beginning to teach composition to younger students, try to give them the feel for a word and its meaning. Ask each student to select a word that he will have to work with until the next paper. He will have to join it to other words, make it into a sentence, add related sentences, and finally construct a paragraph. Building a finished paragraph by this gradual process will increase understanding of the importance of words and provide a better knowledge of how a composition grows. For example, the word might be "occult." After writing a few sentences bordering on definitions and gradually expanding them until he develops an informational paragraph, the student, curiosity aroused, could hardly be prevented from writing an entire report on "occultism."

306- I   (Discover/Tutoring) "PTA/Peer Tutoring Approach"

Vocabulary learning is more enjoyable if students teach one another. Each student selects several words to teach, using pictures, records, collages, and the like for reinforcement. After one student has taught a set, he switches roles with his partner.

307- I, C   (Discover/Tutoring) "Word-a-Day"

Students should assemble their personal word-definition list from words they encounter in reading. Each day throughout the semester one or two students present a new word. They write each word on the board, read a sentence or the context in which the word was found, define the word, and explain its derivation. Vocabulary quizzes may be given using a student-assembled list of words presented during the week.

308- T   (Read/Chalkboard, Words) "Chalk Up a Few"

If any new terms or words are going to be used during the lesson, write them on the board while the students are still getting into their seats. Discuss the words briefly. Besides being a good way for students to acquire new words, this approach eliminates having to clarify new words in the middle of a lecture or discussion.

309- I   (Read/Dictionaries) "Not a Miss Match"

Challenge the students' interest in vocabulary study by giving
them a list of words without definitions. Distribute a separate
sheet containing the definitions. Students match the clues and
words (numbers and letters). Given a week to do this, they
must check various sources to make sure they have correct
matches. This process can build into timed or untimed contests for individuals or teams. One ultimate requirement is to
be able to paraphrase a definition of any word when asked.

310- I   (Read/Dictionaries) "Words in the News"

To increase vocabulary and motivate slow learners, pick a
weekly topic based on student interests, e.g., cars, grooming
hints, or sports, and have them bring in current magazine or
newspaper articles dealing with that topic. From their sources
compile a list of names such as these for the auto topic: Cougar,
Gremlin, Maverick, Wildcat. Each student must find a dictionary definition of one word and write an explanation of why
that particular word is appropriate for a car.

311- C   (Research/Bulletin Boards, Words) "Three for the Book"

Each day post three vocabulary words on a Vocab Section of
the bulletin board. Students copy them as a continuing list in
their notebooks. They must be prepared to define and use
them correctly in sentences on request at any time. A brief
weekly quiz on the fifteen new words will help keep the
slackers on their toes.

312- G   (Research/Dictionaries, Discussions) "Quintet Query"

Divide the class into groups of five. Give each group a list of
words to look up and report on. Instruct each group to use
several dictionaries. They must also consider the use of their
words in various contexts. For two days allow groups to meet
during class. On the third and fourth days each group presents
a fifteen-minute panel discussion revealing what they have
discovered about the words on their lists.

313- G   (Research/Lists) "Synonymously Speaking"

The growth of our system of language hardly knows any
bounds. We can illustrate this by pointing out that Roget's

Thesaurus lists more than 175 synonyms for money, such as: kale, shekels, wherewithal, wampum, jack, chips, gingerbread, and wad. Students will enjoy an exercise listing all the words for some very familiar terms. Turn it into a contest.

314- C   (Research/Lists) "Operation Cooperation"

INTEREST VOCABULARY

SEX MUSIC ART SPORTS

Rather than assign vocabulary lists, let groups devise lists. Each group should contain students with similar interests so the vocabulary study will be profitable, e.g., science buffs, mechanical experts, or literary types. Valuable terms and concepts can be learned if each member finds, defines, and uses the words correctly and trades information with other group members.

315- I   (Research/Lists) "What's New?"

To sharpen students' awareness of the importance of vocabulary, distribute file cards or a small notebook for jotting down new words they encounter. Periodically collect the cards or notebooks to make up a class vocabulary list. This helps assure that new words are connected with experience of the youngsters. Opportunities to use these words in sentences should also be provided.

316- I   (Research/Mixed Media) "Wordy Class"

Increased exposure to mass media, particularly periodicals, broadens vocabulary. Each day students find and cut out one paragraph containing an unknown word. They paste the paragraph in a notebook, above the newly found definition which they have looked up. After several weeks when the notebooks are completed, the class might enjoy sharing their knowledge by comparing lists and sources. Possibly the most frequently appearing words can be placed on a master list for some formal or informal testing later.

WORDS

317- C   (Discover/Games) "Reacting Adverbally"

This game can be used to introduce the value of vivid language in writing. One student leaves the room. While he is gone, the class decides on an adverb which the student must guess, for example, "angrily." When the student has returned and asks questions about the word, the class answers in the manner the adverb denoted, in this case, angrily. This continues until the student guesses the word. Then the turn is passed on. Naturally, the most difficult of all the adverbs to portray is "naturally."

318- C   (Discover/Games) "Whozit?"

Introducing adjectives and their best use need not be dull. Describe a person in class (or an object) by beginning with one general adjective such as "big." Then list more descriptive adjectives, moving slowly from abstract to concrete until someone in the class guesses who or what is being described.

319- T   (Observe/Artwork) "Real Abstract"

A comment which frequently appears on evaluated compositions is "Unclear" or "Be specific!" A clear writer recognizes abstract words and realizes they often need more explanation than concrete words. Art can help illustrate the difference between abstract and concrete language more vividly than the ladder of abstraction. Students view two paintings, one abstract and one realistic. The ensuing discussion helps formulate ideas on what is concrete or abstract and on how art and language express ideas.

320- C   (Discover/Paragraphs) "Reaching Extremes"

Write a paragraph describing a walk or some other activity using no adjectives or adverbs. Then write two more paragraphs, one using as many descriptive words as possible and another with a judicious number. Distribute copies of all three paragraphs and discuss the most effective and the reasons why.

321- C   (Read/Paragraphs) "Modified Writing"

To demonstrate the importance of adjectives in composition,

copy a particularly descriptive paragraph, such as one in *Treasure Island*. Remove all adjectives and then ask the class how the passage may be improved. Compare their versions; contrast them with the original.

322- I   (Research/Dictionaries) "Turn on the Rajio"

Many words used in foreign countries are strictly American words only slightly modified. For example, in a Japanese-American dictionary there are such shared words as *rajio* for radio, *inki* for ink, and *hankachi* for handkerchief. Students list as many of these words as possible from foreign language dictionaries. Besides being fun, the exercise helps students realize how widespread the English language has become.

CHAPTER
6

DELIBERATION

DIALECT

323- C   (Analyze/Models) "Soul Searching"

After an introductory study of dialect, ask students to bring in examples of the following: regional variations (language differences in various geographical areas of the United States); social dialects (language based on social status); functional or temporal (changes which conform to the formality or informality of the occasion). Samples may be found in the media, films, and folk songs. For added challenge, suggest folk etymology (vocabulary changes due to prolonged use).

LINGUISTICS

324- C   (Analyze/Discussion) "So, What's the Difference?"

To emphasize differences between oral and written English, two students describe the plot of a short story. One reads the plot summary he has written, the other gives a summary aloud. The class then analyzes the obvious differences (structure, sentence variety, organization, or formality) between the two presentations.

325- T   (Analyze/Sentences) "Two Plus Two"

Most teachers are familiar with traditional sentence diagramming often used as a tool to explain how words in a sentence relate. Linguists theorize that diagrams which force words out of their natural order serve to confuse students. They suggest the immediate constituent approach to sentence diagramming: the idea that each part of a sentence can be divided into two parts. Each part can be additionally divided by two until only single words remain:

> Several rude people in the audience/laughed very loudly.
> Several rude people/in the audience · laughed/very loudly.
> Several/rude people · in/the audience · laughed · very/loudly.
> Several · rude/people · in · the/audience · laughed · very · loudly.
> Several · rude · people · in · the · audience · laughed · very · loudly.

Sentence analysis proceeds with discussions of each cut and how the structures function in the sentence. For example, the first cut yields the complete subject and the predicate. The functions of the additional cuts, although they should be obvious, can be highlighted by colors or various forms of brackets.

326- C   (Experiment/Chalkboard, Sentences) "Born Linguists"

In learning the parts of speech, native speakers can rely on their own use of language. Write a sample sentence on the chalkboard: The athlete _____ well. Each student supplies a word for the blank. The result will be a long list of verbs (except for a few errors). Do the same for other sentence parts. Students prefer implementing their innate knowledge of language as opposed to memorizing grammar rules.

327- C   (Experiment/Talks) "Body English"

To gain experience using many dimensions of oral language, class members pair off by two's. Each pair prepares and presents an impromptu conversation using and repeating only one word like "anthropology" or a phrase like "from one to another." The audience must guess the nature of the nonsensical message by listening carefully and observing the only communication clues: gestures, facial expressions, and vocal inflections.

328-C,G (Organize/Chalkboard, Sentences) "Participatory Sentence"

When diagramming sentences (either traditionally or linguistically) divide the class into small groups, each representing a part of speech. As each sentence is placed on the chalkboard, the groups decide which words are of their type and must be prepared to list all such words from this and other model sentences. Over a period of several days the groups can be changed.

MECHANICS

329- C (Analyze/Poems) "Punctuation Cummings and Goings"

Students read and discuss several poems by E. E. Cummings, who omits conventional punctuation. Talk about the effect on the reader. The class will gain a greater appreciation for studying punctuation.

330- C (Experiment/Paragraphs) "No Nonsense Punctuation"

In a punctuation unit, the students need to understand why they must know the rules. Frequently, paragraphs without punctuation or capitalization are given for practice. An interesting variation is a passage containing nonsense words. Students fill in the needed punctuation marks according to their knowledge of standard sentence patterns and vocal inflection. Vigorous discussion about changes of meaning through different punctuation patterns is a healthy sign.

OVERVIEW

331- C (Analyze/Chalkboard, Sentences) "Clearly Unclear"

Although students may not know all the rules of grammar, they do know what they can or can't understand. On the chalkboard write some ambiguous sentences. The class analyzes each for word choice, word order, and modification. They can also make up their own grammar rules based on the samples.

332- C   (Analyze/Magazines) "Discussing the Issue"

Obtain an issue of *Hot Rod, Seventeen,* or any other magazine for adolescents. Remove one or several short articles, retype them, and deliberately make strategic grammar mistakes in the process. Duplicate copies for each student or project the articles. Correct the examples in class as a demonstration exercise. When students are unsure of an answer, the teacher does not supply it. They must consult the original printed article and explain the discrepancies themselves.

333- I   (Analyze/Mixed Media, Sentences) "Media Messages"

Grammar can be made more relevant by examing sentences in newspapers, magazines, and speeches for differences and similarities in structure and style. Analyze various news articles reporting the same incident to see how the information can be stated different ways. Sentences out of the media, by their very nature, create student interest in a way that conventional materials cannot.

334- C   (Analyze/Newspapers) "Quantity Not Quality"

Have students count the quantities of the various parts of speech used on the front page of the newspaper. Compare front-page counts among different leading newspapers. See, for example, if some publishers use more modifiers than others. Many other "accounting" analyses can be done to help characterize publishing philosophies.

335- C   (Consolidate/Books) "Student's Own Golden Rule Book"

Rather than working tedious grammar lessons and memorizing rules, advanced secondary students could help each other write a handbook summarizing in their own words what they have learned. Such a project, though time consuming, provides purposeful writing experiences as well as increased familiarity with grammar. Writing groups, well-informed about particular areas, can write sections of the booklet.

336- C   (Experiment/Cartoons) "Funny Grammar"

For variety, instead of continuously assigning exercises from a grammar text, have students identify grammatical principles in their favorite comic strips. Balloon talk is usually grammatical. For something more sophisticated, let them analyze or write captions for single panel cartoons.

337- I   (Experiment/Mixed Media) "Grammar Search"

When students have some knowledge of basic grammatical concepts, allow them to prove how many they can find in printed messages on matchbook covers, cereal boxes, giant highway billboards, and the like. They must note the source as well as the concept when they report.

338- C   (Restructure/Models) "Applying Self"

Give students the opportunity to see the practical use of English by supplying them with standard business forms, catalogue order blanks, job applications, and college admission forms to fill out. Selections should require more than simply checking off items or numbers. Emphasize succinctness and accuracy in word choice and sentence structure.

SEMANTICS

339- C   (Consolidate/Bulletin Board) "Semantics Antics"

Following an introduction on clarity in communication, design a bulletin board around such ambiguities as: (1) Son sending his mother a telegram reading, "Twins arrived tonight. More to come." (2) A puzzled boy with a fishing pole stands by a stream posted, "Fine for fishing." The class can write some of their own and then locate and correct errors. Include magazine pictures to illustrate the ridiculous interpretations.

340- C   (Consolidate/Demonstration) "Back to Blocks"

Place two desks back to back in front of the classroom. On each, place an identical supply of multishaped children's blocks. A student occupies each desk while the class observes. The student on the right assembles a simple structure using the

blocks on his desk. Then he tries to communicate the design so
that his partner behind him can assemble a duplicate structure.
The first student or sender must be precise, but the receiver is
allowed to ask questions, especially to find out whether the
order is reversed. This activity emphasizes the need for clarity
in language.

341- C   (Consolidate/Lists) "Loaded List"

Start the class thinking about the importance of referents by
having them compile a list of words which usually have no
referents and denote abstract concepts—words such as "big
business," "prosperity," "free world," "democracy," and
many others which are found in speeches and periodicals. Additionally, discuss why these are sometimes called "loaded
terms."

SPELLING

342- T   (Consolidate/Models) "My Pal, the Principal"

PRINCIPAL   Mnemonic devices as memory aids can help
improve spelling. Here are some association
ideas. Make up some others.

all right   *All* right is better than *all* wrong.
parallel   *All* railroad tracks run para*lle*l.
principal   The princi*pal* is our *pal.*
separate   Each *rat* will *rate* a sepa*rate* cage.

343- T   (Experiment/Lists) "Spelling Step by Step"

Suggest that students learn lists of spelling words not simply
by writing each word five or ten times but also by studying
it carefully, analyzing it syllable by syllable, affix by affix, and
writing it in sentences.

SYNTAX

344- T   (Analyze/Sentences) "Compose v. Decompose"

Teach sentence structure by providing models of good sentences rather than so many poor ones. If visual impact is

important to learning, students should be getting positive experiences.

345- C   (Analyze/Sentences) "Winning Context-ant"

Distribute a duplicated sheet with several sentence pairs, each set employing a word which sounds the same in both sentences. Ask the class to identify the homonym or homophone (see below) by using the clue in parentheses and by examining the context of the sample sentences. Then have them correct any which are wrong, as in the second set.

(witch, which)

1. This is the book (relative pronoun) I read last night.
2. For Halloween she was a (noun) on a broomstick.

(would, wood)

3. She went to the (auxilliary verb) shed to get firewood.
4. Every evening Uncle Louie (adjective) smoke his water pipe.

The exercise draws on knowledge of grammar, word definitions, and syntax.

346- C   (Analyze/Skits) "Living Language"

Role play correct sentence structure by letting each student represent a part of speech (approximately 40 percent verbs, 30 percent nouns, 10 percent adjectives, 10 percent adverbs, a few determiners and some prepositions). Each one holds a small poster on which the name of a part of speech is printed. Secretly the student chooses a word which might be used as the designated part of speech and prints it on a large note pad attached to the reverse side of the poster. With any short sentence in mind, a volunteer chooses and lines up students bearing the appropriate parts of speech, arranging them in correct syntactical order. He then reads the sentence he had in mind. Finally, as a humorous finish, each student in the lineup shows his own word for the part of speech by turning the poster around. This results in some very unusual and comical sentences but does teach syntax.

347- C, I   (Consolidate/Definitions) "Whatsa Sentence?"

Do students know what a sentence really is? For a quick impromptu exercise, ask them to define a sentence. The variety of responses will be interesting. Finally the class and teacher agree on a definition.

Here is a possible definition. Is it a good one? "A sentence is an uninterrupted utterance that lies between silence and a terminal upward or downward voice pitch and, whether stated or implied, contains a subject and a message about that subject." Perhaps that's a bit exaggerated, but it's better than "A sentence expresses a complete thought."

348- C   (Consolidate/Magazine Pictures) "Snip of a Tip"

This idea could be used for a younger class. Cut out magazine pictures, one for each student. Class members write at least one sentence about the picture using a noun with two adjectives and one without, one verb, and one adverb—or any other combinations to gain needed practice. Sentences are read aloud while corresponding pictures are held up for viewing by the class.

349- I   (Experiment/Audiotape) "Off the Record"

Use the tape recorder to aid sentence development in this extemporaneous approach. As each student goes to the microphone, he is handed a card on which are printed four words. He must use them in a sentence which conveys a complete idea. He has one minute to produce a sentence on paper before he has to read it for immediate playback. Through this type of analysis, the student quickly sees written and oral language interact.

350- I   (Experiment/Audiotape) "Sound Writing"

Student writes a paragraph on a given topic. Then he reads the paragraph aloud while recording it on tape. After playing it back and listening to weaknesses which seem to be magnified by recording, he rewrites the paragraph, records and listens again, repeating the process until satisfied.

351- I   (Experiment/Paragraphs) "Topic Quartette"

After studying the four types of sentences (declarative, imperative, exclamatory, interrogative), students write four paragraphs using each of the four sentence types. Other experiments can include the four sentence patterns (simple, compound, complex, compound-complex). This will provide more viable models for discussion than most textbooks.

352–C   (Experiment/Sentences) "Feeling Sklurophy?"

Encourage the class to create new words. With each new word they write a complete definition and use it in a sentence. The meaning of the word, of course, should be made clear through the context of the sentence, its position in relation to other words, or by inflected endings. This exercise is a good introduction to etymology and syntax.

353- T   (Experiment/Sentences) "Resourceful Sentence Source"

Student-originated sentences provide a valuable source of exercise material when studying syntactical structure. Dictate a list of key words. Ask students to write a sentence using each key word as the subject or main idea. Then when you need to develop practice exercises or tests, you'll have a good supply of student-written sentences on hand. Five classes of 35 students will create a pool of 175 from which to select.

354- C   (Organize/Sentences) "Know the Combination"

Redundant words and phrases often characterize student writing. Practice in combining short sentences will help pupils recognize and eliminate this problem. Give sentence kernels such as the following and ask students to combine them into one good sentence. For this pair, suggest imbedding a prepositional phrase:

> Detroit is an industrial city.
> Detroit is located in Michigan.

With the imbedded prepositional phrase, the sentence might read:

> Detroit is an industrial city in Michigan.

Other kernel sentences can be offered along with signals for other types of combining: compound sentences, various compound structures, subordinate clauses, and verbal modifiers.

355- C   (Organize/Sentences) "Something Different"

Show students how to vary their sentence structure by placing each subject in a different position from the original. Stress that the order must sound both pleasant and natural. For this practice let students rewrite about a dozen such sentences.

356- C   (Restructure/Books Sentences) "Being Stylish"

Compare passages from such authors as Conrad, Faulkner, Hemingway, and Steinbeck. Study the syntax which is characteristic of each. Predominant patterns can be identified and frequencies compared. For practice, students rewrite the passages by using different grammatical structures. This exercise not only reinforces the compositional aspects of grammar, but it also enhances literary perception.

USAGE

357- C   (Analyze/Models) "Just Write for the Audience"

Provide two writing examples about the same incident. One might be in pedantic prose style, the other appropriate to a newspaper. Discuss differences in usage and diction. Analyze how the writer fulfills his intentions for a particular audience.

358- C   (Analyze/Newspapers) "Pages of Misusages"

Ask students to read the front page, the editorial page, and one page of the sports section of any metropolitan newspaper. Have them note misuses of English. Students discuss and correct errors, compare sources to try to determine in which paper most of the weaknesses occurred, and advance possible reasons why, What one might consider an error a writer may have needed to convey a particular idea or nuance of meaning.

359- I   (Analyze/Talk) "Listen and List"

After an introduction on how language varies from place to place and person to person, urge students to listen critically to the language found in their daily lives and to list these samples. Suggest a variety of sources in which oral communication is vital: in class, to or from school, around the dinner table, or on the phone. Discuss the similarities and differences among the samples found and the appropriateness of the language for the occasion.

360- G   (Experiment/Lists) "Remodeling Old Cliches"

To learn more about clichés, small groups make up lists of

cliches and try to determine the source of the original and its intent. Then, they write it in a different way. For example, "nose to the grindstone" means "to work hard." Which is more effective? Why? What is a better saying, more current and descriptive?

361-C   (Experiment/Papers) "Say It Again"

Suggest that the class write two versions of the same event. In the first version they write in colloquialisms and in the second, formal English. This exercise helps to illustrate that both forms are effective in the proper situation: colloquialisms for everyday communication and formal English for an unseen, relatively well-educated audience.

362-G   (Experiment/Role Playing) "Comedy of Errors"

Have the class think about situations in which a working knowledge of good grammar would be beneficial (interviewing for a job, introducing people, entertaining the boss, or making court appearances, for instances). Divide the class into groups of three or four to role play situations illustrating use of good and bad grammar in any social activity. Allow members to speculate on the simulations. This approach emphasizes the importance of good English in everyday situations.

363-I   (Restructure/Paragraphs) "To Be or Tain't So"

You art had it !

When reading a play by an Elizabethan playwright, assign each student a pertinent passage to be rewritten using the vocabulary common today. This will increase knowledge of how and why language changes.

364-C   (Organize/Dictionaries) "Id-tionary"

Let students compile a dictionary of the specialized vocabulary and idioms they use. This attempt to define fresh and vigorous expression dramatizes the continual changes in vocabulary and helps the teacher understand the rather private language of the students.

VOCABULARY

365- C   (Analyze/Talk) "Watch Yer Pronounciation!"

Aside from vocabulary tests, students often have little motivation for developing vocabulary. To keep the class alert, intentionally misspell, misuse, or mispronounce "big" words, inviting
students to make corrections.

366- C   (Consolidate/Bulletin Board, Pictures, Words) "Picturesque
Words"

Motivating students to learn the meanings and use of new words
can be difficult. An enjoyable way to learn vocabulary is through
picture association. Devote a portion of the bulletin board to
lists of words (coded) on one half and pictures (similarly coded)
representing the words on the other side. The idea is to match
the words with the correct pictures. For example, the word
"corpulent" could be matched with a picture of an extremely
obese person.

367- C   (Consolidate/Lists) "You Said It!"

Here is an idea to stir up a little action when things seem to be
getting dull. See who can come up with the most synonyms
for the word "said." There are easily 75 to 100.

368- C   (Consolidate/Puzzles) "What's That Again?"

Kindle enthusiasm for vocabulary development by having
students rephrase famous quotations. With the help of a
dictionary or thesaurus, "One small step for man; one giant
step for mankind" becomes "A micromotor ambulatory progression for a featherless biped; a macromotor ambulatory
progression for featherless bipeds."

369- I   (Experiment/Dictionary) "Used Words"

A word becomes part of an individual's vocabulary only if
it is used frequently after the initial contact. Suggested dictionary practices are: (1) Find an antonym for the word
and compare the meanings. (2) Ask a question using the
word. (3) Supply another form of the word (synonym). (4)
Use the word in a sentence.

370- T (Experiment/Games) "Monday List; Friday Test"

Many students regard vocabulary building as dull, tiresome memorization. And even if they work hard at memorization, all they receive is a dull test on Friday. Suggest that each study a few words for fifteen minutes a day. Then to assess achievement on Friday—or any day—use a crossword puzzle, a fill-in passage, flash cards, anagrams, dictionary hunt, "baseball" or "football" game, Scrabble, or other word games. Use a different approach each week. For additional ideas see Games in the Index.

371- T (Experiment/Games) "Well-stocked Larder"

For vocabulary studies, keep a box or preferably a file drawer stocked with motivation tips: original or collected crossword puzzles, word games, and exercises. Offer these, affixed in folders for easy filing, as challenges for students who find time for additional practice.

WORDS

372- C (Analyze/Books) "Writer Psych-out"

Analyze the use of syntactic patterns, dialects, and favorite word choices and expressions of famous authors, noting how these elements reflect their own thoughts and personalities so important to the themes of their works. By this approach students gain insight into their own writing styles.

373- C (Analyze/Paragraphs) "Prune Verbiage Like Foliage"

To become familiar with the function of modifiers, students read a supplied descriptive paragraph. Then they rewrite the information as a telegram which they "will send" for a limited cost, say two dollars or ten cents a word. Stress the "cost" of excess verbiage and that the main idea of the passage must be conveyed without loss of meaning. Later students can analyze the value of deleted material to the message.

374- C   (Analyze/Sentences) "Like It or Not"

Instead of asking students to demonstrate grammar knowledge by labeling and defining terms, give one sentence in which the subject or verb is underlined. Then introduce a second similar sentence in which students must choose the word which is like or accomplishes the same purpose as the underlined word in the first sentence. This method, if used consistently, teaches word function concepts without students having to memorize grammatical terms.

375- C   (Consolidate/Chalkboard, Sentences) "Oral Moral"

After teaching the parts of speech, write any subject and verb on the chalkboard. Then ask students for an adjective, adverb, preposition, and so on, to form a simple sentence. Example: "Dog barked" is written on the chalkboard; then this type of exchange follows between teacher (T) and class (C):

T: *Adverb?*	T: *Article?*
C: Suddenly	C: The
T: *Article?*	T: *Noun (or Object)?*
C: The	C: Truck
T: *Adjective?*	T: *Preposition?*
C: Big	C: At
T: *Oh, you can do better than that!*	T: *Article?*
	C: The
C: Enormous	T: *What next?*
T: *Another adjective?*	C: Noun (or Object).
C: Red	T: *Give one.*
T: *Preposition?*	C: Policeman
C: In	

Resulting sentence: "Suddenly the enormous, red dog in the truck barked at the policeman." (An interesting related discussion could uncover an imaginative reason for the sentence.) This technique can also be used for teaching compound and complex sentences, but in this case expand each sentence by having the students offer the entire clauses and phrases.

376- C   (Consolidate/Chalkboard, Sentences) "Fun Free-for-all"

To arouse interest in a grammar lesson have a little fun with the

parts of speech. Construct sentences on the chalkboard by
calling for words from different students. When each student
gives his word, he identifies its function in the model sentence.
While learning a lesson in grammar, students can create some
very absurd, humorous, sentences.

377- G (Experiment/Bulletin Board) "Board with Words"

During a unit on parts of speech, groups of students create
bulletin board displays clearly depicting the parts of speech
in use. Displays may be original posters, pictures, cartoons with
captions, or collage or montage paste-ups with appropriate
titles and inscriptions. Since displays remain over extended
periods of time, the chance to drive home a grammatical concept is enhanced.

378- C (Experiment/Lists) "Driving Differently"

An interesting way to practice using verb tenses is to select
two words such as "I" and "drive." Students list as many variations as possible using only the two words and the additional
words required by a change of tense.

379- C (Experiment/Mixed Media) "Fill-in Assignment"

Skillful use of the parts of speech is required for this exercise.
Students bring in news articles or short short stories from magazines. Working in pairs, one obliterates key words throughout
his article. He asks the other student to think of a noun, adjective, verb, or whatever is needed to fill in the blanks. Any
word can be used as long as it fits the sentence pattern. Compare the originals with the rewrites. Some of the funnier versions can be saved to share with the class.

380- C (Experiment/Movies) "Moving Grammar Lesson"

Show the class two or three short ten-minute sports films illustrating actions. Keep the sound low. Students then write every
verb (and adverb, if desired) which they can associate with the
actions as they occur. This list can serve as the basis for a paragraph on motion or may be incorporated into a short vocabulary lesson.

381- I (Experiment/Sentences) "Modification Vacation"

To avoid the routine of traditional grammar lessons on

modification, give students a "map" to follow with directions to fill in the blanks with the needed information.

> *Time*—The speaker arrived _____; *Space*—The building is _____; *How something is done*—The mouse moved _____.

382-C   (Organize/Games) "Telling Storease"

The purpose of this game is to reinforce the learning of a particular part of speech, in this case a verb. Each student in succession tells a portion of a story built around a familiar experience. Each player adds one sentence and must use a different verb each time to score. Sentences continue until a satisfactory story ending is reached.

CHAPTER

7

EVALUATION

DIALECT

383- C (Extrapolate/Books) "Tain't Proper"

How successfully students can locate regional vocabulary can readily be determined by having them scan the writings of Faulkner, Twain, Huxley, Lardner, Steinbeck, Hughes, and others. Each student examines one portion in detail, picking out examples of dialect, coined words, and other terms unusual to their own speech. This approach leads to further evaluative discussions on how, where, and why certain words are used.

MECHANICS

384- I (Restructure/Paragraphs) "Guided Tour"

Select a brief writing sample calling for a variety of punctuation marks. Type and duplicate the passage, omitting all punctuation and capitalization. At the bottom of the page, however, place a checklist covering what has been omitted. This list might read:

Beginning/End	*Internal*
Capital letters: 30	Commas: 15
Periods: 27	Semicolons: 2
Question marks: 2	Colons: 1
Exclamation marks: 1	Dashes: 1
Quotation marks: 6 sets	Hyphens: 2

The student must return all the marks of punctuation to their proper places and capitalize as needed. They can keep track of their progress by tallying on the list. In this exercise, if the student knows he must use a certain number of semicolons, for instance, he will be forced to carefully consider the rules governing their use.

OVERVIEW

385- I   (Identify/Plans) "Grammar Contact Contract"

After some form of diagnosis or assessment, have students prepare written contracts stating what each must learn to improve and use language skills more effectively. This employs accountability in the classroom since the students state specifically what they want (need) to learn and, by accepting the contract, the teacher indicates what will be taught.

386- T   (Identify/Problems) "Start at the Start"

Some teachers forget that students do not learn to express themselves well in a total composition through osmosis, but that there is a series of important learning steps needed to reach such a level. A student who has difficulty reading and writing words or putting them into recognizable thought units cannot deal with sentences, paragraphs, and total composition. Therefore, he should not be frustrated into defeat by requirements to write a total composition. No one writes at a higher skill level than present ability to read or deal with grammar. Thus, it is important to determine where a student is in language development before starting an instructional program. A few diagnostic tests or writing samples will establish a starting point.

387- C   (Identify/Problems) "The Big Three"

Here is a useful test approach to see if a student comprehends important sentence elements and how they are used. Advise the student to set down three column heads at the top of a sheet of paper: *Element, Use,* and *Relationship.* Then present at least ten sentences with a word or several key phrases underlined. The student places the underlined word(s) in the first column and then fills in the other two columns appropriately.

Example: The *hungry* boy was waiting for his lunch.

Element	*Use*	*Relationship*
hungry	adjective	modifies boy

The test also works with linguistic terminology.

388- G   (Judge/Chalkboard, Paragraphs) "Group Attack"

After studies concentrating on one aspect of grammar, devise a paragraph incorporating several errors and write it on the chalkboard. Divide the class into any number of groups. Each group competes to find the most errors and to make the proper corrections. The group that presents a perfect paper in the least amount of time wins.

389- G   (Judge/Papers) "Big Change Exchange"

Save on correcting time by allowing pairs to evaluate each other's compositions for particular grammar problems recently under study. Usually pairs will need some guidelines if the textbook does not provide them. This greater involvement by students provides a better sense of cooperation and mutual understanding as well as a better grasp of standard grammar rules. For each error noted, the evaluator must suggest a corrective grammar rule and cite the source from among several made available. The writer refers to the rule and rewrites accordingly. Further justification for this approach is that evaluating someone else's writing is easier than checking one's own.

390- G   (Judge/Papers) "Grammar Is Not Dead"

Divide the class into small groups to exchange and judge papers (based on recently learned grammatical principles). For variety, use an overhead projector. In addition, an anonymous theme or sentences collected from several themes may be projected and then corrected by the class.

391- I   (Judge/Papers) "Read-a-long"

If a student has a consistent writing problem in grammar or punctuation such as incomplete sentences or comma faults, read a weak portion of his paper aloud to him during a conference. Listening to these mistakes, the student will readily become aware of the need for improvement and will probably try the same procedure for the next paper.

392-I   (Restructure/Puzzles) "Ruleword Puzzle"

Students can study grammatical rules by completing a crossword puzzle. To answer, complete the blanks and reveal the rule. A much better learning incentive than simply reading the rules, this game forces the student to think.

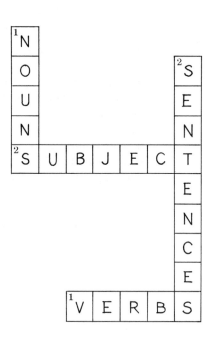

ACROSS

1. _____ appear in the predicate and tell what action is taking place.
2. The _____ is who or what the sentence is about.

DOWN

1. _____ are words that name the subject.
2. _____ have both a subject and predicate.

When a puzzle is completed, have the students prepare a summary statement: *nouns* usually name the *subject* of *sentences* but *verbs* never do this.

393-C   (Judge/Paragraphs) "Editorial-Eyes"

Prepare several prose paragraphs which contain some obvious

grammatical errors. Duplicate and distribute these to the class and have a contest to see who can uncover the most errors. Later go over the paragraphs with the class and have them give reasons for each correction. This approach gives the teacher a "glimpse" of the class's general ability.

394- I (Restructure/Sentences) "Grammar Is Looking Up"

Combine grammar study with all written work. Code major weakness to match practices in the textbook. When papers are returned, students look up each grammatical weakness, work on the exercises as needed, then place rewritten portions on a special sheet to be returned to the teacher along with the original. A simple checkoff system handled by a room cadet will assure that all work has been accomplished. From time to time, in conference, students explain how they overcame certain writing weaknesses.

SEMANTICS

395- I (Extrapolate/Lists) "Up the Ladder"

Limiting the subject to their own interest area, each student draws the classic ladder of abstraction. An athlete might develop one beginning with *person* and progressing to *Westfield's Quarterback Al Smith.* A student with a medical orientation might design a ladder with the bottom rung labeled *instrument* and the top, *stainless steel hemostat.* Besides proving knowledge of abstraction, this assignment also encourages students to write more precisely. Displays of ladders on the bulletin board create interest among the class members.

396- C (Judge/Magazines, Newspapers) "A What?"

Play a game in which students compete for points by looking for double or ambiguous meanings in headlines or articles from magazine and newspapers. For example, "Flying airplanes can be dangerous." Discuss ways to correct the faults.

SPELLING

397- C (Compare/Lists) "Misspelt Werds"

Divide a list of commonly misspelled words into four separate lists. In each list have a varying number of incorrectly spelled words. Let the students study the lists and place them in the order of least errors, e.g. in the sample groups below, list I has the most errors, list III the least. Sample groups:

I	II	III	IV
rassberry	suround	stinginess	cordinate
knowlidge	parallel	similar	thorough
tradgedy	sufficate	Massachusetts	spectacle
summersalt	reinforce	doubt	psycology
envelop	bisness	trapeeze	surprise

398- C   (Judge/Games) "Bee a Good Teacher"

The old-fashioned spelling bee is still a good activity, and it promotes participation. If spelling isn't the goal, try a grammar or literature bee. Such activities are especially useful when the class is restless.

399- C   (Judge/Games) "Monopoly on Words"

Divide the class into two teams for Word Monopoly. Team I will represent the "words" and position themselves along the perimeter of the room, about five to a side. In the four corners will be placed brightly painted signs indicating *Go, Jail, Free Parking,* and *Go to Jail.* Team II will be the first contestants. At the *Go* corner will be a stack of shuffled cards numbered 1 through 12. Each contestant picks a card to determine the distance which must be traveled during his turn. When the player lands on a "word" (student facing student), the "word" person announces the word. It must then be spelled correctly on paper first, then orally, to win a "dollar" or point for the team. If the word is misspelled, the "dollar" is subtracted from the team's bank account. An additional step could involve using the word in a sentence for two "dollars." This process contin- ues until each contestant has had two or three turns. The game will usually take an entire class period. The next day the two teams reverse positions with a new set of words. As in the actual game, players must obey the *Go to Jail* distractor, requiring an extra turn to move out and perhaps spell an additional word. One student serves as banker and scorekeeper.

400- C   (Judge/Games) "Spell-down Switch"

This version of the popular spelling contest helps the poor

speller more than the usual form. Set up like the conventional spell-down, this approach allows everyone to remain on the team, but each incorrect word counts as one mark against the team. Each time a word is misspelled, it is written correctly on the chalkboard. The entire class then pronounces it several times emphasizing the syllables. The word is then erased and is repeated later in the contest.

401- C   (Restructure/Games) "Up Front"

Here is a game for assessing the spelling skills of middle or junior high pupils. Give each class member a small placard with a lower case letter on it. One student comes to the front of the room and is given five minutes to form words by combining his letter with the letters various students are holding. (It may be wise to assign students several of the same vowels and frequently used consonants.) When the timekeeper calls "Start," the participant picks out the letters he wants. Those students come forward and place their cards on the chalk rail as directed. This continues until the time is up. At the end of the class period, whoever made the most correctly spelled words is the winner.

402- C   (Restructure/Games) "Scramble a Few"

Learning new spelling words becomes more interesting when they are presented in different forms. Scramble the letters of each word for the students to reassemble. Also try hiding the words in vertical, horizontal, or diagonal lines of random letters formed into a rectangle as in the popular word-finding puzzle. Students must know how to spell, to find, and encircle the hidden words. Even though he is given the list of words to locate, the student is forced to look at single letters and combinations rather than to look at a word superficially.

403- C   (Restructure/Games) "That Puzzles Me"

When spelling and vocabulary can be feasibly integrated (all vocabulary words do not necessarily have to be spelled), try a "game test." To pass the test, students complete a crossword puzzle and succeed in getting at least 75 percent of the words correctly spelled and correctly defined.

SYNTAX

404- I   (Extrapolate/Papers) "Improved with Age"

The student rewrites a composition he originally wrote for an earlier assignment. In so doing, he follows instructions and suggestions attached to that assignment. Both the old and new copies are then handed to the teacher who evaluates the *degree* of improvement.

405- C   (Extrapolate/Sentences) "Charting the Way"

See if your class can recognize good sentence structure and parts of speech through patterns and word inflections. Have them form sentences by substituting real words for nonsense words.

	Adjective	*Noun*	*Verb*		*Noun*
The	frilby	sard	dowked	the	lod
The	hungry	bird	swallowed	the	worm.

Make this activity into a game by asking for (1) the most "almost real" sentences, (2) the most unusual sentences, and (3) the most imaginative adjectives, nouns, and verbs. Some of the best sentences can be used as future composition topics. Other sentences with errors provide models for proofreading.

406- T   (Judge/Sentences, Paragraphs) "Bare Sentences"

One way to determine whether or not a composition communicates the message intended is to pare down the verbiage to the bare essentials. Simple subjects, verbs, and complements carry the message of any sentence. After students have written a composition, they write on another sheet of paper: *Skeleton Sentences.* For each sentence in the original copy they write only the simple subject, the verb (and helpers), and complements, if any. If the skeleton sentence does not convey a basic message, the original may have some emphasis problems. These weaknesses occur when students hide main ideas in dependent clauses and modifying prepositional phrases. Sentences which are questionable are then revised.

407- C   (Judge/Songs) "Hop on Bop"

Analyze the sentence structure of published popular songs and decide if each is written in the most effective way or if it should be reworded. The objective is to get the full impact and meaning in a minimum number of words. Some results will take away from the lyrics. Discuss whether grammar should be sacrificed for effect in art and entertainment.

408- C   (Restructure/Games) "Gramplify"

Understand grammar with a game called Gramplify. First, make flash cards for the different parts of speech and punctuation. Then have the students build sentences in the following manner. Distribute cards to the entire class. Call on one student to go to the front and hold up a card. If the card contains a noun, a student with a verb usually follows in typical sentence order. The students use their own judgment as to what part of speech is next. Have the class be alert for errors and correct them as the sentence develops. Because so many sentence variations can be made, the process is both fun and instructional.

409- C   (Restructure/Games) "Grummy"

This card game helps assess knowledge of sentence structure. Make a deck of cards containing words which can be subjects, predicates, adjectives, conjunctions, objects, and prepositions. The total number of cards is optional. The object of the game is to make one complete sentence with as many words as possible by discarding and picking. The more words the sentence contains, the higher the score. Members of the class can formulate their own rules; writing them would be good practice.

410- C   (Restructure/Games) "Sentence Carpenters"

Play a game called Sentence Builders. The instructor asks the first two students to give the simple subject and verb of what could be a sentence. Each student in turn (on a team perhaps) must add a word or phrase, each time repeating the entire sentence. If someone adds something which destroys sentence unity, he is disqualified. Set a time limit so that the sentence does not become too unwieldy. More capable students can name the type of grammatical construction they are adding before saying the words.

411- I   (Restructure/Paragraphs) "Scramble Two"

Ask the students to rewrite two paragraphs that have been intentionally poorly written. One paragraph may exhibit faulty sentence structure and misuse of the parts of speech. Another may be characterized by ambiguous meaning, improper emphasis, and weak word choice. This exercise will help pinpoint the strengths and weaknesses of student writers when their revisions are compared with the originals.

412- C   (Restructure/Sentences) "Comic Ally"

For a change of pace, allow students to use some popular comic strips as a "textbook" for studying sentence structure. Select comics with a fairly high level of vocabulary. Then from the "balloon" dialogue students select and write on a separate sheet of paper, the simple subject, verb, and complement (when present) of each conversation. Then from these basic parts, the students could write their own versions of the conversation without looking at the comics.

USAGE

413- G   (Compare/Models) "Find the Worstest"

By individual and group efforts, students collect and study examples of incorrect usage found in books, everyday contacts, and in the media. Through group discussion each sample is revised until it is in its most effective form. Both the original and revised versions are then presented to the entire class for evaluating the degree and type of improvement.

414- C   (Extrapolate/Lists) "Stale Language"

An interesting activity to sharpen students' abilities to recognize stale, trite language is to have them list all ineffective, overused expressions they hear among family, friends, and classmates. For example, "eats like a horse," "barrel of laughs," "hard as nails," and "flatter than a pancake," are but a few they might collect. Discuss the importance or unimportance of these expressions in conversation. What do they reflect about the person using them? Have the students write original and creative replacements.

415- C   (Identify/Games) "Picky, Picky"

To determine knowledge of grammar principles, initiate a long-term game in which the students try to catch each other's oral or written usage problems. One way is to form small groups. Have them engage in occasional oral discussions or paper exchanges on self-selected or assigned topics. (Though the noise level may be high, things are being accomplished.) Collect errors on slips of paper. A contest manager can be appointed to gather and tabulate the errors, list the students who committed them and on what occasion. After a set length of time, perhaps two weeks, the student with the least weaknesses gets some recognition along with the student who catches the most mistakes.

416- I   (Judge/Essays) "Up for Inspection"

Whether or not a student has a working knowledge of the principles of grammar can be revealed by letting the students critically review and correct someone else's essay. Each student should be ready to justify corrections. It is easier to see weaknesses in someone else's writing than in one's own. Finally, the teacher may assess the work of the writer and the reviewer.

417- T   (Judge/Journals) "Proof in the 'Putting' "

Student journals have many uses, not the least of which is to determine language improvement. For example, journals can show if a study of effective modifiers (or any grammatical aspect) has carried over. Of course, they also show what needs more work. This fact need not be announced (so that student writing remains relaxed). The approach can be used to assess any learning in language improvement, since whatever is applied naturally depicts true learning.

VOCABULARY

418- C   (Compare/Games) "Dictionary—a Game?"

Check familiarity with dictionaries (*Roget's Thesaurus of the English Language in Dictionary Form, Funk and Wagnall's Standard Handbook of Synonyms, Antonyms and Prepositions* (Fernald), and *Webster's Dictionary of Synonyms*). Create games which employ these aids. In one approach two opposing team participants each guess a word definition. Several impartial judges look up the word to discover which participant's meaning is closest to the real meaning.

419- C   (Extrapolate/Games) "Beat the Clock"

This is a good game for low verbal, middle or junior high level students. here quantity is more important than quality. Use a stopwatch for best results. Give time intervals (thirty seconds to one minute) in which to write as many words as possible in a given category—adjectives, kinds of animals, or famous people, to name a few. Or pair up the students to say them aloud to each other. Each partner keeps score. A cummulative record of scores each week will show improvement.

420- C   (Extrapolate/Games) "It's a Mystery"

Convert the process of vocabulary assessment into a game. Give the class a short list of new words to define and use in sentences. On the following day recognize the student who uses one of the words—the "mystery word"—in the proper context of the discussion. Although students know the particular list of words, only the teacher knows which one is the mystery word.

421- C   (Identify/Games) "Bowl 'em Over"

Test vocabulary background by forming the class into teams who choose a college to represent—any college from Yale to Podunk Junior College. Then each team is given a definition for which they must supply the word, or vice versa. Working in teams gives the students the incentive to learn new vocabulary. Scoring, of course, is by points for correct answers.

422- G   (Identify/Games) "Concentrate on Concentration"

Number one side of thirty index cards with large-sized numbers 1 through 30. Using manuscript form and not block, or capital letters, list fifteen selected words, one on each blank side (two sets of the same words). Two players set up the cards in six rows, five cards per row. The numbers are arranged consecutively. One student turns over two cards. If they match, he leaves them face up and scores a point if he can pronounce them, two if he can define them, three if he can look away and rewrite the word, and five points if he can write the word in a sentence. When two cards do not match, he places them face down again and relinquishes to an opponent who proceeds in the same manner. Game continues until all cards face upward. The player with the most points wins that round. This game helps improve memory, spelling, and vocabulary.

423- C (Identify/Games) "Define a Fine Word"

To give practice in using new words and to check on understanding, divide the class into two teams. The captain of Team One chooses a word from a list being studied. He calls on the first member of Team Two to use the word in a sentence. The Team Two captain then chooses a word for the other team, and the teams continue to alternate. Each word must be used correctly within thirty seconds. The same sentence may not be used twice. One student serves as timekeeper and another as scorekeeper. The teacher is umpire and decides whether or not the word is used correctly. The team with the highest number of right answers, of course, wins.

424- C (Identify/Games) "Defining Bee"

Instead of the typical spelling bee, hold a word-defining bee. One person gives a definition of a word, then the teams try to guess the word. An extra point is given if the word is spelled correctly. (Requiring students to correctly spell all words which they can read and understand can be a defeating exercise. Few people are able to spell all the words they can read.)

425- C (Identify/Games) "Let the Hunt Begin"

Hold a word scavenger hunt. Select a set of words which appear in ten different articles from current periodicals. The words chosen should challenge the mental abilities of the students but should not be beyond their capabilities to understand. The teacher then lists the articles by magazine title, date, and page numbers and prepares a list of definitions: "A

word which means a sudden forcible overthrow of a government."
When the lists of articles and the definitions are distributed, the
hunt begins. It may last any desired length of time, with different rewards. (Some articles should be distractors but worth
reading.)

426- C   (Identify/Games) "Password Word Game"

To evaluate vocabulary development, play "Passwords." Words
should be on various levels of difficulty and emanate primarily
from previous studies. Words are printed on small cards, two
copies of each word. The teacher or a student, as master of
ceremonies, gives one card to a member of each two-person
team. This member tries to elicit the word from his partner
by issuing clues, usually synonyms. There is a timekeeper for
each round of one or two minutes. Each word starts at ten
points, and each time an incorrect guess is made, one point is
lost. The first pair to get twenty-five points wins the game.
Play the game a few times each week until all members of the
class have participated.

427- C   (Identify/Games) "Stump of Approval"

Students make a list of words and definitions which they don't
understand in their reading assignments. At the end of the week,
they play "Stump the Class." A student reads a word from his
list. Volunteers from the class try to define it for one point. If
none can, the questioner gets a point after he defines the word.

428-C,G   (Identify/Games) "Triple Threat"

An associations test could be used as the basis for a vocabulary
game. The object is to find a word which unites three other
words such as *day, load, master.* The answer is *pay* (payday,
payload, and paymaster). Some others:

man	dog	word	_____	(watch)
work	land	sick	_____	(home)
eat	work	sleep	_____	(over)
fare	lock	dance	_____	(war)
long	fall	mare	_____	(night)

Divide the class into two teams. Each produces ten or fifteen of these triads. The lists are put on the board for each opposing team to identify. The team which completes its list first wins.

429- C   (Identify/Games) "Wild, Wild Weird-One"

To discover if students are learning the vocabulary, play a game based on the onetime classic, "Hangman." Pick a list of words which should be known. For each word place a series of short blank spaces on the chalkboard, one for each letter. Ask each game participant to guess the word which fits a blank in a sample sentence; or he or she may ask questions to get clues. For each wrong answer, another class member adds a part of a monster (left to his imagination): first the head, then the trunk, followed by the legs, arms, and the rest of the body, one at a time. If the monster is completed before the word is supplied, the participant loses the point. To help in the word building, include one or two letters for the longer words.

430- C   (Identify/Sentences) "No Losers"

Every student brings in a new word each day, knows its meaning, and can use it in sentences. The class tries to guess the meaning of the new word from the way it is used in several sentences the student makes up. If no one guesses correctly, the meaning is revealed. These words can be filed on index cards. At the end of a designated period, the class might be asked to write a short paper using some of the new words. The teacher may purposely use the words while teaching. The entire process allows the teacher to evaluate vocabulary skills.

431- G   (Judge/Sentences) "Mean Words"

Check vocabulary knowledge by having the students place words new to them (introduced in the day's lesson) into sentences. Divide the class into groups. Each member of a group must use his new word in an interesting sentence, and the sentence must somehow relate logically to the previous person's sentence. Some could be recorded for playback to the class.

WORDS

432-I   (Extrapolate/Models) "Combination Composition"

Combine grammar with composition. Through assignments
in written description, have the students apply knowledge
of modifiers. Beginning with simple one-word modifiers, students
write how they feel about a situation or describe a set of objects
or pictures. Their work will soon prove whether or not they
know the basic important grammatical concepts of a sentence.
The same situation, objects, or pictures can be used again when
the students write more sophisticated modifiers: phrases and de-
pendant clauses. The fact that they have already written many
sentences from the same stimuli will increase their written
output.

433-C   (Extrapolate/Papers) "Big Combo"

Evaluate the class's knowledge of the parts of speech while they
are practicing composition skills. Students write a short composition beginning each sentence with a different part of speech,
labeling each in parentheses. Besides providing sentence variety,
this practice helps to assess knowledge of grammar.

434-C   (Identify/Games) "Homing in on Homonyms"

This simple game will amuse students and reveal if they know
homonyms. Two students are asked to choose two homonyms,
e.g., *bore* and *boar*, which the rest of the class must try to guess.
Each student gives clues about his homonym saying, for example,
"I am a personality." The other might say, "I am an animal."
The two presenters must continue giving clues (sometimes in
pantomime) until the words are guessed. Scoring, if desired, can
be based on the length of time the two can continue giving clues
without tipping off the class. The couple which lasts longest wins.
(The teacher may find it necessary to supply a list of homonyms
to speed the action.)

435-I   (Identify/Papers) "Join the Evolution"

After studying how our language originated and evolved, assign
a noun to students. Ask them to write a one-page paper on the
word giving its origin, evolution, current usage, and related
points. This exercise will disclose the writer's knowledge and
understanding of etymology.

436-C   (Identify/Paragraphs) "Novel Approach"

The teacher provides each class member with a duplicated copy of a short descriptive passage from a novel or short story, preferably one being studied in literature. Each student takes a turn reading a sentence aloud, first as it appears originally and then without adverbs and adjectives. The class will monitor accuracy. This exercise demonstrates the important function of the modifying words in speaking and writing and determines knowledge of them.

437-C   (Identify/Sentences) "Those Blankety Blanks"

Hand out a list of sentences, each with several key words removed. Students fill in blanks with suitable words, based on context and pattern, and identify the part of speech.

438-C   (Restructure/Games) "Acronymania"

One participant or team member must choose a noun and print it vertically on the chalkboard. The other members of the team must place an adjective horizontally, one for each letter. The adjective may begin with the letter or, for an easier version, include the letter anywhere. For example, using the nouns of equal length like *"child"* or *"house"* might result in these adjectives:

C uddly	c H eerful
H appy	c O ld
I rritated	ha U nted
L aughing	un S ightly
D rooling	E mpty

Teams take turns. The rounds are timed for fairness, and points are based on how many adjectives are completed within the time limit, usually one point for each.

439-I   (Restructure/Sentences) "Try an Additive"

Have students add interesting adverb phrases to very simple sentences. After writing the assignment, the class should read their sentences aloud to prove they can use modifying phrases to expand and clarify the basic idea of a sentence. Sentence samples to expand: The sun rises. Silence falls. Charles leaves.

CHAPTER

8

APPLICATION

OVERVIEW

440-I   (Construct/Mixed Media) "Between the Words"

Words are only one medium of communication and can be skill-
fully juxtaposed with other forms such as art, dance, films, and
music to develop interesting perspectives on ways to create a
message. Assign the problem of developing a project which
combines visuals and words. Preparing a motion picture script
or writing a movie review, for example, requires thoughtful
consideration and use of all communication skills.

441-C   (Write/Newspaper) "Start the Presses"

Correcting and proofreading help
improve language skills. Students
can check each other's writing.
Facilitate this motivational approach
through a class newspaper project.
The paper would chronicle happenings in and around the school. In
compiling articles students will need
to read the articles carefully, putting
into practice their knowledge of
spelling, vocabulary, sentence structure, puncuation, and so on.

442- I   (Write/Papers) "Experience Grammar"

Find ways to relate language study with student experience.
Have students write 50 to 100 sentences about themselves, not
in any sequence, just random thoughts. Include in this assignment some required grammatical applications such as asking
that eight to ten sentences contain a predicate adjective
describing the writer's personality. Or asking that at least five
sentences begin with a prepositional phrase such as "At home
I am usually. . . ." To help an evaluator locate these grammatical principles, suggest they be underlined and labeled.

443- I   (Write/Papers) "Short Circuit Grammar"

To integrate grammar and literary skills, assign the writing of a
short story. Part of the final evaluation would be based on
correct use of grammar and mechanics. Another aspect would
require narration in standard English and dialogue in dialect or
informal speech.

SYNTAX

444- I   (Write/Paragraphs) "In the Eye of the Beholder"

Each student is given a series of objects or illustrations to
describe (one paragraph for each). Lists of verbs, nouns, and
modifiers may also be supplied. This exercise presents an opportunity to apply knowledge of description and paragraph organization.

USAGE

445- I   (Write/Books) "Expression Collection"

In a three-ring notebook, each student keeps a "dictionary" of
once-popular sayings or expressions. Each sheet—one word to a
sheet—includes the expression, its meaning, when or where it may
have originated, and an illustration of its use. Students are expected to do some research and then discuss their lists. Room
and hall displays combined with appropriate illustrations will
generate interest in language and how it changes.

446-I   (Write/Papers) "Slanguage"

Invite written compositions which employ slang expressions.
English purists object to this corruption of the English language
and lose sight of the value of slang in a youth's world—anyone's.
Many times a slang word or phrase expresses a nuance of meaning
for which there is no substitute. The class can engage in an in-
depth study of slang, even picking out instances where famous
authors or speakers have used slang to add color, humor, or
emphasis.

VOCABULARY

447-I   (Write/Lists) "Adopt or Adapt"

After a vocabulary study, students
compile a list of words adopted and
adapted for our contemporary
vocabulary from (1) foreign expressions; (2) clothing and household
items; (3) scientific and professional
jargon; (4) multi-ethnic sources;
(5) religions; (6) slang; (7) sports;
and (8) the theater. Have students
define each word briefly and illustrate some with pictures or drawings.
Share and discuss information.

WORDS

448-I   (Construct/Pictures) "Eye-catchers"

Follow up a word study unit by launching a media search for
dynamic, attention-getting words. Encourage students to look
for words being used effectively by news reporters, advertisers,
and writers to attract an audience and in some way to move that
audience emotionally. As they read newspapers and magazines,
then, students can clip the effective words (with accompanying
illustrations if available) or just copy them for use later. Then
on a sheet of poster board, each student prepares a montage of
both pictures and words, pictures which clearly depict the word

choices. Lines of contrasting cellophone tape or paper strips can be affixed to connect each word to an appropriate illustration. Words recopied rather than clipped can be drawn on small strips of contrasting construction paper. Later the student could write a brief paper justifying the choice of these particular words and telling what, if anything, was learned from this project.

449- I   (Write/Lists) "Facing Up"

Most people can think of adjectives like "happy," "pretty," "sad," or "smiling" to describe a face. For more interest, authors use synonyms for these words. Have students prepare lists of words which could be used to describe "face" other than simple, obvious ones. Finally, ask the students to write a short paper using as the central idea the word they like best to modify "face."

450- T   (Write, Speak, Solve, Perform, Construct/All Vehicles) "All Mixed Up"

Perhaps the best idea which can be offered in this section is to suggest that grammar and language are best studied as an integral part of all communication, not as a separate entity.

PART 3

literature

literature

INTRODUCTION

Chapter 9
Drama 143
Humanities 146
Media 147
Novels 149
Overview 153
Poetry 158
Short Story 163
Vocabulary 164

EVALUATION

Chapter 11
Drama 175
Humanities 175
Nonfiction 176
Novels 176
Overview 184
Poetry 191
Short Story 192
Vocabulary 193

DELIBERATION

Chapter 10
Drama 165
Humanities 166
Novels 167
Overview 169
Poetry 171

APPLICATION

Chapter 12
Drama 195
Media 198
Nonfiction 200
Novels 201
Overview 205
Poetry 207
Short Story 210

CHAPTER
9

INTRODUCTION

DRAMA

451- T   (Discover/Demonstrations) "Backing a Play"

Drama study can be much more interesting with proper groundwork. Choice of plays is the first concern. They must have good plots and plenty of action for today's television-nurtured youngsters. The background of the play should be discussed before the reading begins. Along with discussion and some lecture, bring in appropriate media: music, pictures, and playbills of professional productions to accompany presentations.

452- C   (Discover/Discussions) "What's in a Name?"

Greater insights into literary characters can be obtained by examining their names. Some writers use names which denote special meanings which may or may not be significant for characterization. Some names are chosen because the sound reflects the character, others because the name alludes to a personal characteristic. For example, Willy Loman in *Death of a Salesman* may well be described by some student as "low man on the totem pole"—a "has-been" in society. Students discuss names of characters in both drama and fiction for allusions, derivations, and meanings. They will soon realize that selecting names is as much of a craft as plot development.

453- T   (Discover/Inventories) "Variety Shows"

Before teaching Shakespeare in high school find out which other of his plays the students have read. Most likely it will be a tragedy such as *Julius Caesar* or *Macbeth.* If so, this time choose one of Shakespeare's comedies or historical plays like *Richard III* or *Henry IV.* His plays covered too many aspects of life to neglect any one.

454- T   (Discover/Models) "Learn the Lexicon"

The problem many students have with understanding Shakespeare is relating what is said to how it is said. Instead of making the lexicon—the special vocabulary of the age—become an unavoidable drudgery, go through a linguistic set of drills to aid recognition of certain speech patterns. In addition to the exercises, explain what the words and expressions meant in Elizabethan times. Interject peculiar themes and patterns which Shakespeare commonly used. From here students read the play with greater enjoyment and better understanding.

455- C   (Discover/Models) "Noting Nothing Changes"

When studying any period in literature, whether Greek, Elizabethan, or Modern, the class examines one play from each period, noting the similarities and differences. For example, one thread running through all the plays might be the one characterizing the "flavor" of the times. Excerpts from Sheridan or Molière can capture the comedy of Restoration period manners. These can be compared with preceding and later social customs.

456- C   (Listen/Records) "Romeo and Julie Go West"

Study *Romeo and Juliet* and *West Side Story* together. Compare the modern day version with that of Shakespeare and discuss the social conditions which may have brought about both plays. Classical music may also be introduced through the sound track of *West Side Story* and then Tchaikovsky's *Romeo and Juliet.* Besides simply listening to the easily discernible themes and lilting melodies, compare Maria and Tony's musical themes with those of Romeo and Juliet.

457- C   (Listen/Role Playing) "It's a Draw"

Having students read a play aloud is usually a good way to interest the class in drama. Most of the dramatic effect, however, is
lost because students may be self-conscious or unprepared. For
better reading, students can draw for parts the day before the
play is read in class. With a chance to study the characters and
practice their roles, students will do a better job in presenting
the characters they drew.

458- C   (Observe/Field Trips) "Trip Tip"

Inevitably, during some part of the school year a great movie or
play will be presented in your community or within driving
distance. If it relates in any way to material being studied, organize a theater party as an introductory or culminating activity.
Besides generating class interest, such an event will be a new experience for some. It also provides a chance for a teacher to
display some personal qualities not easily revealed in the classroom.

459- C   (Observe/Role Playing) "Off and On the Record"

Obtain a recording of the play or poem assigned to aid students
in reading aloud with proper intonation. In the case of drama,
it is interesting to compare an actor's interpretation of a role
with the class's. Some students may want to engage in some
mime, mouthing the words along with the record while performing the appropriate actions.

460- T   (Research/Authorities) "Philosophically Speaking"

Since the Greeks first introduced dialogue into their religious
rites, drama has been considered an accurate key to people's
thought processes in any age. An indispensable aid to understanding the true meaning of a play is to have an historical and philosophical perspective of the era. To assure that no student
misses this background, teachers must accumulate the necessary
information explaining why drama over the years took the form
it has. A team of English teachers could prepare a helpful companion text for the plays being studied by combining explanations of events with notes on the pressures of a class philosophy
which strongly influenced the authors. For instance, a brief
summary of the Irish Revolution—not only battles but also the
effect of the prevailing Lockean philosophy of the people—
would make the plays of Synge and O'Casey more interesting

to study and more rewarding to the uninformed observer.

HUMANITIES

461- T   (Discover/Demonstrations) "Constant Struggle"

Demonstrate the persistence of common themes which occur in the various media. Man's struggle to organize and understand his experiences can be shown in a multimedia approach to a particular theme. This diversity of expression, for example, can approach the odyssey theme through various forms of lyric poetry (Homer's *Odyssey*), modern poetry ("Telemachos Remembered"), modern prose (*Ulysses*, James Joyce). Add to these some famous works of music and art.

462- C   (Observe/Slides) "Safe on a Slide"

Often, relating the literature of an age to art and architecture can be very frustrating because illustrations are lacking or hard to find. Sometimes pictures in art books are passed around the class. A better approach is to use slides. First obtain a simple photo copy stand and a 35mm camera (single lens reflex is best) with close-up lens. Then photograph pictures from books and magazines to be made into slides. These may be accompanied by narration, music, or both. If used for an individual class on a limited basis, such reproductions will not lead to copyright problems. If there is a question regarding copyright, send a permissions letter to the publisher.

463- T   (Research/Books) "Killing Two Birds with One Library"

Unless a program of unified studies is being followed in a school, the English department and the social studies department should attempt a coordinated program. Studying a book such as Upton Sinclair's *The Jungle* is a good start. Or if the Civil War is the subject of the social studies class, Harriet Beecher Stowe's *Uncle Tom's Cabin* or Stephen Crane's *The Red Badge of Courage* could be used in English. In a study of the post World War I era, such classics as Frederick Allen's informal history *Only Yesterday* or Fitzgerald's *The Great Gatsby* would be excellent. By this method the class is not only studying literature and poetry but are learning more about an era and the people in it.

MEDIA

464- T   (Discover/Discussions) "Light Side of the Dark Ages"

Students often think literature is something in thick, dust-covered volumes. They would enjoy a long-time classic more if they saw it not as something which is dead but as a very live form of entertainment reflecting the times. Discuss how people's ideas of having fun (being entertained) have changed over the years. Using TV and films along with contemporary literary works, and then "progressing backwards" in time, will help make the point.

465- T   (Discover/Television) "Electronic Boom Boon"

As television becomes more and more a part of every student's life, teachers are capitalizing on the medium as a study aid. Reserve one unit a semester for studying television genres such as the detective story, the family situation comedy, or the western. These forms can be traced to early literary works: Arthur Conan Doyle (detective), Clarence Day (family situation), Louisa May Alcott ("soap operas"), and James Fenimore Cooper (western). This experience can serve as an entree to literature.

466- T   (Observe/Bulletin Board, Mixed Media) "Not Bored with Board"

Initiate a unit on satire by placing on the bulletin board examples of parody, irony, satire, and others from everyday conversation and the mass media. These can be either quotes, paintings, photographs, caricatures, cartoons, or whatever fits. Such concrete examples help clarify the often difficult literary devices.

467- T   (Observe/Movies) "Open Your Film Cans to Frame Number. . ."

Movies are frequently mentioned as a way to implement a study of literature, but how about studying the movie for its own sake? An interesting unit might combine film viewing with readings from any current film "anthology." If the students are aware of varous film techniques such as camera angle, panning, cutting, montage, superimposed images, dissolves, or cuts, they will approach discussions on character development, plot structure, and theme more enthusiastically. Later cinemagraphic development can be compared or contrasted with the literary method. When interest has grown, begin a Film Society, charge dues, and rent films.

468- C   (Observe/Movies, Slides) "Tic-Tac-Toe the Mark"

Using audio-visual equipment can be a waste of time if the students use the darkened room as an opportunity to sleep or carry

How does Jarvis	act	feel	think
When he flies a plane ?			
When he lands a plane ?			
When he is grounded by bad weather ?			

on conversations. Movies and slides can restore enthusiasm and vitality, but students must get more than enjoyment out of a film. So provide viewing guides which can be used to teach content without preventing the watching of the presentation. One easy-to-follow guide is the tic-tac-toe graph pictured in sample form here. Write the questions alongside as in the diagram. If large writing areas are provided, even in subdued light the class can take notes while watching the film.

469- C   (Read/Magazines) "Tonal Qualities"

A bad magazine article can teach more about tone than a week of essays on the subject. Get something which the students readily agree is bad. Have them tell why. Their very good reasons will be enough on which to build at least one good lesson on tone in literature.

NOVELS

470- C   (Discover/Discussion, Slides) "Inquire Within"

Using the inquiry method in discussing literature helps sharpen perceptions concerning mood and characterization. Bring to class some colored slides (or prints). Then through student questions and teacher's "yes-no" replies, pick out a character or author who best relates to the qualities in the illustration.

471- G   (Discover/Discussions) "Speed-Read Whizz Kidzz"

The following reading plan helps to cover many more books than the single common-study novel. A seventh grade accelerated class, for example, met one and one-half hours a day and covered five novels in two weeks. The class had been divided into five nearly equal groups, each assigned one of the five books. Then groups decided how they would participate in a panel presentation. One person handled plot, another characterization, and so on. Students not on a presenting panel ask questions about unclear ideas.

472- C   (Discover/Discussion) "Titles Only Skin Deep"

Make a list of interesting titles of novels, plays, and critical works which the students may have heard about but not read: *Death of a Salesman, Lord of the Flies, The Return of the Native.* Ask the class to guess the possible content from the titles. The variety of opinions will interest students to find out what the books are really about.

473- T   (Discover/Pictures) "Simple Symbols"

The abstract concept of symbolization is often difficult for a student to comprehend. A number of devices can be used. The world is full of readily understandable symbols such as flags, coins, paper money, the holy cross, the star of David, the eagle, and even Santa Claus. Don't forget the status symbols either. Mount these samples or prepare slides. Students discover that interpreting symbols is easy. They do it every day.

474- C   (Discover/Talk) "Sound and Sense"

Oral interpretation, a long-time speech department or forensic
activity, offers a valuable approach for appreciating and understanding literature. Volunteers select particularly emotional
pieces to present in class. From this experience the student discovers both the importance of the oral sense and the literary
understanding. The entire class, unhindered by print, can empathize with the shared experience.

475- C   (Listen/Authorities) "Live and in Full Color"

Many students cannot conceive of a writer as a living, breathing,
human being. They somehow believe works of literature are
created by some omniscient force. If at all possible, bring to
class an author of a book currently being studied. Urge him to
express his views on the book and to answer student questions.
Soon they will realize that works of art are created by people
just like themselves. If an author is not readily available, choose
an interested, capable student to study the life of the author
thoroughly enough to role play as a guest author.

476- C   (Observe/Bulletin Board) "Feeling Down"

An artist in class can develop cutout sketches of each character.
Mount on the bulletin board. As the story goes along, and characters interact, the characters are moved accordingly. The class
can easily see character involvement and movement as each
incident unfolds. This helps clear up some of the complexities
between plot and characters and groups of characters.

477- C   (Observe/Displays) "Dressed-up Literature"

Often a student fails to understand the meaning of a novel simply
because he is not able to picture the characters or the settings,
and consequently the action means nothing. To accentuate the
visual, use some object which will orient the reader or reflect the
times and fashions. For *A Tale of Two Cities* someone could draw
a rough blueprint of the prison or find a picture of the carriages
used in the opening scene. Certainly the architecture is also a
prime visual subject. For a novel like *The Deerslayer* someone
could dress up in a costume of the early frontiersman. Any creative ideas which clarify the scene and the characters add meaning
and fun to the study.

478- C   (Observe/Pictures) "Scenes Not Heard"

Use pictures to demonstrate abstract ideas in novels. To illustrate,
the vague setting in *The Bridge of San Luis Rey* makes the novel
appear more universal in appeal than through a specific setting.
Show students illustrations of both obscure and well-defined
settings for contrast. They will readily see how more people
could "step into" the indefinite setting and feel at home. Thus,
they see how an author can manipulate audience appeal through
setting—a concept students often overlook.

479- T   (Read/Books) "Out with Overkill"

A novel's appeal and enjoyment can
be killed by overteaching. A good
book practically teaches itself. Before discovering the hard way how
much analysis the class can accept
and appreciate, let them enjoy the
book first; then find out what
else the book has to offer.

480- C   (Read/Myths) "Literature and Myth"

Before taking up a work of literature, the class may find it helpful to study the mythology on which much literature is based.
Key myths and fables can be introduced before reading the work
rather than afterward or concurrently. Students will then have a
better background for archetypal problems.

481- T   (Read/Tales) "Short Tales and Long"

A fascinating literary device which keeps recurring and which
can be readily studied is that of fantasy and fairy tale. Recall
how often fairies and the fantastic happen in *Beowulf, Canterbury Tales, The Faerie Queene, Gulliver's Travels, Midsummer
Night's Dream, Paradise Lost, Romeo and Juliet, The Tempest.*
Besides reading articles and books by authorities on fantasies
and fairy tales, study the tales themselves for devices, plot
structure, and themes which strongly resemble those in novels.

482- T   (Research/Authorities) "A Real Dig"

Some students find it easier to read a novel if given a historical
background. Instead of a term paper or lecture approach,

expose class to the history of an era by locating old newspaper articles, editorials, criticisms, movies, and recordings. Try to relate this background to our current social and political trends—even inviting a speaker to prove that some pieces of literature have set a foundation for recent events, e.g., Swift's "The Drapier Papers" and the era of religious quarrels in Ireland.

483- T   (Research/Authorities) "This Is Their Life"

An entire course could focus on the different ways of life in the United States as represented in fiction such as *Grapes of Wrath, The Jungle, Main Street, Native Son, Not Without Laughing,* and *Tobacco Road.* Symbolism, style, and craftsmanship, and all the usual facets of literature study might be purposely played down. The student learns instead the customs, moral values, and the sociopsychological structures of people with a different life style. This course, a kind of sociology of fiction, would help the student recognize the differences among people and at the same time become more tolerant—a desirable goal for English or any subject.

484- T   (Research/Mixed Media) "Looking Glass Class"

A profound and interesting literature study can be based on the all-time children's favorite *Alice In Wonderland.* Numerous journal articles have been written on the social implications and symbolisms in this novel. Besides this resource, library vertical files often contain ready supplies of bulletin board illustrations of *Alice.* There is also at least one filmed version of this great classic.

485- G   (Research/Libraries) "Division of Labor"

Novel study needs a novel approach. Divide the class into various groups, each with a chairman to report progress to a central coordinating committee which works out a group presentation involving the entire class. Suppose a unit on *Oliver Twist* was underway. One group could look into the historical times of the novel, another into character analysis, another into Dicken's life. The students do specific assignments within their groups.

Those working on plot summaries might present a skit. Those working on character analysis could organize a panel discussion on the relative good and evil of the novel's characters. This committee approach gives everyone a feeling of being a major contributor and, therefore, a participant in their own education rather than an observer.

OVERVIEW

486-T   (Discover/Books) "Going, Going, Gone!"

Many of the most entertaining and informative books cannot be covered in an English class because of lack of time or funds. Set aside the first five minutes of class each day for an "auction" of one or two books from the instructor's personal collection or from used book sales. First students are introduced to the books. If they wish to read one, they bid for it. In an above-average class, highest bidder is whoever offers to read the book in the least amount of time. In an average or heterogeneous class, bidding may be by tokens which the teacher converts to party treats at the semester's end. The more bids, of course, the more food will be available. Students may "purchase" only one book at a time. Upon its return, the book may be reauctioned if there are any bidders. This procedure effectively introduces students to a wide array of authors and subjects. Sharing the plan with parents is recommended.

487-T   (Discover/Discussion) "Current of Current Events"

By keeping abreast of current events a teacher can increase student interest in literature. Book lists and discussions are then developed to coincide with world happenings. This makes reading more meaningful to each student, particularly for those who see little value in it.

488-T   (Discover/Discussion) "Start Young"

Begin a study of literature with current themes and modern writers. Students usually know more about the new authors, so they will contribute more freely in discussion. Determine similarities and differences between the modern authors and earlier ones to be studied. Then, when the earlier writers are studied in depth, students soon understand that authors write primarily about the same subjects but in their own times.

489- I   (Discover/Displays) "Share and Share Alike"

Many students would read more if they were able to read books on subjects they enjoy. Since teachers usually don't have time to assign specific books to individuals, the class might match the right books with the right people. One approach is for students to write advertisements touting books they have read and to share these comments with the rest of the class. Since students know each other and their personal tastes, peer suggestion is probably the best "sales pitch" a book can have. This also helps the teacher check on reading progress. (See related idea 34 on determining class interests.)

490- T   (Discover/Inventories) "Clues from Kids"

The first day of class ask each student for a list of five books (or some other quantity) which he might like to read. Chances are, if each turns in a substantial list, certain books will appear repeatedly. Reading groups can then be set up around these popular selections. The books can be related to literature themes or genre being studied by the entire class.

491- T   (Discover/Lists) "Best of the West"

For added motivation in literature classes, post the current best seller list. (This list can be expanded by adding past best sellers.) In another version, make up a list of English or American titles which have been best sellers in much earlier days. Or allow students to compose their own "Top Ten" or "Fabulous Forty" book lists. These are, surprisingly, often very well-conceived.

492- T   (Discover/Plans) "Black Lit is Beautiful"

If your high school has not yet established a course in Black Studies, you can easily plan a unit of your own with such works as: *Go Tell It on the Mountain* (Baldwin); *Manchild in the Promised Land* (Brown); *Soul on Ice* (Cleaver); *Yes, I Can* (Davis); *Invisible Man* (Ellison); *Nigger* (Gregory); *A Raisin in the Sun* (Hansberry); *Stride toward Freedom* (King); and *Freedom Ride* (Peck). Also include selected poems of Dunbar, Hughes, and Jones. Use an inductive approach first, relating literature to individual experience. Then advance to a higher abstract level such as comparing philosophies. Even try a multiethnic approach to include many other minority authors.

493- T   (Discover/Self) "On Being Yourself"

Emphasize how important it is to be aware of effect on self when reading a piece of literature. All good art creates a feeling or reaction in the reader or viewer. Knowing this increases enjoyment of any art form. Since some children need some guidelines for this, study a few different art forms and trace their artistic similarities. (Also see idea 531.)

494- T   (Listen/Authorities) "Resource-full Classes"

More than ever before, schools are using community resources to supplement instruction. Speakers are often available gratis. Many parents have skills and knowledge on certain subjects being covered in class. A farmer or a lawyer certainly can give more useful information on farming and law than the average teacher. This applies to English also. If a play is being studied, a local actor or actress who once acted in that play could discuss it in class. Parents may have slides of places visited in England or in Mark Twain land—Hannibal, Missouri. A lecture by such a person would give both students and teacher a change. Urge the school to send out a resource speaker questionnaire.

495- T   (Listen/Books) "Read It and Weep"

Literature has a beauty which many teachers fail to point out— sound. Many authors create certain moods and feelings which come alive only when their works are read aloud. If the teacher doesn't care to read, student volunteers can be used or original tapes played so as to share the sounds of literature.

496- T   (Listen/Lectures) "Put That Down"

In some high schools the pure lecture technique in English classes is not used enough to prepare students for its more frequent use later, particularly in college. Occasional lectures can be effective to give introductory information or background of a poet, author, or literary period. Students should be required to take notes on these lectures to learn the procedure for picking out key ideas. Later, college-type blue book exams might be given to evaluate information gained from the lectures. This gives students practice answering essay questions, a skill in succinct writing which has many fringe benefits in and out of education.

497-I   (Read/Books) "Call a Sub"

Instead of requiring everyone to read the same novel, poem, or short story, give them a choice of reading thematically similar works. For example, *A Portrait of the Artist as a Young Man* instead of *David Copperfield,* or *Dover Beach* instead of *Ozymandias.* Include research on the authors and the locale of the work.

498-I   (Read/Books) "Ethnic Pick"

After discovering and discussing the many nationalities and races represented in the class, have students read at least one book (fiction or nonfiction) which features characters—even situations—which parallel their own family backgrounds. This introduction can lead into many interesting, related activities as students share experiences.

499-T   (Read/Books) "Get the Point?"

All students need the experience of reading a book to meet a personal need. These needs vary, student to student, day to day. To encourage individual reading, eliminate the required book list in favor of a free-choice approach. Display a chart listing students' names and titles of all books they read. Students record their own books on the chart. Each book is assigned weighted points by type: two points for easy reading (fiction, romance, or "hot rod" stories); five points for medium hard (biographies, autobiographies); ten points for difficult (lengthy fiction, nonfiction in a historical vein). Students are "rewarded" according to the number of points they earn.

500-I   (Read/Books) "Read—It's Free"

As they often claim, many students actually do not have time for reading on their own. Homework for other classes, part-time work, athletics, and socializing consume what free time they have outside the classroom. As a valuable service to students, allow generous amounts of class time regularly and permit each student to read according to individual interest and ability levels.

501- T   (Read/Books) "Spacing Out"

Junior high students are interested in adventure and the unusual. To arouse reading interest in slower students, provide them with something they will want to read: good science fiction, detective stories, mysteries, and tales of the occult. Include some of these in the classroom library so they will be available for those who are not ready for reading the classics. Order these high-interest books from paperback book clubs or travelling library collections.

502- T   (Read/Books) "Time to Browse"

In communities where sources of reading matter are limited, sell the better periodicals and paperbacks at a school bookstore. If the operation is a nonprofit venture, prices can be reduced significantly. This is a convenient way for the teacher to order and assign a class novel. The reading and buying habits formed are likely to have carry-over value. Perhaps a bookstore such as this could be set up and staffed by the student council as a service project.

503- T   (Read/Book Reports) "Paperback Backing"

Arrange a display of paperbacks contributed by both teacher and students. On 3 x 5 cards the contributor writes a description and evaluation of each book and places it in a book pocket. This will help others select books which meet their interests. (Also see idea 863.)

504- C   (Read/Handouts) "Coming On Live"

Way to get your lumps

When studying any type of literature, supply students with information on the writer's life. Since literature usually reflects the author's life experiences, the class will be interested in facts such as these: Alexander Pope, in pain most of his life, was a 4'6" hunchback; Jonathan Swift was so energetic that if the weather kept him indoors, he ran up and down his deanery stairs; Samuel Johnson once threw a glass of lemonade out the window because a waiter who gave him a lump of sugar had dirty fingers. Through such anecdotes students come to realize that writers are human and that their humanity affects what they write.

505- T   (Read/Models) "From Mistakes of Others"

A legitimate goal in general literature courses is to be able to make distinctions between good and bad art. One approach is to present some fiction and poetry which are decidedly poor quality. In doing so, be convincing and persuasive in showing why a selection is bad. Some good examples of bad literature have been cited in Laurence Perrine's *Literature: Structure, Sound, and Sense* and *The Stuffed Owl: An Anthology of Bad Verse*, edited by Wyndham Lewis and Charles Lee.

506- I,G   (Research/Discussion) "Theme Teams"

World literature can be effectively studied through a thematic approach. Groups (or individuals) could be introduced to three or four themes in Western literature and a similar number in Eastern literature. An obvious advantage of the thematic approach is that students can become so knowledgeable in one area that they want to trace their new-found interests through many types of literature.

POETRY

507- C   (Discover/Discussions) "Activated Poetry"

For a group of juniors or seniors who seem to favor the activist approach to life, present a unit on the revolutionary ideas of the Romantic poets. For example, Blake shows church condemnation and government regimentation ("Holy Thursday" and "The Human Abstract"). Shelley gives a brilliant analogy between revolution and the changes of autumn in "Ode to West Wind." Students will be surprised to discover that many of their so-called *new* causes have been dealt with in earlier times.

508- G   (Discover/Discussions) "Diverse Verse"

Use a great variety of verse so individual students are not excluded from participation by being included in "mass-think" exercises. A grab-bag of titles will provide a variety of poetry to read, explicate, paraphrase, love, despise—not in isolation but in small groups, each having drawn the same poem. This procedure allows for a bit of competition through community opinion and, luckily, counter-opinion.

509- T   (Discover/Discussions) "Poetry: Three Deep"

In teaching poetry to high school students, discuss a poem on
three levels: *surface*, *subsoil*, and *in-depth*. The *surface* level of a
poem is its direct translation—the story line. The term *subsoil*
has psychological connotations. It suggests something beneath
the conscious, roots piercing downward, or the base of the iceberg below the waterline. The term *depth* also has psychological
implications, suggesting the deepest soil beneath the oak's tap-
root or the water below the iceberg. But the term *depth* also
connotes darkness which can, in turn, suggest something evil or,
paradoxically, something holy as in the phrase, "dark night of
the soul." This conscious division of a poem helps students
understand that poetry is often written with several different
meanings in mind. This formula can be applied successfully to a
poem like Robert Frost's "The Road Not Taken."

510-T   (Discover/Discussion) "Textbook Writers, Take Note"

Often, too much time is devoted to teaching and discussing the
mechanical or technical aspects of poetry, such as meter, rhyme,
or metaphor. To help students learn and remember these important devices is a troublesome problem. Thus, to leave more
time for the experiential and inferential levels of poetry (see
idea 707), English department members should get together,
decide on the basic poetry for each grade level, and prepare a
parallel study handbook bringing in poetic structure as it becomes useful to create a mood or build an idea.

511- C   (Discover/Discussion) "To Each His Own"

Before moving into a more formalized study of poetry, promote
and hold class interest by giving students a choice of the poets
and poems on which they can concentrate. Some class periods
may be used as library days, others for discussion, comparing
likes, dislikes, types, elements, and problems. As an eventual
follow-through, the end-of-the-unit test should also be unstruc-
tured to allow each student to demonstrate in his own way what
he has learned.

512- C   (Discover/Discussion) "Typical Typo"

This exercise focuses on the questions of if, how, and why typography is part of poetry. Pass out a sample with two sentences

on it, each written to emphasize the typography (poems of E.E. Cummings illustrate this technique). Take one of the sentences out of a prose selection, the other from an actual poem. Students decide which is poetry and discuss the questions above, after which they practice writing some visually expressive lines of their own.

513-T   (Discover/Field Trips) "Poetry Renaissance"

One way to stimulate the enjoyment of poetry is to get out of the formal classroom. A number of alternatives are available: group poetry readings after school in a relaxed environment, attendance at a lecture by a visiting poet, or viewing a good program of poetry reading on television. The essential component is to try to recapture that feeling of camaraderie which people once experienced through the medium of poetry.

514-T   (Discover/Lists) "Prove It"

The announcement of a poetry unit often results in a chorus of groans. One way to handle this problem is to ask each child who doesn't like poetry to list all the reasons for feeling this way. If desired, ask the others to list reasons they like poetry. These lists are used by the teacher to compile a master list of the most frequently mentioned reasons and to find poems which refute each negative reaction. This collection is read aloud and/or placed in a notebook for future poetry haters.

515-T   (Discover/Talks) "Off to a Good Start"

Before beginning to study poetry, many teachers feel compelled to defend poetry because they assume most students hate it. Instead of taking the defensive, teachers might take a more positive approach. One way is to organize a discussion on "Why a study of poetry is of value." Or use the same topic for a paper. A teacher with a bent for drama may encourage students to dramatize a poem either through choral reading or by rewriting it as a play. Poems such as "The Highwayman" or "The Pied Piper of Hamelin" can serve as starters. Some lines may need some changing; others need to be added, but soon the poem can live—with sound effects and even scenery.

516-C   (Listen/Audiotapes) "Teaming with Poets"

Introduce surrealistic poetry, which borders on stream-of-consciousness, by the following method: assign the name of one of three parts of speech (adjective, noun, and verb) in that order to each student. Each child says a word for his part of speech—any word which comes to mind. One student tapes as the activity moves along. Replaying the tape results in a form of surrealistic poetry. (Bring in a surrealistic painting to compare with the poetry.) Often the results are really very good if each response genuinely influences the next one. At any rate, by observing the disastrous results of haphazard choices, students realize that precise word selection is important in writing poetry.

517-C   (Listen/Music) "Notes About Lyrics"

Employ a careful study of lyrics from popular songs, past and present, to introduce and illustrate poetry. Ballads like "Barbara Allen," "John Henry," "Ode to Billie Joe," "Frankie and Johnnie," are good choices. The fact that almost everything which has happened in the past happens today in some form or another comes clear when the older ballads are compared with those of the modern-day balladeer. Students usually put aside negative reactions toward poetry when they realize the songs they like are really poems set to music.

518-C   (Listen/Recordings) "Now Hear This"

Locate recordings of professional announcers and actors reading poetry, perhaps poets reading their own works. Besides making poems easier to understand, this auditory approach makes poetry come alive by attaching it to human emotion rather than words on paper.

519-C   (Listen/Recordings) "Sing Us a Poem"

When introducing rhythm, have students choose a particular poem which they will read accompanied by musical instruments. If live music is unavailable, the reading can be backed by appropriate recorded music. Listening carefully to the tempo, crescendos, and decrescendos of the music, the reader can better attribute proper vocal inflection, intensity, pitch, and rhythm to the poetry. Setting the poetry to music gives an empathic feeling which cannot be obtained any other way.

520-C (Listen/Recordings) "Sound Al'round"

In teaching the various elements of poetry, acknowledge things with which students are already familiar. Poetic sound combinations, for instance, are used in slogans by politicians to appeal to all sorts of people. Advertisers, too, recognize the attractiveness of such poetic devices as the alliterations in "Surround it with Saran," "Reach for the Red Refresher," "Jolly Green Giant"; the rhyme in "Look for the Seal on the Peel," "Hate that gray? Wash it away"; and the onomatopoeia in "Snap, Crackle, Pop." Bring in tape recordings of these and many other commercial excerpts and start a unit on "Found Poetry."

521-T (Observe/Displays) "See the Light"

To create a mood when reading poetry in class, try using a colored spotlight. When certain poems suggest softness and romanticism, for example, bathe the room in soft blue light. Or use the light-show technique of hand-colored transparencies or slides. What a difference in mood!

522-T (Observe/Displays) "Stop, Look, and Listen Poetry"

Poetry can be more dramatic if read aloud with proper voice inflection. To create a particular mood, project slides of appropriate magazine illustration backgrounds on a large, light-colored wall or screen. Add some music. Students listen rather than read along in their books. Few will ignore the impact of this multimedia presentation.

523-C (Observe/Slides) "Seeing Is Believing"

To illustrate a poet's use of imagery, metaphor, or simile, show some appropriate slides on the subject. For instance, if the class has difficulty understanding Emily Dickinson's "I'll Tell You How the Sun Rose," show slides of sunrises and sunsets while reading it. This helps students visualize and appreciate the poet's word-picture.

524-T   (Read/Models) "Made In Japan"

The Japanese verse form haiku has become popular in America during the past few years because of its appeal to all age groups. This form can be introduced in classrooms as early as grade school and can be continued through high school and beyond. An interesting approach for high school is to include the haiku in a study of an American poet such as Robert Frost. Frost poems such as "Design," "Dust of Snow," "Nothing Gold Can Stay," and "Spring Pools" use complex juxtapositions. One is unnatural whiteness and the natural life-death cycle. Both are re-flected in this original haiku:

> *Bedded patient, dead*
> *Still, white in a sun-drenched gown,*
> *Grasping sheets of white.*

Thus, the student gains both a clearer understanding of Frost's images and the single-impact haiku. (See idea 42.)

SHORT STORY

525-C   (Listen/Recordings) "Sounding Off"

When reading a short story orally in class—especially descriptive passages—have some students provide a background of appro-priate sound effects, live or on tape. Record distributors often have sound effects albums. A good introductory selection is John Steinbeck's "Flight"—Pepe's escape into the mountains.

526-C   (Research/Libraries, Role Playing) "Full Immersion"

This activity is recommended for middle or junior high students when studying short stories about ethnic groups. After some library research on social customs, particularly special foods, have a banquet featuring the authentic foods and styles of cook-ing. Whether the cooking is done in school or at home, the point will be made strongly that American society is truly pluralistic. Some classes have even donned costumes for the occasion. The history behind the characteristic menus also makes an interesting study.

VOCABULARY

527- C   (Discover/Chalkboard, Words) "Take It from Lit"

Difficult vocabulary in literature—obscure or archaic phrases, allusions, and new words—should be clarified before the reading begins. At the start of each lesson, place a few of the day's difficult words on the board. For full enjoyment of a poem or other work, discuss and define these stumbling blocks. But spend only a short time on this phase, since the main reason for reading literature is not the vocabulary study.

CHAPTER
10

DELIBERATION

DRAMA

528- T (Analyze/Discussion) "Shakespearean Sin"

Sometimes, in teaching Shakespeare, we find ouselves concentrating too much on the plot and obvious action. Instead, we need to delve into Shakespeare's genius and analyze the deep beauty and meaning of his plays. Such discussions, quite naturally, will enhance interest and understanding of the past as well as the present and future of our society.

529- C (Experiment/Field Trips) "Orchestra or Loge?"

While doing a theater unit, plan a field trip to see a community or civic theater production of an appropriate play. Possibly a special matinee performance can be offered to combined English classes. Make arrangements for the cast and/or stage manager or director to speak to the classes after the performance. Perhaps this could include a costume, prop, or make-up demonstration and an opportunity for the students to ask questions.

530- G   (Interpret/Role Playing) "Living Arts"

Have groups present key themes or character studies from a play, novel, or short story. Students pose in tableau-like positions which symbolize the way these characters relate to each other. For example, one group might portray the prevailing theme in *A Raisin in the Sun* by joining hands and forming a circle facing stoically outward, away from a frustrated student placed in the middle. Another couple might portray Hester Prynne (*The Scarlet Letter*) standing tall above a genuflecting Dimmesdale. Add a bit of competition through a contest in which students guess the play or key scenes within a play through these tableaus or simple charades.

HUMANITIES

531- T   (Analyze/Artwork) "Literature in 3-D"

Review the methods for analyzing the visual arts and music and then have students apply the same principles to literature. One approach, emphasizing line, form, and space, is to show how each work of art incorporates design, differences, and dominance (the 3-D theory): design through repetition, differences through contrasts and variations, dominance through a device such as prevailing colors, forms, or themes which holds the work together to give it purpose. The effective use of all three aspects differentiate between any art and good art.

532- T   (Consolidate/Instruction) "Multi-Lit"

Encourage reading which parallels current studies in other subject fields. For example, every period of history has had its writers who reflect the age. Many books are based in lands being studied in geography. Civics classes consider many themes found in novels and short stories. Foreign language classes can quite naturally tie in with world literature. Science courses can introduce a host of biographies, novels, and short stories. To accomplish this goal ask other subject matter teachers to forward their future plans to allow time to research titles and sources. Then allow students to make free choices which will eventually help them consolidate these seemingly divergent but actually very similar sources.

NOVELS

533-I   (Analyze/Books) "Mirroring the Images"

Following a discussion of the concept of imagery in literature, provide activities which will encourage students to look for repeated images in a novel, e.g., water imagery in Hemingway. A good starting point would be a study of the author's life to provide a possible clue to the strong images. The teacher can help students in developing this study of imagery by providing lists of strong image words. Such an approach provides some relief to the usual ways of analyzing a piece of literature.

534-C   (Analyze/Discussion) "Parallel-o-Greats"

This game involves character analysis. Start with a group discussion and proceed to a deeper exercise of individual thought and research. Taking one character at a time, work up a list of a half-dozen one-word character traits. Then for *each* trait decide what famous person in history or entertainment might epitomize this trait. From here move to a guessing game by merely leaving out the character's name; list just his traits and name the famous people who epitomize each trait. For example, one personality trait of Odysseus is being crafty or cunning which might be compared with someone like James Bond, Dick Tracy, or a famous militarist in recent history.

535-I   (Analyze/Notes) "Psych 'em Out"

Students are often asked to write character sketches for novels or short stories they are reading. To create a deeper interest in such an activity present this exercise. Each student becomes a "psychoanalyst." As the story is covered he writes on-going observations about a main character and then, through analysis, draws some conclusions about the individual's personality which were not brought out in the text.

536-C   (Discover/Discussion) "A Novel Approach"

This idea works best if the assigned novel has not yet been read. For one of the primary characters, list behavioral traits, appearance, attitudes, and so on and state briefly the character's relevance to the novel. Then the class considers what type of person the character is and how he or she will probably act within the novel. With this preliminary discussion, the students should be anxious to start reading the novel to find out if they are correct.

537-C   (Experiment/Tales) "Twice-told Tales"

To experiment with style, students select a popular fairy tale and retell it in a well-known style, e.g., Chaucer, Melville, Hemingway, Joyce, the Bible, or a news magazine. This exercise helps to illustrate that style is a very personal literary attribute and that anybody who writes frequently begins to develop a style even if at first it is copied.

538-I   (Interpret/Cartoons) "Comical Characters"

Practice how an author creates a character. Each student reads a comic book. On paper they describe the main character as completely as possible using material from the comic book to support contentions. Have the students discuss the complexity of these characters in relation to what they think makes a real or great literary character. Many similarities exist between character development in the comics and good literature.

539-I   (Interpret/Papers) "Calling All Careers"

Capitalize on the need to bring more career education into the classroom by taking an inventory of the students' career interests and combining this information with the need to read. After students have decided what their life ambitions might be, they will read at least three novels in which the main characters are also engaged in that same career. Then each student writes a paper drawing the parallels between knowledge of the career and the books' versions, concluding with an interpretation of what such a career may be like.

540-I   (Interpret/Papers) "Who's Who?"

Lengthy novels often contain so many characters that it is difficult to remember them. Selected students or volunteers could read ahead, each writing a brief description of one particular character including appearance, speech habits, moral traits, and eccentricities as well as the character's function in the novel. When each new character is first introduced, the paper may be read orally and discussed. These thumbnail sketches, which can be illustrated and placed on the bulletin board, serve to crystallize characters so they will readily be recognized as the plot unfolds. Whenever anyone has a question concerning a character, the student who researched the character is called upon as a resource.

541-G   (Interpret/Paragraphs) "Subbing"

To help everyone keep track of what is going on in a long novel, write a plot outline on the chalkboard showing the main plot and various subplots. Then divide the class into groups, assigning each one of the subplots. As each subplot occurs in the study, ask the group to summarize it in one paragraph and then read it to the class. Discussions can occur when time permits to consider how the subplots relate to the main story line.

542-C   (Organize/Games) "Who, What, When, Where, Why—and How!"

This simple game helps develop the concept of plot. Place five members on a team, one member for each of the five W's. They first establish a few characters and a simple plot. On signal, one team member writes a word or sentence answering "who." He folds over his response and hands the paper to the next person on his team who writes a "what" to go with the "who," etc. A story will develop for each team and is read aloud immediately. In awarding points for teams, the class uses some criteria: Does the story have a plot? Does it make sense? Is it complete?

OVERVIEW

543-C   (Analyze/Games) "Four for Metaphor"

When studying a novel or play which has many characters, such as Galsworthy's *Man of Property*, students may find it difficult to understand and recall the aspects of each personality. To better explain the characters' actions and importance, try a game of "Metaphors." A team of three or four students leaves the room briefly while the rest of the class chooses one fictional character for the team to guess. Returning, the small group suggests a category from a selection decided earlier such as favorite color, clothes, transportation, furniture, or books. Volunteers give clues which fit the category and would most likely represent the character in question, e.g., the type of clothing he would probably wear to a party. Someone writes these suggestions on the board to aid recall. If the character has not been guessed by the time limit, the name is given. Discussion to clarify may follow. Teams can participate in timed competition.

544- C   (Interpret/Books) "Going My Way?"

When teaching literary criticism, keep in mind the following notions. There is no single "right" method to handle literary approaches or to uncover all the significant truths of a work. Although scrutinizing various literary theories is a useful philosophical activity, the full understanding of literature does not always depend on such theorizing. Try to have students construct their own sets of valid, simple statements to clarify the nature and quality of a work and thereby increase appreciation.

545- I   (Interpret/Books) "Stitch in Time"

Use proverbs to bring out the theme of a book or story. Encourage students to either find a proverb or write their own describing what was said in a work under study. This helps reduce themes to a sentence rather than forcing the all-too-common paragraph or report. To illustrate themes and interacting subthemes, more than one proverb may be found, or one major proverb and several related. For example, Frost's repeated line in "Stopping by Woods"—"And miles to go before I sleep"— will evoke several interesting explanations.

546- T   (Organize/Talk) "Enjoying by Joining"

Start an English Club composed of students whose interest in literature is reflected in their scholastic achievement. At the beginning of the fall semester hold a social meeting with a short program aimed at encouraging membership. Club members elect officers and plan programs focusing on dramatic presentations, readings by guest poets, debates, lectures by visiting authors, the production of an original play, or a language arts exhibit for the entire student body. The club could also help promote use of the school library.

POETRY

547-T   (Analyze/Discussion) "Meritorious Poetry"

Time and again when students analyze poetry and prose they
are subtly coerced to agree that a poem or play is good because
it is by Carl Sandburg, Bob Dylan, or someone equally famous.
It is easy, then, for students to think literature is good only if it
is written by a well-known author. This idea makes it more
difficult for new writers and poets to be read and accepted.
Teach students what true poetry is, what makes good poetry.
Then bring to class poems which are good regardless of who
wrote them. Encourage students to bring in little-known poems
they feel are worthy. Discuss these poems for content, not ever
mentioning the poet's name.

548-C   (Analyze/Discussion) "Poets Who Know It"

The teacher reads aloud two contrasting poems without comment. The class discusses the subject of each poem, the authors'
attitudes, likenesses and differences, the sound of each poem and
the relation of sound to tone, and the tone in each and how it is
achieved. With the students themselves providing the answers,
they will soon realize that they really do know something about
poetry.

549-C   (Analyze/Models) "Air and Compare"

Analyze the effect of poetry upon the listener by duplicating
some song lyrics and several poems. See if students can tell
which are which. Delete a stanza of a poem, or substitute either
words or entire stanzas. How quickly do students note a change
in effect? Then ask different students to read a short poem aloud
to show its dramatic quality and prove that the effect varies
with each reader. Each time a poem is read, others reading the
same poem should be out of hearing range.)

550-C   (Experiment/Chalkboard) "Chalk One Up for Poetry"

To better understand how a poem is created, the class will
write a poem and post it on the chalkboard. First, list poetic devices as reminders—alliteration, meter, metaphor, rhyme. Then
the class chooses the topic and suggests content. Even if the
poem isn't too good, it helps develop a working understanding
of poetry.

551- C   (Analyze/Music) "Class-ick Hit"

Students become very interested in poetry when it is current. Before delving into the classics, duplicate songs by popular lyricists from albums students bring to class. Examine how these songs follow patterns. Urge everyone to try writing his own lyrics—really poems. Then, later, if time permits, students who want to put forth the extra effort might work with the music department (or musically talented within the class) to put the words to music.

552-I   (Experiment/Essays) "Saying It Like It Is"

Ask students to paraphrase a poem in their own words, in prose as in an essay. Selections are read orally and compared with the poem. Besides developing some poetic and rhetoric insight, students will also see poetry as the better way to express some thoughts.

553-C   (Experiment/Poems) "Graffoetry"

To stimulate experimentation in poetry have students create "found" poems consisting of words, sentences, or phrases found anywhere (billboards, newspaper articles, advertisements, recipes, even some walls). Arrange items in poetic form. Words may be left out or repeated, but no words are added. Share results.

554- I   (Interpret/Audiotapes) "For the Record"

Let each student choose a favorite short poem to read into a tape recorder. Several practice readings before taping will improve results. Play back all the readings, making certain the words for some of the more difficult poems are available to read while listening. This approach is a good opening for discussion of oral interpretation of poetry.

555- C   (Interpret/Discussions) "Clash of Symbols"

A relatively mature college prep class would benefit from the following idea illustrating there is no final interpretation of any poem, not even the author's. Write a poem yourself, then write out your own interpretation of it. Present your poem to the class as an anonymous poem and have them interpret it. They will be able to find and support meanings and symbols that you had never considered. When they are finished, reveal what you have done, show your interpretation, and explain how their versions are superior to yours.

556- I   (Interpret/Mixed Media) "Cut Out the Dissection"

Awakening student sensitivity to poetry can sometimes be a problem. One way to sharpen interest is to avoid the usual explicative phase, at least initially. Assign a specific poem for each member to interpret in his own way. This interpretation may be in the form of an original painting, dance, music, a prose essay, or even another poem. This procedure encourages the student to explore poetry for its between-the-lines message.

557- T   (Interpret/Poems) "Going My Way"

When studying poetry, a teacher can unwittingly antagonize students by foisting off a teacher interpretation when there really is no way to know. If a student tries but comes up with a different interpretation than the expected one, he should be encouraged to know that his opinion is as good as the next person's. Similarly important, use care when commenting upon written papers which offer interpretations.

558- C   (Interpret/Recordings) "Auditory Imagery"

To aid in understanding poetic imagery—symbol, simile, metaphor, and so on—bring in some record albums of image-rich songs. Any songs popular with youth are good. Play the song, perhaps several times. Hopefully, the students would be acquainted with the words. Then they can pick out the images, tell what they might stand for, and comment on effectiveness.

559- C   (Interpret/Talk) "Greek to Me"

To illustrate the role of sound in poetry, the teacher (or

another bi-linguist) reads several poems in any foreign language with which most students would not be familiar—even in "Jabberwocky" nonsense words. Through voice inflection, pause, rate, and other devices, the reader tries to project the general ideas and moods of the poem. See if the class can empathize on the basis of sound alone. Experiments in phonetic symbolism indicate that this can be done with a high level of accuracy.

560- G   (Listen/Audiotapes) "Reading between the Lines"

Poetry is often characterized by the saying: "What counts most is not what is said but what is not said—what the reader must discover." The student of poetry should be able to recognize how a message moves across the vacant space between images in a poem. To demonstrate, a small group can tape a word-association discussion outside of class. Members of this group speak spontaneously but use only one word at a time which has been suggested by the previous word. The tape is then played to aid discussion of the logic behind the flow of conversation: What single thought connected each image? Why did one word or image inspire the next? What were the cognitive aspects of the discussion?

561- C   (Listen/Recordings) "Folk-singing Young Folk"

Analyze the poetry used by contemporary folk singers, noting the interrelationship of words, rhythm, and rhyme. Suggest putting some poems to music. Discuss the fit of both meaning and rhythm. Also try some original poem writing which could be sung by a student guitar-playing folk singer.

562- G   (Read/Poems) "Togetherness"

Let the class experience the fun of reading poetry through choral reading. Selections by Kipling, Poe, and Service are good starters. Encourage the class to work out some groupings to achieve special effects after they have learned how to read in unison effectively.

CHAPTER

11

EVALUATION

DRAMA

563- G   (Judge/Role Playing) "Try Tryouts"

When studying any play, encourage students to act out key scenes. Have a contest between several groups (casts). This is a good way to analyze the characters' motives, emotions, and other traits and to encourage creativity. The rest of the class decides which group (and individual) did the best interpretation.

HUMANITIES

564- C   (Compare/Games) "Humani-tease"

To determine if students comprehend the correlatives of the arts, literature, philosophy, sociology, technology, and so forth of an age, play a random drawing game. Call it "Humani-tease" or something better. Provide six small boxes which will hold 3 × 5 index cards. Label each box with one of the following: Traits and Ideas, Literature, Architecture, Sculpture, Painting, and Music. Place in the first box a number of cards each bearing a key trait of a period, say the Romantic, e.g., emotionalism, individualism, and nationalism. Then place the names of titles of various works of art (or artists) of the period in their respective boxes. Assume at least two teams of six players each. Each team player is caretaker of one box while his team has its turn. The first card drawn gives a trait or idea. Each of the other players must go through their boxes until they find a work which reflects that idea or trait. (Cards may be filed in alphabetical order to save time or may be in a jumbled state.) The chosen cards are then compared with a master list held by a monitor or the teacher. Allow one point for each correct card among four. The game progresses until a team reaches the preselected top score.

565- G   (Extrapolate/Demonstrations) "Renew the Review"

A literature review can even become exciting if the class is divided into committees, each of which is responsible for producing a fifty-minute program characterizing the literary period which the group selects to cover. The groups use art galleries, libraries, museums, and other sources to gather material. Their programs might incorporate filmstrips, slides, records, appropriate costumes, pictures of literary figures, puppets, or other props. After the shows have been presented, the best ideas could be worked into a program for other English classes or even the entire school. Of course, students can be evaluated on their contributions.

NONFICTION

566- C   (Identify/Biography) "Propped Up Book Reports"

Everybody in the class independently chooses a biography to read. They must, as part of a book report, illustrate, nonverbally with gestures and props, the famous person. The class must guess who the book is about. Some type of prize could be given to the person(s) with the most successful guesses. This activity requires good character analysis.

NOVELS

567- C   (Compare/Cartoons) "Charlie Caulfield v. Holden Brown"

Compare comic strip characters with people in books. Students can learn much about Holden Caulfield (*Catcher in the Rye*) by comparing him to Charlie Brown (*Peanuts*). Let the class cut out specific comic strips or cartoons which illustrate a point they want to make about a book character. The similarities can be amazing.

568- G   (Compare/Games) "Miss or Match"

The object of this game is to match a character with a well-defined personality trait or a situation with its significance in the story. Two sets of cards are prepared. The name of a character or description of a situation appears on each card in one set. The personality characteristic (or significance) is written on a card in the second set. The cards are distributed randomly throughout the class. Then one player with a character (or situation) card reads it and waits for a classmate to complete the matching trait (or significance). The student who thinks he can, reads his card when called. If there is a match, that student gets a point; if not, the point goes to the student who first reads a card. It is important to have unambiguous clues.

569- G   (Compare/Skits) "Characters in Search of Plot"

This exercise helps develop understanding of the interdependence of characters and plot. Two different groups present for the class an improvised scene based on a single idea supplied by the teacher, e.g., a crowded bus, a supermarket checkout counter, an ice cream parlor. They will work independently of each other and give their performances at different times (neither seeing the other's). Each group usually gives a different improvised interpretation of a single-idea plot, and the characters take on different personalities. A strong similarity between the two performances still provokes good comparison discussions on how the plot was altered through the characters' different personalities. If both presentations could be videotaped, the two groups could share each other's effort.

570- I   (Extrapolate/Books) "Plot-It-Yourself Kit"

The plot, almost always interesting and usually neglected because it is so obvious, should be used to develop an understanding of the novel's theme. One approach, when giving the next day's reading assignment, is to tell the class not to read beyond the assignment but rather to imagine the rest of the plot and jot down anticipatory notes. Since through plot direction the students must frequently change their idea of the theme, they gain a greater understanding of the term. Both teacher and student, then, can check on understanding.

571-I   (Extrapolate/Cartoons) "Comic Pick"

In just about any daily or Sunday comic strip, one can find the literary devices used in structuring a novel. Evaluate ability to pick out such elements as satire, irony, and allegory as students see them exemplified in various comic strips. Each example can be pasted at the top of a short explanation of how the strip illustrates the particular element.

572-C   (Extrapolate/Games) "For the Game Room"

This game is a technique for checking on understanding characters and plot details in drama, short story, the novel, or even poetry. The idea is to create nonsensical allusions, obvious puns, or outrageous similarities, or find song titles that will match and identify the predetermined list of titles and characters drawn up by the teacher.

Examples:

Giants in the Earth—"The Sounds of Silence"
The Iliad (referring to Helen)—"That face, that face, that marvelous face"
Moby Dick—"The Impossible Dream"
The Odyssey—"Bill Bailey, Won't You Please Come Home"
The Odyssey—(referring to the cannibal Laestrogonias) "People Who Need People"
The Old Man and the Sea—"One in the hand is worth two in the bush."

573-I   (Extrapolate/Papers) "Extra, Extra!"

A quick way to discover if students understand the basic plots or themes in novels is to let them write headlines:

"Soldier Missing in Action Returns to Fight" (Plot)
    (*The Red Badge of Courage*)
"Youth Finds Self up a Tree" (Theme)
    (*A Separate Peace*)

This technique can be expanded to writing a news article about the event, using facts from the novel. Or the teacher can make up headlines for a matching section in a literature test.

574- I   (Extrapolate/Papers) "Moving Bulletin Boards"

When teaching long, thematic units using several sources, keep track of the basic points by building a progressive bulletin board. As the unit moves along, list the elements of the novel across the top: Plot, Characters, Setting, Style, Emotional Effect. As each element is studied, a few students at a time write very short summaries (1) defining the element and giving its function in the novel and (2) telling how the element affected them. Their papers are then placed on the board under the proper headings.

575- I   (Extrapolate/Tests) "Self-tests"

Students can prove they understand the novel under considera-tion by preparing a test, with answer key, which checks on familiarity with characters, basic theme, and plot. The teacher then selects the most comprehensive test and administers it to the class. If desired, the teacher may do a little editing to im-prove a question. The test writer then helps the teacher evaluate the results.

576- I   (Identify/Discussion) "Conceptual-eyes"

To elucidate an abstract concept in a literary work, ask each class member to write his own definition of the concept in as few words as possible. Faith, honor, courage, patriotism are some of the concepts that might be examined. This statement could be the starting point for comparing and contrasting stu-dent ideas with an author's. Not only does this activity stimulate discussion, it also allows the shy student to share his ideas in a relaxed atmosphere.

577- C   (Identify/Discussion) "Drawing Blanks"

Spice up a literature review and generate interest in new authors by distributing to each student short passages from famous authors. Obliterate the main characters' names. By analyzing the unknown author's style, structure, apparent opinions, and other clues, the class narrows the piece to a particular literary period and then to a particular author. For some classes it may be necessary to use works of authors already studied.

578- C   (Identify/Discussion) "Slipping into Lit"

As a review of the impact of·a novel, ask each reader to write
on a slip of paper some key questions or feelings about the
novels. These slips of paper are collected and then used as a
springboard for class discussion. Each student draws one slip
and leads the class in discussing whatever it introduces. The
procedure is repeated as long as interest is maintained. The
best questions can be saved for final testing.

579- I   (Identify/Displays) "Cool Coats"

After a reading unit on *King Arthur: Tales of the Round Table,*
allow students time to explore their interest in legendary em-
blems by designing their own coat-of-arms. A student's emblem
will reveal many things about his beliefs, self-concepts, interests,
abilities, and needs, and will reflect historical knowledge about
his family. These designs can then be placed on book jackets,
lockers, sweaters, and blazer jackets.

580- C   (Identify/Games) "English Inquisition"

This game enables students to review literary facts and develop
the skill of asking questions. One student thinks of a certain
author or character and gives the rest of the class the first letter
of the name. They then begin to ask questions to identify the
mystery subject. Whoever guesses the word gets points and
begins another game. The vital clue to solving the mystery name
is in the questioning procedure, so some time should be spent
prior to playing the game on how to ask questions which move
from broad generalities to narrow categories very quickly. This
approach gives everyone an opportunity to participate and gives
the teacher a chance to hear how everyone thinks.

581- C   (Identify/Games) "He's a Card"

A valuable literature review game can be created by listing about
a hundred facts pertaining to different fictional characters.
Enter each fact on a card and shuffle cards. Each participant
randomly chooses an equal number of the fact cards. The remaining cards are placed in one stack. In a round, a player puts
down a card, reads the fact on it, and identifies the character.
For each card handled successfully, he is able to draw another

from the stack. He continues until he misses. Then the next player continues. Scores are based on the number of cards each player has before him when an agreed-upon time limit is reached.

582- C   (Identify/Games) "Panting for Pantomime"

Relying on their own reading background for material, students play a game of charades with the following categories: authors, characters, titles, and quotations which the teacher or a student committee prepares on slips of paper. One team tries to guess whatever one of their team mates draws to pantomime. Before beginning the game it would be helpful to review the useful pantomime gestures such as ones to identify categories and certain insignificant words.

583- C   (Identify/Games) "Slip Me the Answer"

Limiting their activity to books familiar to the class, pupils draw up lists of questions about authors, titles, plots, themes, characters, and settings. They write on small slips of tagboard and place the questions in a box. Someone acting as questioner draws a slip from the box and reads it aloud. Each class member who answers correctly can keep the slip. At the end, the person with the most slips wins the game.

584- I   (Identify/Notes) "Spicy Review"

This literature review is a cooperative effort and particularly effective with slow learners. A number of volunteers choose characters from one or several novels and make up three clues about each choice. In turn, these are presented orally to the rest of the class who make notes about the clues. Using their texts if they wish, the class brings in a list of the correct characters the next day.

585- C   (Identify/Paragraphs) "Author Bee"

Discover if pupils have developed a concept of style through an "Author Bee." Divide the class into two teams. Read a paragraph written by one of the authors studied. The teams must guess who wrote it. Each member who answers correctly gets to sit down. (Why should the winners suffer on their feet?) The first team to seat all its members wins.

586- G   (Identify/Role Playing) "Role It"

To see if students can identify characters, persuade them to act out key scenes or to interpret dialogue from selections under study. Encouraging them at times to give their own free interpretations promotes discussions about the controversial adaptations.

587–G   (Judge/Conferences) "Take Five"

Gear literature study to include both rapid and slow readers even though the class is reading the same novel. The first five students to finish the novel have a group conference with the teacher. They are then assigned another novel based on the same theme or topic. The next five to finish have their conference and are assigned a shorter novel or even a group of poems which relate to the novel. Each five to finish confer with the teacher and receive additional assignments which can be completed in the remaining time. In this way the slow readers can read at their own pace and not be inundated by more work than they can handle. Everybody is challenged to the extent of his ability. Then at the very end, the whole matter can be brought together through several days of panel discussion on the various materials covered by groups.

588- I   (Judge/Papers) "Texture Titillation"

To capture a student's overall insights into a novel's plot, imagery, and symbolism, assign key chapters or sections to each student on which he writes a short critique. These papers are shared orally before the class and act as a catalyst for class discussion.

589- I   (Restructure/Notes) "Dear Diary"

Students fabricate a diary which might have been kept by the most or least likeable character in a novel which the class has read. The specific selection of notes will tell whether they have learned the technique of characterization. Instead of being written in one or two sittings, the best diaries develop over a period of several weeks during which time the student "lives" the character's life.

590- T   (Restructure/Journals) "New Heights for Wuthering Heights"

When teaching the culturally disadvantaged, nonreaders, school haters, and so on, don't force upon them books like *The Scarlet Letter*, *Wuthering Heights*, or other works which may further alienate them. To begin, offer a choice of contemporary selections more in keeping with their particular social and cultural concerns: *Viva Chicano* (Bonham), *The Chocolate War* (Cormier), *The Outsiders* (Hinton), *Lisa, Bright and Dark* (Newfeld), *The Chosen* (Potok), or *Native Son* (Wright). Give them previews of each book on the suggested list, and let them choose which ones they prefer to read. Have students keep journals in which they record their daily personal reactions to the reading. Stress that the journals are not to be graded and that the students are free to discuss their book in any manner they please, as long as they write a certain number of pages weekly. When a student completes a book, have an individual conference which might begin by discussing journal reactions—positively, of course.

591- I   (Restructure/Plots) "Summarily Speaking"

Unfortunately, some teachers assume that they alone can handle the summarizing of major and minor events in works studied. In an exercise which calls for plot summaries, students write down in chronological order the main events of a section they have just read. This gives the teacher an indication of how well pupils are keeping up with reading assignments. Let the summaries serve as springboards for discussions.

592- G   (Restructure/Skits) "Lit Skit"

To evaluate student understanding of character development in an assigned novel, let two or more students present a skit dramatizing character-revealing scenes from the story. For example, in Salinger's *Catcher in the Rye*, Holden and Mr. Spencer consider Holden's exam. Holden does not want it read aloud; Mr. Spencer insists on it. Two students build on this impromptu scene, each trying to keep his character in the role.

593- C   (Restructure/Skits) "Skit-Lit"

The learning accomplished by accurately and successfully portraying character development in a skit (as in idea 592) can be
transferred into an original, relevant situation reflecting modern
day crises. The entire class can then discuss how well each character was interpreted. The best situations grow from areas of
student interest: relating to peers, getting along, socializing, examining the weird and grotesque, or finding an inner peace.

OVERVIEW

594- C   (Compare/Games) "Concentration Creation"

Especially helpful and entertaining for junior high classes is a
literary game much like "Concentration." In this simplified
form, the students match author cards or questions, with the
correct title. Each correct match uncovers a section of a rebus
puzzle which, when fully revealed, depicts either a notable
quotation from one of the works studied or from another
famous title. To win the game the student must also guess the
rebus. Of course, the game can also cover short stories and
poetry—or any other forms. Use large sheets of tag board or
newsprint mounted on the bulletin board for overcoming the
logistics problem.

595- I   (Compare/Papers) "Pardon My Melancholy, Baby"

If teachers expect students to be creative in their written work,
they would do well to phrase assignments imaginatively. The
return on an assignment like "Write an 800-word paper on 'How
Lavinia in O'Neill's *Mourning Becomes Electra* Can Be Compared
with Her Legendary Greek Counterpart' " predictably is going
to be dull and repetitious. But asking students to contrast their
personal knowledge of or direct experience with one instance of
Lavinia's behavior is assurance that there will be as many uniquely
individual papers as there are students in the class.

596- C   (Extrapolate/Games) "Abstraction Attraction"

A lively way to approach understanding of metaphors so frequently used in literature is a game called "Abstractions."
Everyone guesses which class member is the subject a player has
in mind by asking him questions such as "What magazine is he

most like?" or "What would he like to do on a vacation?" Then the class can discuss what traits were conjured up by certain abstractions and why. The teacher observing this activity will be able to tell if the students are understanding the concept of metaphor.

597- C   (Extrapolate/Games) "Team Up"

In the manner of charades, divide the class into two or more teams. Give one member from each team the name of a character or describe a situation. The member whose team is up first chooses someone from his team who most resembles the character to be guessed (or the characters involved in a situation). He then gives stage directions to his character(s) for carrying out activities which will help other members of his team guess the right answer. The "actors," of course, do not know the answer either and must follow through in the same impromptu manner as the "director."

598- I   (Extrapolate/Illustrations) "Can You Picture That?"

As an alternative to the usual written report on a piece of literature, each student draws or locates pictures for a collage to illustrate the main theme of his selection. Pertinent quotations may accompany the illustrations. Display finished projects on the bulletin board. By this approach the student reveals if he has caught the essence of the literary work. Best of all, the typical and overused written book report can be omitted.

599- I   (Extrapolate/Journals) "Logging Literature"

Although using journals has become an academic fad, they can be very useful in teaching and evaluating literature as well as composition. Instead of asking students to write extensive papers, allow them to keep journals in which they record anything they want—opinions, emotions, anger, arguments—while they read their assigned or free readings. Several times each term set aside a class period to share these ideas. The instructor reads the journals, regularly writing comments to encourage additional exploration and development.

600- I   (Extrapolate/Papers) "Pick a Card"

Don't let the belief that each book requires a written book report limit the number of books read. Yet some reading record should be kept. Many teachers find this successful. In a file box on the teacher's desk, each student places 3 × 5 cards summarizing books read. At intervals the teacher chooses any book card in a student's file and makes up a question for an impromptu paper. This is an acceptable way to monitor reading when book conferences are not possible. (See related idea 606.)

601- I   (Extrapolate/Pictures) "Unfolding Personalities"

To determine if students understand the role of characters in a play or novel, have each student prepare a file folder on one character. These personality folders include on one page a montage of pictures portraying the subject's personality— appearance, likes, dislikes, interests, occupation, and the like— on one side, and on the other a detailed explanation of the illustrations. When completed, the picture portion of each card or folder is displayed for class discussion and identification. How well the pictures reflect the role of the character will reveal how well the student understood the character. (See related idea 34 for student personality folders.)

602- C   (Extrapolate/Role Playing) "In-quiz-itive"

Instead of the usual written quiz to find out who has or has not read the assigned novel or play, try this role-playing approach. Assign main character roles to several students who must answer questions asked by the class. The class asks such questions as why a character acted or felt a certain way. To ask perceptive questions, class members would have had to read the material. And certainly the "characters" would indicate by their answers whether they have read or understood the material.

603- C   (Identify/Games) "Enveloped in Lit"

Test knowledge of novels or plays through subjective or objective questions in this game approach. Write a series of questions on slips of paper placed in sealed envelopes (sealed for heightened suspense), one for each student. Progressing in some sequence, each student opens his envelope at his turn and gives an impromptu answer. If he cannot reply, the question is offered to the class. This becomes a good method for assessing preparedness before a test, for a review, or as a game. The students may even be graded on answers.

604- C   (Identify/Games) "Pair of Aces"

After reading the works of several authors, the class can play "Who Am I?" Before the class begins, each student writes several sentences about an author. Then either in pairs or two or more teams, participants try to guess the author. The score is based on the number of statements needed to identify the author. The fewer the statements, the higher the score. This same procedure can be used for characters or any other aspect of literature study.

605- C   (Identify/Games) "This Is Your Strife"

Pupils need involvement and opportunities to express themselves in the classroom. A "This Is Your Life" review provides that opportunity and will also show who is informed about authors, poets, playrights, and artists studied in class. A skillful group can lay the groundwork by preparing a number of biographies listing key events in the lives of those studied. Through the type of conversational dialogue used in the popular television show, the clues are given so two teams can compete for points in making the right guesses to identify the "mystery person."

606- I   (Judge/Book Reports) "Box Hunches"

Instead of having students write book reports, allow them to use this time for more reading. Require very short reports on 4 × 6 file cards which each student can keep in a small accordion card file. Whenever students finish reading a book, they enter the author, title, subject, and brief commentary including reactions. The cards are kept in the classroom for other students to examine. The teacher also uses them, not only to check progress but to locate ideas for planning future lessons, e.g., getting students to share what they have read when it relates to the lesson at hand.

607- I   (Judge/Conferences) "Do-It-Yourself Reading"

To enhance those free reading periods which allow students to pursue their own reading interests, some adjustment to environment is needed. If books or funds are available, provide a special reading room or arrange for converting a section of the library for this purpose. Contacts with publishers or distributors will often succeed in obtaining a supply of free or very reasonably

priced, appealing paperbacks. Changes in evaluation may also be
in order. Students should be told they will be evaluated on the
amount of reading, on the quality of choices, and on their understanding. Individual conferences are the most effective because
they allow for differences both in ability and interest. Most of
all, students learn best by doing what they enjoy most. Book
reading is no exception.

608- T   (Judge/Questions) "Why How?"

In directing literature discussions, ask "how" and "why" questions, not "who, what, when, or where." For example, "How do
we know what will happen at the end of the story?" not "What
happens at the end of the story?" Or ask "Why does Santiago
want to catch the giant marlin?" and not, "Who is Santiago?"

609- C   (Judge/Talk) "Debate is De Bait"

Debate—the intelligent, constructive exchange of ideas and
opinions—is one of the most valuable learning and sharing situations the classroom can help develop. Used in the right manner,
it can be a most effective way to criticize literature. In this
activity the teacher can act as Socratic guide, Devil's advocate,
prompter, arbiter, and interpreter, offering alternative opinions
rather than giving the "correct" one or "the truth."

610- G   (Restructure/Discussion) "Past In Review"

Divide the class into small groups, each responsible for a particular author the class has studied during the term. On an appointed
day, each group presents its panel giving in-depth analysis of the
author. They may wish to conclude with a brief quiz. In this
way students do their own reviewing.

611- C   (Restructure/Games) "Exciting Citations"

Covering literature in a classroom need not be routine. For instance, at appropriate times the class can be divided into two
groups. The teacher (or student) gives clues (questions, statements) to elicit information about key episodes in the novel. The
group which gives the best response and actually cites the desired portion of the story gets two points. The group reaching
twenty points first is the winner.

612- C   (Restructure/Games) "Jeopardy Party"

Based on a game approach called "Jeopardy" in which contestants give a question having heard an answer, this game serves as
a good review. The teacher has prepared a section of the chalkboard with five or six columns each headed "Authors," "Settings," "Characters," "Quotations," "Plots," and "Themes."
Each column also contains eight empty boxes as for a graph. To
keep track of progress in each category, X's are inserted in the
boxes when a correct response is made.

Two students take turns each round to represent their
teams. Each can choose a favorite category. For example, if the
category is "Characters," the teacher might give an answer from
a prepared list such as "He changed the lives of the Starretts."
The student correctly answers "Who was Shane?" As long as he
replies accurately, the participant keeps playing—usually down
a preferred category column, but he could switch since the items
further down the column are harder than those near or at the
top. The first correct response in a column gives one point; the
second, two points; and so on. These points are totaled for each
player or team at the end of the set time. Team participants can
be changed or retained.

613- G,C   (Restructure/Games) "Lit Wits"

Following several weeks or possibly an entire semester when
students engaged in outside readings, the class divides into two
equal teams for competition between those who prefer modern
and those who prefer classical literature. All students working in
groups within the two large teams prepare questions on all
aspects of their preferred readings: comprehending form, plot,
implied meanings, and themes; clarifying settings and characters;
and judging craftsmanship. Each group preparing questions gets
an identifying alphabetical letter to place on all its questions so
they won't get called upon to answer their own. Then the questions written on cards with answers on the back are collected so
that a quizmaster or mistress on whom everyone can agree can
ask selected questions to the large teams, each participant taking
turns in some planned way. Points are tallied, and the winning
team is treated to a party by the losers.

614- C   (Restructure/Games) "Question My Answer"

Here's a literature review game which all ability levels will enjoy.
Make up five categories within the work of literature being

studied, e.g., Characters/Settings, Story Line, Main Plot, Subplot, and Implied Meanings. Five teams frame four questions and answers in an assigned category. When called upon, one team member draws a question from each of the other four teams. His group must answer these within a time limit. For each question they answer correctly, they get one point; for each incorrectly answered question, the team submitting it gets two points. At the end of the playing time, the team with the most points wins.

615- C   (Restructure/Games) "Play Ball"

Middle or junior high students enjoy this game in the spring when baseball is in the air. Divide the class into two teams standing on opposite sides of the room. The teacher "throws out" questions to the first team: questions on authors, their lives, and their works. Each question answered correctly is a base hit, if incorrectly, an out. Three outs for the first team give the other team members a turn "at bat." Use an overhead transparency of a baseball diamond to show progress.

616- C   (Restructure/Puzzles) "Sometimes a Crossword"

Instead of the typical ways to review short stories, plays, novels, or poetry, involve the students in building games and puzzles. Since the crossword puzzle has proven to be a great brain teaser and a good way to approach study questions, teachers spend hours constructing them. Let students build these puzzles, singly, in groups, or in pairs. The best ones are chosen for the class to work.

617- C   (Restructure/Puzzles) "Switchword Puzzle"

As a variation of the regular crossword puzzle approach to review titles, characters, authors, and the like, pull a switch. Bring to class a puzzle already filled in. Ask the students to make up the clues to the answers. This provides variety when crosswords may be overused.

POETRY

618- I,C   (Identify/Discussions) "A Quo-Test"

Some students like to memorize entire poems. Others should be
encouraged to attempt memorizing portions of popular, well-
known poems. The satisfaction gained from being literate among
peers and family will outweigh for some the necessary practice
to improve ability to recall. The memorization can be shared
effectively through class discussions in which one student recites
a memorized portion and the others guess the source from a background of poetry studied in common during the year. Additional
discussions can cover such matters as meanings, figurative language, sensory images, sounds, rhythm, and tone of the lines
presented.

619- C   (Judge/Audiotapes) "Orally Speaking"

Before the class meets, volunteers who are some of the better
readers tape record individual interpretations of the same poem.
After hearing the tapes, the class selects the best interpretations,
giving reasons for their choices. This exercise covers many hard-
to-get-at items for poetry understanding.

620- G   (Judge/Music) "Five by Five"

Since musical lyrics are a form of poetry, go music. Five groups
of students review the lyrics of the five most popular hits—one
for each group. First, among themselves, each group criticizes
verse quality based on what they know about poetic structure.
They may even rewrite the lyrics to improve the verse, keeping
in mind the music. Then the class is given the opportunity to
react to each group presentation.

621- C   (Judge/Recordings) "Can You Beat This?"

In your next poetry unit, encourage
students to build a room library of
their favorite record albums. Over a
period of time, by class vote and a
process of elimination, select the
four best songs. Rate them 1 to 4.
Write the lyrics on the board and
have the class assess the qualities
which make these songs so good:

the rhythm, beat, lyrics, emotion, or whatever. Then find poetry with these same qualities and follow the same procedure as above. If one of the students plays the drums, let him bring his sticks and practice board to beat out the time for some selections. To assess learning let students write comparison papers showing how both mediums have many of the same qualities but how poetry has greater artistry of language, more depth, and deeper feeling.

622- C   (Judge/Sentences) "Nice and Concise"

When reading shorter poems such as Emily Dickinson's works, the students can write one-sentence summaries of what seems to be the main theme. Pass these around for class reaction. This is a good way to judge understanding and to start discussion.

623- C   (Judge/Talk) "Inner Action"

Poetry is the product of a mind sensitive to innermost feelings and to both natural and supernatural worlds. Encourage students to become aware of this sensitivity. Also emphasize an oral approach to poetry. Either assign a short poem or a passage in a longer poem to be memorized or read for a presentation to the class. Allow choices from the class anthology or anyone's favorite. The class then evaluates each presentation, noting the reader's manner of capturing and conveying the intended feelings of the poet. This method calls for close examination of what lies behind each poem.

624- C   (Restructure/Poems) "Scramble One"

Type or write selected scrambled stanzas from popular poems on separate pieces of paper. Pass out one complete set to each class member. Ask them to reorganize stanzas into their original positions. Although this activity relates most to "story line," it can also be used to check on structure.

SHORT STORY

625- I   (Compare/Models) "Keep Plotting Along"

After some study of the short story, use the following to see if students can discriminate between good and trite plots. Begin by describing a typical plot. Then provide three endings: one improbable or even trite, another fairly predictable, and the third original and very unusual. After rating them 1, 2, and 3, students will hopefully show that they prefer the original rather than the trite endings. Have about a dozen examples—originals or from little-known short stories.

626- C (Judge/Lists) "Plotting the Plot"

To quickly check on the students' understanding of plot, hand out a list of incidents from a short story. The students are to check only those which they feel are important to plot development. These checked items then form the basis for a discussion of plot development. Once the plot is well in mind, students can proceed to other aspects of the work.

627- C (Restructure/Models) "Loose Interpretation"

If a short story doesn't seem to have been well-liked and the class is dissatisfied with it for any number of reasons, try this. Let them see if they can do better by changing the characters and plot to the way they would have liked the story to happen.

628- C (Analyze/Movies) "Seen and Heard"

After reading a short story in class (for which a film is available), decide what the main points of the plot are, how they are sequenced, and why they are important to each other and to the entire story. In the next class meeting, review these points and show the film. Students compare the events of the film with those of the story, discovering similarities and differences. Considering "why" can be very interesting and informative.

629- C (Experiment/Role Playing) "Playing Up the Ending"

A useful device to give students practice in thinking "on their feet" is a modification of the old *commedia dell'arte*. After a short story involving a few characters has been briefly summarized, have the students act out spontaneously what they think is the climax.

VOCABULARY

630- C (Identify/Lists) "Get the Word"

While reading an assigned book or short story, individuals find words which they cannot define (or even pronounce). Each such word and the sentence in which the word appears (under-lined) is placed on a 3 × 5 index card. These cards are then ex-changed in some appropriate way so that students can help each other figure out a suitable definition. It's noisy but instructional, and the knowledge gained usually remains. The teacher could collect some of these cards for later evaluations.

CHAPTER
12

APPLICATION

DRAMA

631- C   (Construct/Mixed Media) "Scraps of Life"

After a drama unit, find out what students have learned about
life as reflected in the play(s) just covered. The class could prepare one large collection of current events which reflect incidents which are closely parallel to those in the plays. This collection could be placed in a large scrapbook. But each student
could also construct his own booklet to include newspaper or
magazine articles—even advertisements—which make the past
come alive. If *The Crucible* were the play, clippings might include
examples of contemporary "witch hunting" to show that history
can repeat itself.

632- C   (Construct/Newspapers) "Roman Gazette"

After studying certain Shakespearean plays such as *Julius Caesar*,
construct a newspaper with students contributing articles, crossword puzzles, cartoons, and advertising written in the vernacu-
lar of Shakespeare's time. Suggested articles might focus on
Caesar's assassination or on soothsaying, or there might be a
feature on Portia's household hints. Choose a staff which includes an editor, typist, a few star reporters, and an artist to be
responsible for the layout. The final product can be displayed
in class or in a hall display case. It could also be printed and distributed throughout the school.

633- C   (Construct/Pictures) "Seen Scenes"

As part of a drama unit, encourage the amateur photographers
in the class to make a photo story of scenes from the play(s).
Students pose in tableau fashion with minimum props and costumes. It is surprising how effective a bedsheet can look in a
black and white picture. Make a hall bulletin board display using
quoted lines from the play to identify each scene.

634- C   (Perform/Play) "Mirror, Mirror"

Drama, it is often said, is a mirror of life and ourselves. After
reading one or more plays, students assume roles of characters
in the play but not in the context of the play. Instead, they
must justify their conduct or actions in the play based on the
demands of modern society.

635- C   (Perform/Play) "Play Day"

One way to create interest in any play is to update the script
for a class presentation. After reading a good family play like
I Remember Mama or a one-act play such as *Happy Journey to
Camden and Trenton*, the class can recreate the key scenes or
the entire play using any modern ethnic or regional approach.
Keep the basic theme and characters' names but change their
personalities and lines. This helps foster the slice-of-life about
good drama.

636- I   (Perform/Play) "Putting Them On"

After studying plays, choose a good
one-act play for the class to act out
instead of reading it in the usual
fashion. Members of the class do the
tryouts, directing, acting, and producing. Some might design simple
backgrounds painted on large sheets
of wrapping paper. If the finished
product is good, put it on for the
entire school.

637- C   (Perform/Recordings) "For the Record"

Plays are often more meaningful to actors and an audience
when read silently. Suggest several one-act plays, one to be

chosen by the class for a tape-recorded radio performance or videotape. Students must plan narration, sound effects, background music, and so on. Tapes could be exchanged between two classes for sharing.

638- C   (Perform/Videotapes) "Dry Run"

If the school has a videotape recorder, student film makers will find it useful for running through scripts and trying out camera angles before committing the action to the permanency and expense of movie film.

639- G   (Solve/Mixed Media) "Switcheroo"

Divide the class into small groups and assign a particular scene from a play being studied to each of the groups, who will present the material in any way other than a dramatic script. Some may choose a short story format, others a photo essay, still others may write a radio script or a series of tableaus. Each group then presents the new version for the class. It is interesting to see the different interpretations of plot and character.

640- I   (Solve/Mixed Media) "The Play's Their Thing"

When working with students of widely varying ability levels, allow for a variety of applications of learnings. The entire class can study the story line and characterizations. Abler students can go on to learn the basic theater conventions which enhance the understanding and enjoyment of drama. The most advanced can study the technical aspects of play production. They might do a research paper on costuming or scene building. The many facets of drama accommodate individual differences.

641- I   (Speak/Discussions) "Review the Reviews"

After seeing or reading a contemporary play, students search newspaper library archives to locate reviews of the play when it was first produced. Some reviews can be shared through discussions. This approach encourages students to work with back issues of periodicals or microfilm copies.

642- I   (Speak/Role Playing) "Behind the Scenes"

Naturally, before a play can be performed on stage, it must be developed through a series of steps. Select a popular play as the hypothetical model. Assign each student a position: stockholder, theater manager, ticket manager, costumer, advertiser, producer, actor, and others. Each student must research how his role works in the real situation. They then share this information with the rest of the class. Very often this aspect of drama is left out. It shouldn't be.

643-I   (Write/Papers) "Hand Them a Line"

On cards the teacher presents famous lines from plays (identifiable by the quotations). Even though several students may have different quotes from the same play, each student gets a card and must write a short paper explaining such lines as Biff saying in *Death of a Salesman,* "I'm a dime a dozen," or Frankie in *Member of the Wedding* saying, "All people belong to 'we' except me." These can be shared by the entire class.

644-I   (Write/Plays) "Being Play-writes"

Motivate aspiring actors and writers to try their wings by following these simple directions. On a half sheet of paper sketch an imaginary scene, complete with props and characters. Underneath, list the characters involved in the picture and write a brief description about what is happening. From this sketch, each one then writes his own one-act play or one scene using that setting and those characters. Several plays are selected for staging. The authors are their own directors. Finally, the plays may be judged by the class for qualities discussed earlier.

MEDIA

645-I   (Construct/Book Reports, Mixed Media) "Nonbook Report"

Sometime surprise a class by suggesting they read whatever they want. Their book reports, also, might take just about any form: collages, photographs, scrapbooks, or poems, or if they desire, the usual "I read _____ by _____ . It is about _____ . And I like it because _____ ."

646-C   (Perform/Role Playing) "An Inner View"

Following the reading of a novel, play, short story, or poem, two members of the class pose as author and literary critic on a radio interview show. By projecting themselves into these roles, students will have a nearly first-hand experience of coming to grips with and articulating the intentions of the work. They will also apply past learnings to forming useful questions for examining a piece of literature. This process may be handled in small groups or with an entire class.

647-I   (Speak/Book Reports) "Bringing Out the Artist"

WOOPS!

Let students create an art project (pictures, dioramas, models, sculptures, even cartoons) demonstrating an important aspect of each book they read. This approach is effective in spicing up oral book reports or critiques. Not only does the student get a chance to express his creativity, but the audience has something more interesting to observe than simply listening to three days of "The name of my book is _____ ."

648-I   (Speak/Television) "TV by the Week"

As a regular Monday assignment ask one student to report on worthwhile TV movies or specials scheduled through the following Sunday. Very often these television specials and documentaries tie in with much of the literature studied in school. The reporter can strengthen his oral presentation by having available printed materials supplied by newspapers or network broadcasters. The focus might be on the purpose of the programs, originality of plot, effectiveness of settings and special effects, quality of the acting and dialogue, or the application to our own lives.

649-I   (Write/Book Reports) "Boost or Bust a Book"

Since most students are very familiar with the format of television commercials, let them adapt this method for "pushing" or "panning" a book or any type of literature which they either like or dislike. They should include some quotes from the work itself. This style of book reporting sparks new interest in an old subject.

650- I   (Write/Commercials) "Getting Personal"

As a means of emphasizing the concept of personification, draw students' attention to the many TV commercials that employ the device: "Pink Pad, you're all washed up in this town" (scouring pads); or "Meet the sharp shooter" (camera). Students will be able to suggest many more. Following this activity each student creates a hypothetical product for which he writes a commercial employing personification.

651- I   (Write/Critiques, Films) "Film Extras"

For extra credit, students review films adapted from novels or plays. They write critiques which include how the film and the story differ, how certain elements were kept intact in the film version, how characters remained or didn't remain true to the originals, and so forth. Such an exercise serves to sharpen literary perception and to focus on the different techniques.

NONFICTION

652- I   (Speak/Book Reports, Discussion) "Friendly Persuasion"

A study of persuasive literature and techniques can be a vital experience when students are given a stake in planning and carrying out the activities. A student chooses, reads, and shares a book with the class by defending or rejecting a certain point of view expressed in it. Lively debate ensues when the class's ideas clash. The fringe benefits of this assignment are discipline in logical thinking and the demand for exact verbal expression.

653- I   (Write/Biographies) "VIP Lit"

Develop a "Great Persons" unit to give each student an opportunity to explore the life of an author he has read and admired. Culminating activities may run the gamut but should include some writing. As he locates all the books and information he can find, the student also learns more about using the library and its variety of resources.

NOVELS

654- C   (Construct/Books) "Not-So-Scrap Book"

The class can work together constructing a giant scrapbook. This project could illustrate, through magazine clippings or drawings, the theme, characters, plot, setting, and other ideas about the novel being covered in class. These scrapbooks can be saved to help introduce the novel to a new class.

655- I   (Construct/Display) "Boxing Show"

Students type out a brief description of one conflict or the climax from a chosen novel or short story. Then, in a small cardboard box, they recreate that scene in miniature using toy figures, dolls, cutouts, drawings, or whatever seems to work. They finish the project by covering the box attractively and pasting their name, the book title, author, and the typed description on one side of the box where viewers can see it. These dioramas are then placed on exhibit.

656-I   (Construct/Display) "Novel Film"

As a culminating project encourage students to make a "motion picture" of a novel recently completed. Each chapter becomes a "frame" in which the students draw or find magazine illustrations for the one scene they feel is the most important to that chapter. At the end, when all the frames are strung together, the class will have a pictorial commentary of the novel. Later, these projects could be made into slides, which when shown in quick succession resemble a movie.

657-I   (Construct/Mixed Media) "Scrap of an Idea"

After studying a novel let the students prepare a Character Sketchbook, with each page containing an accurate, easily recognized character sketch. Students may cut out pictures from magazines or draw their own. Below each illustration they might place a caption, possibly a quote from the book or a brief explanation why the picture or drawing is appropriate for the character. Since this activity succeeds well with ninth and tenth graders, this cut-and-paste approach is not to be limited to grade school use.

658- I   (Construct/Discussions, Displays) "Alas, Poor Silas"

One approach to the study of a nineteenth century Victorian novel, in which the development or destruction of one character occurs (*Silas Marner* or *The Mayor of Casterbridge*), would be to discuss how this character might act if faced with the varied problems of today's industrial society. In preparing for the discussion, students make montages or other simple displays illustrating the elements in today's world which would interest the character under study and which would affect him in some way.

659- I   (Perform/Book Reports, Role Playing) "Five Ways Better"

Middle or junior high students seem to favor these approaches to book reports:

1. Your are a television director casting characters from the book. Select names of actual TV stars who would be good types. Support choices by referring to the character personalities described in the book.
2. You are the same TV director but you want a specific actor or actress to play a lead role. Write (or try orally) to persuade the star to accept by explaining the story's value and the merits of the part.
3. You are the star the director is addressing in number two (above). Explain why you are or are not suited to a certain role or why the story is not to your liking.
4. Do a "What if" report. Suggest what would have happened if a character in the book had made a different decision at a crucial point.
5. Pretend to be a character in your book and you are being interviewed (by a class member) for newspaper, TV, or radio. The nature of the questioning tells the story.

660- I   (Perform/Role Playing) "Take On the Author"

Encourage the students to apply their knowledge of characterization by letting several pretend they are characters in the novel and are having a conversation with or writing a letter to the author. They may question the author's motivation or reasoning, complain, compliment, suggest ways to make the character look better, offer another way to end the story, and so on.

661- G   (Perform/Skits) "Acting Out"

In conjunction with reading and studying novels, discuss how strongly authors are influenced by the times in which they lived. Then let students put their knowledge to work. Divide the class into groups, one group representing each literary work studied. Then let the groups produce skits depicting situations typical to the era in which each writer wrote. Skits need not be elaborate. (Four chairs with driver in front and two seated behind can be a horse-drawn cab.)

662- G   (Speak/Discussion) "Four on the Floor"

Divide class into four symposia, each to characterize through research and example one of these four areas of English literature: classical, neoclassical, romantic, and modern. Class time can be given to group meetings, although out-of-class work should be encouraged. The final two weeks of the unit are devoted to presenting the symposia research as imaginatively and differently as possible. One group may take a straight discussion approach. Another might videotape a presentation. Others could do a slide-tape program. The possibilities are limitless. Let the students' imaginations reign.

663–G   (Speak/Discussion) "Let Your People Go"

Allow students to form small groups, each group reading a different novel and presenting a panel discussion on the book to the class. Consult a list of novels appropriate to the age and interest level of the pupils to guide choices. By this method the class is introduced to several novels instead of the customary one or two. Invariably students are enticed to read novels on which others report.

664- G   (Speak/Discussion) "Panel the Room"

Give college-bound or advanced classes an opportunity to express themselves orally by arranging a unit in which they work in groups to study additional books having the same theme as a novel read by the entire class. Each group takes a different book and all the information is brought together in a class discussion.

665–C   (Speak/Role Playing) "Opportunity Mocks"

Many classes have had successful mock trials. Students who desire to be lawyers or actors do very well in this activity. Opportunities to use debate skills will occur, for example, in determining the guilt or innocence of a character (before continuing the reading to discover how the author handled it). Another approach would be to try the author for libel or for writing prurient literature for adolescents. Staff the trial with judge, jury, prosecuting and defense attorneys, and others.

666–I   (Speak, Write/Book Reports) "Real Characters"

Each student compares or contrasts a character in his book to a person he knows in real life or someone he has heard or read about. This activity helps students to see that most novels are true to life, and it encourages them to become more critical of reading choices.

667–I   (Write/Papers) "Precise Précis"

Following the reading of a novel, e.g., Hemingway's *A Farewell to Arms* or *For Whom the Bell Tolls*, assign a one-page précis of the novel. Ask students to try writing it in the style of Hemingway or as a book reviewer on the staff of an important periodical. The requirements of précis writing—concise exact expression—demand a thoughtful review of all the material studied.

668–I   (Write/Papers) "Proof Positive"

Provide many opportunities for the class to write brief papers about literature. Have each student write a general statement about an author, a work, a character, the plot, setting, style, or theme. Then he locates and copies a short passage illustrating the generalization. This attempt to be succinct is a readiness exercise for answering essay test questions.

669–I   (Write/Papers) "Take Four or Five"

Throughout the semester individuals read at least four books by the same author. This array can be the basis of a critical paper comparing the several works, tracing trends, similarities, differences, stylistic matters, and so on. By studying one author in depth, students gain a better understanding of how (s)he writes.

OVERVIEW

670- I   (Construct/Anecdotes, Bulletin Boards) "All Aboard"

In the study of a certain historical period of English literature
students are frequently exposed to major facts and happenings
of that era. How these facts and happenings affect the personal
lives of the authors makes the subject alive and arouses student
interest. Encourage pupils to be on the lookout for literary
anecdotes which they can share with their classmates. This
could be a bulletin board project.

671- I   (Construct/Book Reports, Artwork) "Tailor-made Jackets"

For a different kind of book report, students make book jackets
for their selections. Along with the title, they create an illustration of an important incident in the book. They may use any
medium (chalk, crayons, paints, magazine cut-outs). Inside the
book cover, on the two flaps, they are to fasten a brief book
report including a summary of the illustrated incident. The
jackets can be fashioned directly on the books they depict or
can be mounted on the bulletin board.

672- I   (Construct/Book Reports, Displays) " 'Now' Book Reports"

Students prepare a montage of magazine pictures which depicts
an idea, theme, or actual scene from a book they have read.
Around the display they arrange words or phrases which are
appropriate. They should stress vivid modifiers and active verbs.
At the lower left corner they attach a small file card giving the
title, author, publisher, capsule plot, and summary reaction.
Visual book reports such as these help students "see" the key
scenes and grasp the meaning. Students also increase their
vocabularies and learn to make concise descriptions.

673- I   (Construct/Lists) "Shares for Profit"

Encourage students to keep written lists of characteristic and
interesting facts and quotations drawn from readings done in
and out of class. The exact source should be included as well as
an appropriate illustration—verbal or pictorial—to entice others
to read the same book. Lists can be collected in spiral or looseleaf notebooks for all to use.

674-I   (Perform/Book Reports, Role Playing) "Five Pluses"

Let the class present oral book reports in which they impersonate the main character. This exercise has several desirable effects: (1) allows student to empathize with characters and obtain a greater sense of development and mood, (2) helps student relax since he is not himself, (3) serves to interest rest of the class, (4) makes it possible for the teacher to verify student understanding, and (5) allows "characters" to be characters which often spells f-u-n.

675-C   (Construct/Magazines) "Read All about Us"

As a culminating activity to a literature unit, guide the class in publishing a literary magazine. It might contain reviews of books, plays, or essays which have been read by the class or which are original student pieces. All art work, layout, writing, and printing is done by the students. The teacher serves only as a resource person.

676-I   (Construct/Pictures) "Graphic Art Part"

Students illustrate something they have read by creating a montage or photo essay using magazine or catalog illustrations reflecting the theme or other important aspect. Ambiguous visual interpretations provoke good discussion by other class members.

677-G   (Speak/Book Reports, Discussion) "One Will Get You Four or More"

Each of four or five discussion groups chooses a book they want to read. Allow some class time for groups to meet and discuss how they are going to present their book to the class in a panel-type approach. Through this procedure each student reads only one book but learns about three or four.

678-I   (Speak, Write/Book Reports) "Free for All"

Often teachers limit book report lists to fiction classics, their own preferences, or books they think should be read. If a student wants to read a nonfiction book, he should be encouraged. The form of the book report is more easily adjusted than a student's interests.

679-I   (Write/Papers) "Quote Note"

On the bulletin board post a fairly well-known quote from prose or poetry. For extra credit or a continuing contest, students identify the author and the specific work from which it came. Leave the quote on the board for several days so students have enough time to research and discuss it in a short paper. Why is it an important quote?

POETRY

680-I   (Construct/Books) "Saying It Poetically"

Let the entire class join in constructing a poetry scrapbook. Students cut out interesting poems found in newspapers and magazines and organize them into sections of the book. These sections can be on meaning, form, societal struggle, or whatever. Such a project appeals to nearly everyone's interests and motivates them to read poetry other than that assigned or discussed in class. The scrapbook clearly demonstrates the variety of situations put into verse. The completed book can be displayed on a dictionary pedestal in the main hall or be donated to some worthy organization or person.

681-I   (Construct/Pictures) "Poetry Cut-up"

Each student chooses a poem about which he has particularly strong feelings. He draws or locates pictures which interpret his feelings about certain stanzas. These selections usually initiate interesting discussions. This approach lends itself to a sound-slide presentation. If students can be persuaded to donate their efforts, a teacher could have a collection of visual presentations to be used for future study.

682-I   (Construct, Write/Pictures, Poems) "Visual-eyes"

In a comic strip, one-word exclamations and even pauses take on a special significance because of accompanying pictures. Each pupil provides one particularly evocative picture and prepares a visual poem consisting of single words, pauses, and lines formed into designs which reflect the idea or mood.

683- I   (Construct, Write/Pictures, Poems) "Picked Sures"

Have students locate several related pictures which have strong emotional impact. Let this be the motivation to write a short poem attempting to catch the same mood.

684- I   (Perform/Dance) "Let's Dance"

Poetry can be interpreted kinesthetically as well as literally. Let students select a line or stanza from an especially descriptive or musical poem and try to interpret the message, mood, and rhythm through modern dance. If students are too reticent, perhaps a dance class in the school or community would welcome such a creative project.

685- I   (Perform/Music) "Live, on Record"

Music-minded students can choose a favorite poem and apply an appropriate melody to it, appropriate to tone, movement, and subject matter. They can then either sing it, accompanied by a musical instrument, or possibly can record it on tape.

686- I   (Write/Books) "An Anthology and Annotations"

To help create the feeling that poetry is an expression of an individual experience, encourage each class member to make his own anthology of original poems or those written by others. Each selection should be followed by a brief comment on why it fits into the collection.

687- I   (Write/Poems) "Poetry Want-ads"

After they have learned various poetic forms such as the sonnet, ballad, blank verse, and free verse, students write their own verse using words or lines cut from magazine ads— not copied, CUT! The differences in typography adds another dimension to the poem.

688-I   (Write/Essay) "Take the High Road"

Students read "The Road Not Taken" (Robert Frost). Relating the poem to its general theme—blazing a trail v. conformity—the class writes a short one-page paper on how the poem would have ended had the narrator taken the *other* road.

689-I   (Write/Poems) "Good Trips"

To motivate an aesthetic awareness of the beauty all around, arrange a "senses field trip." This could be merely imaginary, though students would undoubtedly prefer an actual trip to a lake, the business section downtown, or a nearby park. Students list impressions at random as they become aware of them. Then each could find or write poems relating to what they felt and experienced. Have students use the flow of consciousness technique activated by their being reminded of a past experience by the sight or sound of something. Perhaps a familiar odor calls forth an early childhood experience. The polishing can be done later.

690-C   (Write/Magazine) "Let's Make Book"

The class reads a broad selection of poems and then chooses several favorites to be included in a poetry "magazine" which is duplicated for each student. Class artists can help dress up the publication. These booklets saved over the years will go a long way toward supplementing the class anthology. Also increased student interest would follow because poems were selected by students themselves.

691-I   (Write/Poems) "Life-lifting Poetry"

It's a common project for students to illustrate a poem with pictures from magazines, photographs, or drawings of their own. Although this helps make a poem more visual and meaningful, more could be done with this idea. For example, some classes have recycled old greeting cards. Using the illustrations, they have replaced the messages with appropriate lines from famous poems or from their originals. The cards were then sent to the elderly, to shut-ins, or the hospitalized. The class artists might do the illustrations as well.

692-I   (Write/Poems) "Poetry in Concrete"

An unlimited imaginative expression of ideas is possible when students write "concrete poems." In this approach the form adds to the meaning. For example, lines in a poem can be shaped into the contour of the subject. Lines may also be written or printed tightly, loosely, or helter-skelter to depict a mood.

693- G   (Write/Poems) "Together We Conquer Poetry"

Pupils need more evidence that poets are ordinary people just like themselves, sensitive to everyday events. Occasionally one of these events triggers a response in the poet which he feels compelled to express in verse. Thus, encourage the class to share similar experiences. At first, limit their audience to small inform-al groups. Each student-poet brings his poem to the group where it is read, interpreted, and changed if need be. This procedure is repeated until a half dozen or so poems emerge from the group. Then they vote to select the best one to be discussed with the entire class. Each group submits one poem and the entire class selects the best one.

SHORT STORY

694- G   (Construct/Mixed Media) "Picturing a Story"

Assign groups of five or six pupils a different short story. Each group decides what the story line is and how best to present it to the class. There are several possibilities: a graphic presentation on a bulletin board, a chalk drawing (traced lightly in advance and filled in as someone tells the story), skit, poem, slide-sound presentation, or even a lecture by a dynamic student.

695- I   (Perform/Mixed Media) "A Moving Story"

Two essential components of a well-written story—dialogue and descrip-tion—are vividly highlighted by the following demonstration. First have the class dramatize a short episode with much dialogue and no stage movement. The second time through let students combine dialogue and movement. Here the value of descrip-tion and narration as related to dialogue is demonstrated. Finally, have the class rewrite the episode using description but no dialogue. A successful attempt proves mastery of many literary techniques.

696– G   (Perform/Play) "Everybody into the Act"

Using a short story with much dialogue, let the class adapt the story into a play. One group does the writing, another plans the costumes and makeup, other groups choose appropriate music and sound effects, and still another group gives the actual performance. After the presentation, a group which has studied the art of criticism presents their critiques of the play and how it was produced. This project exemplifies the type needed to give everyone a task suited to interest and ability.

697– G,I   (Perform/Skit) "Short Change"

Divide the class into pairs, asking each to select a short story to share with the class using only pantomime. After each performance, the class tells or writes what they thought was happening. The best story idea can then be expanded upon by individuals writing a complete short story.

698– I,C   (Write/Essay, Discussions) "Seeing Ourselves in Others"

After reading a story like "The Secret Life of Walter Mitty," students write a short, one- or two-page paper reacting to Mitty. This should help them better understand themselves through their reactions to a literary figure. The variety of student reactions will stimulate discussion on the reasons for such differences. This way they learn to examine literature closely to see what evokes a calculated response and how this occurs.

699– I   (Write/Movies, Short Stories) "Short Subject"

Following a study of the short story, show a short film dealing with a situation in which the students can become very emotionally involved (a chase, a fight, or a race, for instance.) Each student is to imagine himself as having experienced first-hand what occurred in the movie. Then, as an author wanting to share these moments, he writes a brief narrative based on the episode. For useful feedback, discuss the film and the student versions, considering how individual opinions of the facts vary. View the film again to discover the real facts. Discuss what can influence viewer or reader perception and a writer's viewpoint. This exer-

cise helps to illustrate the fact that the reader—and not
just the author—brings meaning to the page.

700-G   (Write/Papers) "Learn by Doing"

Students cooperatively write an original short story after discussing and planning characterization, plot development, theme,
and so on. Some write the beginning, others the middle and the
end. The project is then read aloud and discussed to determine
if the finished product met all of the requirements of a short
story.

PART 4

reading

reading

Introduction

Chapter 13
Journalism 215
Media 215
Nonfiction 216
Novels 217
Overview 218
Short Story 223
Study Skills 223
Vocabulary 225
Words 227

Evaluation

Chapter 15
Exposition 243
Journalism 243
Narration 244
Novels 244
Overview 245
Sentences 248
Spelling 249
Study Skills 249
Vocabulary 251
Words 254

Deliberation

Chapter 14
Letter Writing 229
Media 229
Narration 230
Novels 230
Overview 232
Poetry 233
Study Skills 234
Vocabulary 236
Words 239

Application

Chapter 16
Exposition 257
Journalism 258
Letter Writing 258
Media 259
Narration 260
Overview 261
Poetry 262
Short Story 263
Study Skills 264
Vocabulary 265

CHAPTER

13

INTRODUCTION

Note to Teacher about Part 4: Reading and writing skills should be developed together, each supplementing the other to double or triple the chances of learning in one operation. This section on reading includes hints for teaching both reading and writing, as well as listening and speaking, and is especially for students with learning problems. But ideas could be changed slightly for any ability level.

JOURNALISM

701- T   (Read/Newspapers) "Paper Route"

A unit on the newspaper helps develop the slow reader's ability to think critically about what he reads. It also arouses reading interest in readily available periodicals. A typical unit includes judging the logic of editorials, investigating language use in advertising, studying the appeal of human interest stories, and comparing different treatments of the same news item covered by several publishers.

MEDIA

702- T   (Discover/Topics) "Treasure Chest"

To stimulate the flow of ideas for writing exercises, the teacher can bring to class a Chinese wicker suitcase, a chest, or simply a decorated box loaded with interesting collections of pictures, magazines, flyers, booklets—anything worth looking at and reading. Students can freely add their own contributions so everyone will have a source of usable materials when they need pictures or ideas for writing assignments, covers for homemade books, montages or collages, for instance.

703-T (Read/Mixed Media) "Change in Command"

Are you a victim of "great expectations"? Reading material in the classroom does not have to be the traditional classics. Current newspaper and magazine articles along with contemporary paperback books and even comics can be used more effectively in some classes to achieve basically the same reading skills as those offered by the classic titles. In addition to the useful information and numerous human interest stories found in the periodicals, contemporary novels may encourage more slow readers to read more books. *Huckleberry Finn* may be a classic, but it will serve some no better than *Pickpocket Run*, a story about a boy destined to follow in his dishonest father's footsteps. Both boys and girls can readily identify with Buff and Elaine in *Two and the Town*, a tastefully written novel built around the problem of premarital sex.

NONFICTION

704-T (Read/Circulars) "Souped-up Reading"

A good, economical source of high interest reading material for middle and junior high school boys can be found in advertising circulars, brochures, and booklets supplied by sporting goods, motorcycle, and automobile dealers. Have stacks of such materials available in the room. When possible, base simple assignments on this type of literature.

NOVELS

705-T   (Discover/Definitions) "It's a Plot"

To make the study of literature as meaningful as possible for the
low ability students, try to present literary devices concretely
rather than abstractly. When using such abstract terms as *plot*,
symbol, and *theme*, express these ideas in terms which they can
understand. Students who don't know what "plot" means can
easily tell what "happens" in the story.

706-G   (Discover/Discussion) "At Any Rate"

When teaching a novel to the entire class, a teacher can accommodate various reading speeds by allowing students to read as
quickly as they like and then to form small discussion groups as
they finish. The teacher can meet with one group while the
others read. Those who finish early can be directed into other
activities. (Also see ideas 471, 485, and 497.)

707-C   (Discover/Discussion) "Pet Theory"

Literary discussions can follow a specific format so that the
slower students can participate even if they can't read well. Begin
the discussion with questions on the literal level—the *plot*—so
that everyone knows the story. This can be just a simple summary
by a capable student. Next cover the idea of the relevance of the
material, considering the varying levels of *experience* among the
students. Everyone must feel the selection is worth reading and
does in some way reflect the way things are in this world. Here,
too, students consider the new material within the framework of
past experience. Even the slowest students can enter discussions
at this critical level. Finally, move to the inferential level—the
theme—where the reader must consider what the writer has said
"between the lines" and how he said what he has through the
structure. This is, then, the real message. Thus, compare initiating
a literary discussion to the act of dropping a pebble into water.
The rings radiating outward represent moving from the concrete
to the abstract, from specific to general; thus, from *plot*, to *experience*, to *theme*. This should become the English teacher's
P-E-T discussion approach.

OVERVIEW

708- T   (Discover/Authorities) "Not so Foreign"

A foreign exchange student or immigrant who has achieved mastery in handling reading material by studying English as a foreign language is an invaluable resource to any teacher confronted with classroom reading problems. Such a student's experiences—use of textbooks and other techniques—are all applicable. The handicaps the foreign student has overcome closely resemble the challenge which the average student faces in learning to read and write.

709- T   (Discover/Books) "All Booked Up"

If your school is short of quality books, organize a paperback project. Enlist the aid of your classes to bring in paperback books they have enjoyed. Gather some of your own favorites. Appeal to the community and to book dealers. When bookcases become scarce, construct some of boards and bricks. A concentrated effort usually results in a large, excellent collection.

710- T   (Discover/Books) "Freedom to Read"

A one-period-a-week free reading period when children are allowed to read anything they desire is not a new idea. But have you considered three days of free reading some weeks? This will also provide a good opportunity for one-to-one conferences. To facilitate, provide bookshelves to house free-reading material. To avoid book selection problems, let a student committee, with some adult guidance, approve the contents of this special library. With this approach, slow readers in particular discover that reading can be fun, because they don't have to wait seven days to read again.

711- T   (Discover/Books) "Reading Deeply"

Provide opportunities to acquire and practice the following reading skills for understanding literature:

Follow sequence of events	Visualize characters and
Predict outcomes	incidents
Recognize reality from	Create mental images
make-believe	Recognize mood, tone
Interpret figurative language	Infer from clues
Identify with characters	Recreate settings

Since students do not acquire these skills by sheer exposure, they need competent guidance and practice including a chance to exchange ideas with other classmates.

712- T   (Discover/Problems) "All About Reading"

Reading problems group themselves within five basic areas: (1) word recognition (context, structure, phonics, usage), (2) comprehension, (3) sight word vocabulary (words known without recognition skills being employed), (4) rate and adjustment to reading difficulty, and (5) study skills (following directions, locating information, selecting and evaluating information, recalling and organizing information). Exercises in reading improvement involve all these areas. Working in one area at a time will benefit both the student and teacher.

713- I   (Discover/Selves) "Fifth to Eleventh Eighth-graders"

Usually a wide range of reading abilities exists in any single class. Generally there is about a two-and-a-half-grade span both ways: a possible five-grade spread in a single class. Many teachers, failing to realize this range, force all students to work at the same reading level. This is both unrealistic and unfair. Remember individual differences when dealing with literature. Supply a variety of material from which the students can choose something appropriate to their own ability and interest level. The task of the teacher then is guiding individuals to conquer their own reading problems and to progress as their abilities allow. Discover what community or school help is available for the most seriously incapacitated readers.

714- C   (Discover/Selves) "Last But Not Least"

This idea is a new twist on a frequently used demonstration lesson on why we should follow directions carefully. The key, of course, is to read the *first* instruction and follow it. Individual copies of the test—or call it a problem—are available to each student but are returned after the activity, which, by the way, is less vocal and noisy than some versions of this bit of useful trickery.

A Simple Problem in Modern Math

Directions: First of all, read the full page of instructions carefully.

    1.   For this item and all the others, you will need a sheet of

paper numbered from 1 to 12. For item number 1, look at your watch or the clock and write the exact time without the colon (i.e., 1:15 becomes 115) after number 1 on your paper.

2. Look at five students seated closest to you. How many of them are wearing brown or tan shoes? Write that figure (or 000) after number 2. (You will follow this procedure when answering remaining items. Keep all figures in straight columns.)

3. How many boys in the class are wearing blue shirts or sweaters?

4. How many blonde girls are in your class?

5. Count the number of pieces of gum under your desk or chair arm—not the chair seat—without getting out of your seat.

6. How many students are in your class today?

7. Count the number of individual light fixtures in the room.

8. Look at the student directly behind you (or to your left or right) and count the number of buttons exposed on shirt or blouse.

9. Find a book near you and open it to a center page. Write the left hand page number.

10. Using this same book, open it and stand it upright on your desk to show that you have finished all but one question. Then write the figure 30 after number 10 on your paper.

11. Now that you have finished reading all the instructions, don't do anything. Sit quietly and wait until those who can't follow directions complete the tenth step. For something to do, while you wait, see how long one person takes to get to number 11. Do not reveal the secret of this exercise.

715-I   (Discover/Selves) "Who Is Me?"

Culturally deprived students often have trouble developing a self-concept. Until they have done so, they will have difficulty understanding the feelings and experiences of the characters they read about. The following three suggestions will help give such students mental, auditory, and visual pictures of themselves: (1) Assign a free-wheeling, unthreatening paper which tells what the student's shadow would see when following him

around for a day. (The student looks at himself more
objectively than through the "I am" approach.) (2) Allow
the student to talk into a tape recorder and then to
listen to himself speaking on a subject he knows.
(3) Photograph students working diligently and closely with
classmates on room projects. Find a good reason to place such
pictures on the bulletin board.

716- I   (Discover/Topics) "Unfolding Personality"

Each student receives a plain manila file folder and prints his
name on the tab. In a few days he brings back the folder bulging
with memorabilia: photographs, favorite magazines, souvenir
menus, playbills, concert programs, clippings, box tops—things
that reflect his life-style, hobbies, and interests. The result will
be a veritable treasure house of ideas for suggesting topics to
write, books to read, and ideas to share in discussion.

717- T   (Discover/Tutors) "Learning by Doing"

Be alert for students who can readily explain a word or describe
(demonstrate) a concept to their peers when the teacher may
flounder. Use them as tutors or aides for younger children
(fourth through eighth grades) who need practice in reading.
This tutoring program gives high school students a chance to review reading skills at a lower level and increases their confidence
about their own role as readers. The younger students benefit
from the individual attention.

718- C   (Listen/Audiotapes) "Air That Lit"

To help slow readers, ask several
good readers to tape crucial portions
of the selection being studied. Play
back this tape while the class follows
along in the text. Lacking this possibility, cover key portions orally in
class. Since students understand
more words by sound than by reading or writing, their chances of
grasping and being able to discuss a
selection are multiplied. Being
forced to rely only on reading out-
side of class is terribly frustrating and defeating for the slow
reader.

719- C   (Listen/Discussion) "Little Sir Echo"

The Echo Game is an enjoyable way for students to learn that listening for content is an active, not a passive task. Start a discussion on a subject of special class interest (current events, dating, spectator sports, new fads). After the discussion is under way, interrupt it and tell the class that from then on, before anyone adds a comment, he must first paraphrase what the previous speaker has said to that person's satisfaction. Then resume the discussion. After the game, discuss how the echoing rule affected individuals.

720- T   (Listen/Talk) "On the Alert"

Suggestions for projects often arise from overhearing student conversations or monitoring discussions. A teacher must be an alert observer, a good listener, and a skilled practitioner to zero in on student interests in this manner. But being a bit of a "snoop" will reap benefits through improved student attitudes toward school.

721- T   (Observe/Mixed Media) "Reading en Masse Media"

Teachers often overlook the mass media as an incentive for reading. Books on which movies and television shows are based can be used with great success. Discussions of current events such as items on conservation, public transit, or crime statistics may encourage voluntary reading. Comic books have been used with some success though they are limited in enrichment opportunities and, because they tend to be overused, inhibit progress for cultivating new tastes.

722- T   (Read/Books) "Reading Tree"

Choose a corner of the room offering a cozy place for students to relax with a book. Decorate it with a "reading tree," an actual trunk with branches reaching from the floor to ceiling. Its bare limbs can leaf out again with book synopses written and illustrated by the students after they complete a story. To add interest, let students hang other favorite items from the branches: small pictures of movie or television stars, clever buttons with slogans, and many others.

723- T   (Read/Books) "Teacher Reading Readiness"

The task of improving reading through the subject field is always easier if needs are anticipated and prepared for in advance. These simple guidelines may be helpful:

1. Provide material at suitable vocabulary levels.
2. Select material to include all interests.
3. Offer materials from simple to increasingly complex.
4. Avoid situations which embarrass or frustrate.
5. Plan for a variety of activities.
6. Individualize as much as possible.
7. Use fresh, imaginative methods.
8. Provide for successful experiences.
9. Praise and encourage.
10. Record progress regularly and clearly.

SHORT STORY

724- G   (Listen/Audiotapes) "Reel Short Story"

Assign a small group of volunteers to tape a short story, a play, or skit for other classes to hear. Let one student be the narrator. The others will read the dialogue using as much expression as possible. Ray Bradbury's story "The Playroom" is a good beginning. This is one way to cover a number of stories quickly and effectively if tapes of different stories are shared among classes.

725- C   (Listen/Books) "Hey, Teach! Your Turn"

Try reading to the students, no matter what their ages. Through embarrassment teen-agers may show reluctance at first to be read to, but in a surprisingly short time they will request the reading of exciting, suspenseful stories. Fill the hour with animated reading. This activity improves reading interest and auditory skills. Try to select only those stories which can be completed with the hour.

STUDY SKILLS

726-T   (Read/Books) "Skim This"

Skimming and scanning are valuable skills in improving reading ability. They form the basis of many related reading skills. Skimming is reading rapidly for meaning—just hitting the main ideas. Scanning, on the other hand, involves looking for specific information—rather like looking for a particular name in a phone directory. Easy to confuse, the two words are often differentiated by equating the two m's in skimming with "main meaning." Take every opportunity to get students to practice scanning or skimming. For example, try a Scanning Relay. Divide class into three equal teams. Ask a question about a story; everyone hunts for a sentence or sentences that will give the right answer. As soon as a participant has located the sentence, he raises his hand. He reads it aloud, and if he is correct his team gets five points. The first team to earn twenty-five points wins.

727–C   (Observe/Skits) "Playing Library"

Introduce younger students to the use of the library for locating information by creating a "play" centered on the use of the card catalog. For the drawer fronts, print segments of the alphabet on cards attached to chairs. One simple skit approach is to give each student a card (lettered large enough to read across the room) naming a familiar book and its author. Then tell the students to stand behind the correct "drawers" (chairs) in the proper order of a title card section, then for an author card, finally for a subject card. For the latter they may have to do a little guessing. More elaborate sequences can be planned for other library resources such as the *Reader's Guide to Periodical Literature.*

728- C   (Research/Libraries) "Relaying Information"

This idea requires cooperation from the school librarian who provides a box with book catalogue cards. In the library, arrange students in relay teams of five to ten pupils. Children draw a card from the box, race to find the book, bring it to their team table, and tap the next person who continues the relay. The team which gathers the most books in the set time, wins. Arranged beforehand with the librarian, books obtained could become the room library. This helps instill skills for locating information.

729-I   (Research/Mixed Media) "Armchair Travels"

Distribute picture postcards from various geographical locations.
Ask each student to imagine that he has been to the place and to
write an expository paper about it. Encourage the use of encyclo-
pedias, road maps, and travel booklets. In this writing, the student learns to use and cite resources and increases his knowledge
of English and geography simultaneously.

VOCABULARY

730-I   (Discover/Lists) "Using the Right Type"

Those who are unmotivated by simply copying lists of spelling
words or vocabulary, or sentences containing these words, often
find the typewriter an interesting way to put these lists on paper,
especially if they are unhappy about their handwriting. Typing
will also force the student to analyze words carefully.

731-T   (Discover/Problems) "Text Looks"

Examine class texts for reading problems which may overtake
average and below average readers. Anticipate specific problems
in word recognition skills (context clues, structure, phonics,
dictionary), sight vocabulary, comprehension (literal, critical,
inferential), rate and adjustment, and study skills. For the teacher relatively uninformed about reading, a visit to the school's
or system's reading specialist will be most helpful. A good textbook on teaching reading is invaluable. We tend to take reading
skills for granted until we find some students who don't even
know the purposes and locations of the table of contents,
glossary, and index. Many don't know where to find the copyright date nor what it represents.

732-C   (Discover/Tutors) "Expert Ease"

Assign one or two words from the vocabulary lesson to each student who is then to become an expert on the words and teaches
them to the rest of the class in some interesting way (riddle,
pictures, games).

733-C   (Read/Cards) "Flashy Cards"

Help students enlarge their vocabularies by defining new words in reading assignments. Each day three different students bring to class four unfamiliar words from the assignment. The words are placed on 3 × 5 cards with the word printed in large letters on one side (upper and lower case so that capitalization will be recognized) and the appropriate definition on the other side. These cards can be used for class or individual practice.

734- I   (Observe/Pictures) "Snap into It"

To increase sight vocabulary, take snapshots of familiar objects and people. Attach the appropriate words to them. If placed on small cards, these word builders become flashcards with some visual impact.

735- T   (Read/Lists) "Minimatch Flash Cards"

As new vocabulary is encountered, have students print words (standard manuscript) on small cards which will fit into small match or pill boxes. Have them make the words a little larger than the average handwriting. The teacher uses these flash cards for individual drill in root words, syllabication, or classification, for instance, and the student then also has his own list of troublesome words to carry around in purse or pocket for use when there are moments to spare.

736- C   (Research/Dictionaries) "Box Scores"

Construct an attractively decorated box with a slot in the top. Encourage children to deposit words which they do not know how to pronounce or define. Every few days draw a slip from the box. Place the word on the bulletin board. Then have several students find the pronunciation and write a sentence using the word in each of its various definitions (uses). Have them write these sentences below the word. The results are then discussed in class. The newfound words should then be used as frequently as possible in the regular classroom activities.

737- I   (Research/Lists) "The Big Ten"

To make vocabulary study practical each student takes from a
newspaper ten words which he does not understand. From the
individual lists, compile a master list of the most common difficult words. Have students look up the definitions in their dictionaries or make up their own. Chances are very good that
such a list will be more useful to the students than a literature-
based list.

WORDS

738- T   (Discover/Definitions) "Fear of Fonix"

Phonics in reading instruction often throws fear into teachers
just beginning to learn some of the fundamentals. Terms like
"blends," "digraphs," and "diphthongs" tend—needlessly—to
give the most trouble. Once understood, this aspect of word
recognition problems can be dealt with. Here are some remember-
ing devices:

Digraphs, as *di* denotes, are of two types: consonant and
vowel. The *ph* also illustrates consonant digraphs, two consonants sounded as one. (A vowel digraph is *au* in *caught*.)

The word *blends* has two sets of letters illustrating this
definition: *bl* and *nd* or two letters having two separate sounds—
usually the original sounds of each letter. Blends are associated
only with consonants.

The vowel counterpart of a blend is the *diphthong* (*di* meaning two and *phthongos*, voice). Examples of diphthongs are *oi*
in *oil* and *oy* in *toy*. These two-letter combinations often give beginning readers a problem and deserve to be emphasized in vocabulary and spelling exercises.

CHAPTER
14

DELIBERATION

LETTER WRITING

739- T (Analyze/Papers) "Noteworthy Idea"

If note passing is a problem in your class, capitalize on it as a teaching technique. Announce that you will collect and duplicate all notes as letter writing models for study—and do so! It may not cut down on the note passing, but students will probably write with more discretion.

MEDIA

740- G (Organize/Mixed Media) "Wanted: an Ad"

Advertisements are often overlooked as a source of reading matter. Ask students to bring to class a newspaper or magazine advertisement for a particular product (autos, fashions, or furniture, for instance). The students form small groups and arrange their ads into categories according to type of appeal (economy, prestige, adventure, or quality, for example) and find an appropriate name for each category. The last and most important step is to analyze the effectiveness of the advertisement by answering several questions about each ad: Why is (product) important? How does this product give (category)?

NARRATION

741- C   (Consolidate/Talk) "Chain Reaction"

Study narration by letting the class compose its own story to read aloud. Either the teacher or a student begins by offering an introductory narrative paragraph, preferably involving the classroom or the school and, of course, class members. Going around the room, each student adds a section. A tape recorder is needed unless each student writes his contribution. When the story is complete, it should be one which is within the students' experiences, interests, and vocabulary.

742- I   (Experiment/Myths) "Fabricated Fables"

Most children like fables and myths. After reading some published versions, the teacher reads a simple one (s)he has written. This is usually a good beginning because published myths can be too involved. Students then write their own using the teacher's myth as a model. This assignment helps the teacher detect the more creative children, and they can help the teacher create model materials which will interest even the slowest reader.

743- I   (Interpret/Cartoons) "Filling Balloons"

Select some of the students' favorite comic strips or cartoons. After removing the balloon speeches or captions, duplicate them. Students then write their own versions of what they think the characters are saying. Keen observation of the action (pictures) will reveal the key ideas which the students will phrase succinctly.

NOVELS

744- T   (Analyzing/Books) "Being Critical"

Some practical exercises to improve critical reading involve recognizing certain aspects of plot, characterization, setting, and style. A look at critical questions involving plot will suggest some for other areas:

1. Did the action interest me?
2. Was the action convincing?
3. Did it relate to me?
4. Did suspense build logically and adequately?
5. Was action lively or did it move slowly and unevenly?
6. Was the ending reasonable and inevitable, yet pleasantly surprising?

745- C   (Analyze/Cartoons) "Comical Plotting"

Students take Sunday comic strips (self-contained serials) such as "Blondie" or "Dick Tracy," analyzing them for characterization and plot (rising action, climax, falling action). This is a different way to practice using the elements of fiction. Also, most students enjoy comics even if they don't like to read, yet the basic structural differences aren't that great.

746- G   (Experiment/Games) "Monopolizing Adventure"

In teaching a book like *Tom Sawyer*, emphasize plot sequence by letting the class work in groups to make up a simple game-board game depicting Tom's escapades. The markers, fashioned out of paper, can be key objects from the story, e.g., a tomb-stone. The goal can be Aunt Polly's house. Various problems in the story can be built in as game hazards. As a follow-up writing exercise, each student submits a short paper giving directions for playing the game. The best of these can become the game rules.

747- T   (Interpret/Plots) "Causing an Effect"

Inferences in reading are drawn from cause and effect relation-ships. Students need much practice to sharpen their ability to move from making simple inferences to more complex levels as illustrated here:

1. Find meaning in more complex generalizations than em-ployed at the critical level.
2. Identify the purpose or main idea from what the author has included.
3. Equate certain statements or passages with that purpose.
4. Recognize literary devices such as symbolism, imagery, and allusion as well as historical references.
5. Relate these literary techniques to the meaning of the work.

OVERVIEW

748- C   (Experiment/Chalkboards) "Chalk One Up"

Reserve a section of chalkboard or supply a banner of wrapping paper for a "graffiti wall." A bulletin board for tacking up displays of words and appropriate pictures also serves the same purpose. Students are encouraged to write clever, nonembarrassing expressions and slogans. This activity provides an opportunity for informal writing and reading practice.

749- C,I   (Experiment/Mixed Media) "Fix It"

To speed up reading rates and to increase the amount of printed matter gathered through a single eye fixation, the following suggestions are offered:

1. Match pictures with captions in timed contests.
2. Beat the clock in choosing from the table of contents in a popular youth magazine an article (1) to read first, (2) to read last, (3) for boys only, (4) for girls only, or other categories.
3. Race to pick out in three minutes a previously designated car from a page of classified auto ads.
4. Pick out preannounced key items from classified or display ads.
5. Bracket words which belong together in sentences of varying difficulty; read them as "single words," no pauses between them.

750- T   (Interpret/Books) "Three-tiered Trials"

Reading comprehension occurs on three levels: literal, critical, and inferential. The literal level covers the act of translating the words themselves. Critical skills require an interplay between what is read and the reader's past experiences, while inferential reading involves reading between the lines—determining the deepest meanings in a work. Although all three levels are important for full literary appreciation, plots and story lines must be made clear to slow readers so they can enjoy the discussions at critical and inferential levels. Thus, reading is plot oriented, experience oriented, and theme oriented. (See related idea 707.)

751- T   (Interpret/Talk) "No Put-down"

Do not underrate the intelligence of slow readers. They may be slow academically but not mentally or emotionally. Respect and emphasize the qualities and abilities these students have rather than dwell on what they lack. Slow readers, for example, often compensate for their lack of reading and writing skills by becoming highly articulate in speaking. Thus, if they know the plot or the gist of a selection, they often outdo better readers in critical and interpretive discussion.

752- T   (Organize/Books, Papers) "Up Organization"

The following list contains just some of the elements of organization skills which can be turned into practice exercises:

1. Central ideas through lists of questions
2. Central ideas into headlines
3. Events placed in proper order: chronological, space, importance, deductive-inductive
4. Chapter titles and topic headings
5. Main ideas found in groups of words and phrases
6. Outlines of main and supporting ideas
7. Signal words, e.g., first, then, next
8. Summaries and precise writing
9. Short synopses of paragraphs, pages
10. Titles for paragraphs or entire selection
11. Topic sentences
12. Words and ideas grouped and classified

POETRY

753- C   (Experiment/Word Lists) "Qua-training"

Develop an interest in writing simple original poems by practicing the suggestion below. Write on the chalkboard three lists of rhyming words such as these:

Group 1	*Group 2*	*Group 3*
girl	stop	slow
pearl	shop	mow
say	Ann	walk
pay	pan	talk

Students then write a four-line poem for each group. When the poems are complete, they should be shared and placed on the bulletin board with some appropriate pictures.

STUDY SKILLS

754-C   (Consolidate/Games) "Library Full of Treasures"

Allow students to practice locating information in the library, particularly reference materials. Start a treasure hunt game. At each step along the way students must find a specific bit of information. After finding one answer in the atlas, searchers could be directed to the encyclopedia, from there to the *Reader's Guide*, and so on. Of course, this must be carefully preplanned with simple, easily followed directions printed on small slips of paper.

755-I   (Experiment/Dictionaries) "Things Are Looking Up"

To acquaint the student with the wide range of information that a dictionary offers, look through an unabridged dictionary and make up questions. For example: (1) In what century was Robin Hood supposed to have lived? (2) Why is a weasel like a skunk? (3) Why is "rodeo" a good name for that event? (4) Why is a "doubting Thomas" a Thomas and not a David, Donald, or a Douglas? Have students look up the answers in the dictionary after they determine the key word or phrase in the question.

756-C   (Experiment/Games) "Follow the Flash"

Practice following directions. Divide the class in half. Write a command on the board or use flash cards. Quickly remove the command. Call upon a pupil. If the direction is carried out accurately, then that team gets a point. A typical instruction might be: "Open any book to page 33, then hold up the book."

757- I   (Interpret/Authorities) "Going to the Source"

Give students an opportunity to develop the skills of locating
and selecting information by acquainting them with the *Guiness
Book of World Records* and the *World Almanac.* Late elementary,
junior, and senior high students enjoy looking up the biggest,
most, least, of anything. This activity is interesting, educational,
and fun, and it broadens the students' informational horizons.

758- G   (Interpret/Talk) "Telling It Again"

This exercise provides practice in recalling information accurately.
Although there are many ways to proceed, one approach is to
have one student tell his neighbor something—an event or just an
idea. The listener then tries to paraphrase exactly what he was
told. Whether this is done in pairs as above or in teams, or class
halves, it becomes an awakening event to discover the task is not
as easy as thought.

759- C,I   (Organize/Mixed Media) "No Penalty for Clipping"

Clip short articles from the financial, society, sports, and the
general news section of a newspaper and paste them on cards.
Shuffle the cards and pass them out to class with these instructions:

> *These articles were taken from the newspaper. Arrange them
> under the proper column headings listed on the chalkboard
> (financial, society, sports, news) as quickly as you can deter-
> mine the type of article.*

For variation, students can discriminate between articles which
might be of interest to an athlete, for example, or a banker,
housewife, sixth grade girl, or business man. Summaries of
stories written by pupils can also be arranged in the same manner
using categories such as travel, humor, adventure, fact, fantasy,
or history. This activity allows practice in skimming and scanning
(see idea 727).

760- I   (Organize/Models) "Classy Game"

To develop organizing and classifying skills, students practice
putting together related things. For example, cut out basic car
parts and see if the student can match the part to its name and
description. These can be placed in file folders for storage and
later use.

761- I   (Organize/Sentences) "Mental Telegraphy"

Provide practice in selecting main ideas in a paragraph. The
object is to reduce a paragraph to a telegram format. Give students an imaginary budget of $5 and suggest the cost per word.
They then condense a message until it fits the budget.

VOCABULARY

762- C   (Analyze/Games) "Say and Tell"

Help students develop an awareness of antonyms and synonyms
with this exercise. Divide the class into two or more groups.
The teacher pronounces a word and uses it in a sentence. Each
pupil on a team has a chance to go to the chalkboard to write
a word which has an opposite (antonym) or similar (synonym)
meaning. The teams build points by their correct word choices.

763- I   (Analyze/Pictures) "Words Which Unfold"

Use file folders for this vocabulary building exercise. For example, inside place a picture of a West Coast Indian carving a
totem pole. This provides a clue to a new word—"gouge."
From a list of possible definitions printed on the opposite
page, the student chooses the definition "to carve out, usually
with a metal tool." Students can participate in developing these
exercises by contributing interesting pictures which may suggest new words and ideas. The teacher can hand out blank
folders for this purpose.

764- C   (Consolidate/Lists) "Two Matches"

Vocabulary words may be learned
by matching two lists of words, a
list of nouns representing occupations (e.g., minister, surgeon, author)
and a list of verbs indicating what
these professionals do (e.g., preach,
operate, write). Adding adverbs
would be a natural follow-up.

765- I   (Experiment/Games) "Scrabbled Egos"

"Scrabble" can be used effectively for a word-building game.
But adaptations of the regular rules and procedures can also be
made. For example, players can have two minutes to see how
many words they can make from a half dozen letter tiles (without use of the gameboard). Or various prefixes and suffixes
can be printed on short strips of wood or cardboard propor-
tioned to match the tiles. Each player is given an affix and
must see how many words he can make with a set number of
letter tiles.

766- C   (Experiment/Games) "Teach-Tac-Toe"

The familiar game of Tic-Tac-Toe may be adapted for building
vocabulary, by first drawing two game frames on the chalkboard. In one, print assigned vocabulary words in each box.
The class is split into two teams. Individuals from each team
are alternately called to pronounce and use in a sentence one
of the boxed words not already used. For a correct response
a circle or an "X" is placed in a box in the other game frame.
To win, a team must earn marks in any three consecutive
boxes forming a straight line in any direction.

767- C,I   (Experiment/Mixed Media) "Perfect Practice"

New words should enter the child's vocabulary through neces-
sity. Even an abstract term such as "democracy" can be
thoroughly learned in a series of steps: (1) write the word in
syllables, (2) list word derivations and related words, (3) give
the definition and write the new word in several sentences,
(4) paste pictures from newspapers and magazines under the
heading "Democracy is . . . ," and (5) take field trips to city
or state government offices to see democracy in action.

768- I   (Interpret/Cards) "Cardology"

Capitalize on a student's desire to substitute words when
reading by encouraging a study of synonyms and antonyms.
Prepare flash cards on which are printed the word, a synonym,
an antonym, a definition, and an illustrative sentence. The student reads all of this as it is flashed and, with practice, (s)he
will be able to give synonyms and antonyms by seeing only
the original word stimulus. Another way to proceed is to devise exercises in which more effective and picturesque words

are substituted for those in the original sentence, e.g., "The boy ran quickly from the car." "Dashed" would communicate more feeling.

769- G   (Interpret/Games) "Check Mates"

This checker game is designed for students who need sight-word drill. On the squares of a regular checkerboard paste the words to be learned (the Dolch sight-word list or any other suitable list). The two-color scheme of the checkerboard must, of course, be retained. Students play as in a regular checker game but must name the word on the square to which he is moving or over which he is jumping.

770- T   (Observe/Cards) "Build a Tach"

A useful, do-it-yourself tachistoscope can be made by cutting a slot or several in a file folder. Trim off the tab to form a straight edge and tape this edge to form a sleeve. Cut another folder to form a single sheet or card which can be slid up or down inside the sleeve exposing words or phrases in the windows as slowly or rapidly as desired. To estimate timed exposure of words, count off by thousands to approximate seconds: "One thousand, two thousand, three thousand" is three seconds. Any speeds of less than a second should be confined to commercial equipment.

771- I   (Organize/Lists) "Measure Hunt"

An effective way to teach spelling is to mark off three or four columns on a sheet of paper. Label each column with a desired category (depending upon the subject under study). In lieu of any special categories, suggest "animal," "vegetable," and "mineral." Using dictionaries students see who can place the most correctly spelled words in each of the categories in a specified time limit. This activity also teaches the process of classifying.

772- I   (Organize/Lists) "Words on File"

Encourage students to record new words in file folders which can be stored for review and used by other classes to build vocabulary. Suggest creative ways to arrange lists such as finding meaningful definitions and sample sentences. Occasional pictures from magazines or drawn by the student will add interest and help clarify the words in these personalized classroom dictionaries.

WORDS

773- C   (Analyze/Cards) "Got a Pair?"

This activity helps students having difficulty with any aspect of reading which requires word analysis. On the chalkboard or on a large poster, print word endings: *-an*, *-ould*, *-ead*, *-oop*, *-each*, and others. Prepare another list with initial consonants, digraphs, or blends (see idea 738) which when matched with the correct endings will complete the words. Students are asked to see how many words they can make by matching the endings. Set a time limit. The student with the most words at the end of, perhaps, six minutes reads his list to the class. Other students offer additional words. Then all can apply meanings to unknown words. (Idea 793 will help in a related area of affixes.)

774- C   (Analyze/Magazines) "Be a Cut-up"

Pictorial magazines can provide the stimulus for many aspects of teaching reading skills. For example, to aid in the practice of forming the consonant vowel combinations, (see idea 738) have students cut out words employing whatever sounds are being studied. Sometimes parts of various words can be cut up to form syllables of specific words. The change in type design or size helps accentuate syllabication. Such a collection can be pasted in a scrapbook or notebook. This approach gives an air of practicality which sometimes doesn't come across in the average workbook exercise.

775- C,I   (Experiment/Chalkboards) "Long and Short of It"

For practice in decoding polysyllabic words, prepare a list of phonetically spelled words to use in board drills. Write a word on the board, dividing it into syllables. Some of the syllables will be short words the students can read immediately. Others will have simple sound patterns that they can sound out by relating them to rhyming words. For example, *er* usually has the same sound as the letters *er* in the word *her*. In the word *plan* they can find the word *an*. Soon they also will become familiar with certain common sound patterns, such as *ing*, *ank*, *con*, *pre*, *tion*, and *tious.*, and they will decode these combinations automatically. Here are some examples of phonetically spelled words that can be sounded by breaking them into syllables:

apartment	continental	maximum
apparatus	illustration	operate
buffalo	imitated	peppermint
commanding	importantly	perforate
comfort	insist	pulsating
conductor	internal	satisfactory
confident	ligament	transcontinental
consistent	management	understandable
constricted	manipulate	workmanship

After some practice, have volunteers sound out the words to see if the other students can write them correctly.

776- C,G (Experiment/Games) "Picture Clear"

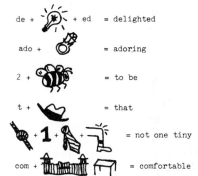

Show students a typical rebus puzzle; then have them make up their own. Working in groups later, students pass around their papers so each has someone else's. Then each attempts to solve the rebus, carefully pronouncing the word. This exercise for learning syllabication can also be expanded to include entire sentences.

777- I   (Experiment/Pictures) "Sound Pictures"

Show four or five magazine pictures (without captions) or place pictures in sets of file folders. Illustrations should suggest adjectives or adverbs. By questions try to elicit the best words. Responses can be oral or written.

778- C   (Experiment/Senses) "Snakes Alive"

Give your class an interesting noun (sometimes with a picture) such as snake. Ask them to think of a sensory word describing a snake. The first replies may be *green* or *long*, but soon the class will use more descriptive words such as *scaly*, *slithery*, and *wiggly*. This can be either an oral or written activity.

779- C,I   (Experiment/Sentences) "Have a Pair"

Write pairs of words which are easily reversed or confused because of similar configuration and sound, for example: *bear-bare, bridge-bribe, flight-fight, hoped-hopped, plum-plume, saw-was, shave-shove, their-there, they're-their, weather-whether.* Encourage close scutiny of each word pair to note differences in form and meaning. Have students listen to these words in sentences read orally and then write the correct choice on paper.

780- C,I   (Interpret/Audiotapes) "Tap a Tape"

To allow students to practice word recognition and spelling skills, tape some oral instructions (different for each student) which emphasize specific words you want them to learn, for example: "*Proceed* to the door, open it and *engage* in a brief *conversation* with the first person you see. Then *write* a note *explaining* what you have just done." Of course, you can modify the instructions to grade level. This exercise, which could be presented as a game, also gives students a chance for practice in following directions—an important study skill.

781- C,G   (Interpret/Games) "Under the O"

Play "Word-o" to develop word recognition. Prepare 8½ × 11 cardboard sheets blocked off like a bingo card with twenty-five squares, five rows of five. Or have each student fold a paper into twenty-five equal-sized squares. The center square is marked "free." Print twenty-five troublesome words or sight vocabulary words in the blocks. Students may do so from lists the teacher provides. Each card will have some of the same words but all will be quite different. The teacher has all the words on a master sheet or on small cards drawn from a box. As the teacher pronounces the word, the players try to locate the same word on their cards and cover it with a marker. The player who first covers five words in a straight line—vertically, horizontally or diagonally—calls out "Word-o" and wins the game. To make the game more challenging, require the winner to use the words correctly in two sentences before he or she can officially be declared winner.

782- I,C   (Organize/Lists) "Three Ways Better"

Here are three reading exercises to help word recognition:

(1) List all the words in this story which are made up of a prefix and a root word. Underline the prefix. (2) List words in this story which begin with two-letter or three-letter consonant blends. Underline the initial blend in each word and so on. (3) List words in this story which have long vowel sounds.

CHAPTER
15

EVALUATION

EXPOSITION

783-I   (Judge/Papers) "Author Authority"

This idea is a variation of one in which the student dictates
a story while the teacher writes it for the student to read
later. This time, however, the student tells the teacher about
an activity, a sport, or procedure about which he knows
much and the teacher knows very little. The teacher then
writes an explanation based on information the student gives.
The student reads the completed draft, usually quite eagerly.
Then both discuss how well the information was incorporated into the composition and who is at fault if the explanation emerges poorly.

JOURNALISM

784-C   (Identify/Newspapers, Questions) "Page One Start"

Below-average ability classes are often motivated to read by
competing, especially competing with the teacher. Short
daily quizzes based on the local newspaper's front page are
a start. Give a grade of A to anyone who can ask a front-
page question which the teacher is unable to answer.

NARRATION

785- C   (Extrapolate/Games) "A and B Stories"

Assess ability to retell a story aloud by using the classic spell-down. As usual divide the class into two teams standing in lines opposite each other. Begin with the first student on side A who tells what happened first in the story. The lead student on side B takes the story one step farther. Students who cannot reply go to the end of the line and await another turn. A second miss disqualifies them and they must sit. At the end of the allotted time, the team with the most students standing wins. A slight switch can be made in this procedure by asking each student to contribute five questions (with answers) on a subject under study. Answers to these questions determine who stands or sits.

NOVELS

786- C   (Extrapolate/Plots) "Predicting the Future"

Assess ability to listen with understanding. After reading some passages aloud, ask: Can you find the turning point in the story? Do the characters act and talk like real people? Illustrate. What is the moral or main idea of the story? Have you read any other stories with similar ideas? Which ones? To do this the student must organize and recall information and use inference. These skills need constant practice.

787- C   (Restructure/Games) "Expertease"

To help develop good reading habits, plan a Stump the Panel game either before discussing a novel (for testing knowledge of plot) or after (for reviewing emphasized points). A chairperson and panel of four reader-experts are selected; the remaining students are challengers. They write questions about the plot—who said certain important things, what some words mean, which are the key passages, and so on. Questions can be on file cards and should be checked for appropriateness. The following day a moderator is chosen to call for questions, and a recorder is picked to total points for either the panel or the challengers.

OVERVIEW

788- I   (Compare/Audiotapes) "A Record Event"

To encourage oral reading practice and to evaluate improvement, tape record a student reading an unfamiliar selection. Then allow the piece to be taken home for oral practice. In a few days record the reading again and compare the difference. There is usually a great improvement.

789- I,G   (Compare/Charts) "Competitive Rating"

Pair all class members. Have them choose some fairly easy reading such as short stories or novels. Each student reads for three minutes while a partner provides a word count and time check. Both teammates compute a words-per-minute rate, and the teacher (or students) charts the scores. Repeat this with similar materials at least three times each semester. Students like to see how their own progress compares with their peers. After learning this charting procedure, students can show progress in spelling, reading comprehension, vocabulary, and even overcoming composition weaknesses. Such charts also help the teacher tell at a glance an individual's progress.

790- I   (Compare/Charts) "Take Ten"

Break word-for-word reading habits. Let the student compete with himself, and chart that progress. The reader establishes a baseline figure for a normal ten-minute reading. For each ten-minute reading exercise to follow, the reader must increase the pages read by one. This continues until the reader can no longer comprehend. Through various assessments such as comprehension tests (with 95 percent accuracy), the reader should be able to locate the most comfortable and successful rate for that type of reading material. Once this plateau is found, the reader can gradually increase rate as long as comprehension does not drop.

791- I   (Extrapolate/Questions) "Going to Press"

Allow each child to write—or dictate for you to write—an important comprehension question for a story being studied. Duplicate these questions for the class. Possibly attach names to each entry. Students are thrilled seeing their names in print along with the question, and the review is invaluable.

792- I   (Extrapolate/Book Reports) "Audio Books"

Allow slow readers to submit reports on books they have *heard*. Prepare an audiotape library of class-chosen selections which slower students can use as they follow in books kept in a special room library. This involves some work for the teacher of a group of student readers. By reducing the usual frustration, this method encourages slow readers to enter literary discussion. This way, they too can evaluate the work's quality, the author's objectivity, and other matters appropriate to critical and inferential reading.

793- C   (Identify/Lists) "Reading in the Round"

Not all work with words and phrases needs be relegated to lists on the chalkboard or on paper. For example, some teachers have had success with practice wheels which can be made of anything from paper plates to plywood. After teaching such useful structural aids as meanings of prefixes and suffixes, provide additional practice through self-study use of the wheels. The following common prefixes and suffixes are among some which can be combined with root words to produce various words with different meanings, illustrating the importance of knowing affixes. This same approach can be used for thought units as well as for sentence parts.

Prefixes	*Suffixes*
ab—from, off	ation—state of
auto—self	ancy, ency—act of
bi—two	ful—full of
con, com—with	ing—act of
dis—apart	ish—resembling
mis—in the way	less—without
ob—toward	ment—state of, act of
pre—earlier	ness—state of
trans—across	ory—pertaining to
un, in—not	tion—state of

794- T   (Identify/Problems) "Dunce Hat Still On"

There is such a person as the much maligned "dumb kid" who is unable to read or learn at or close to the achievement level of the other class members. Some teachers do not understand this soon enough. Some never do. Expectation levels need constant adjustment based on results of frequent evaluation (see idea 713.)

795- C   (Judge/Books) "Once upon a Time"

Motivate middle school or junior high students who read on picture-book level. Encourage them to read aloud to younger brothers and sisters or other children in the neighborhood or school. In addition to the reading, they can also rate the picture books according to the reactions of their youthful audience. Ratings could determine whether these titles should be included in a bibliography of recommended children's gift books. They could also be rated for such elements as horror (whether it is suitable for children), fantasy (whether it is the right kind), or endings (whether they are believable). The final ratings along with brief annotations are published for parents to aid in book buying. How does this help the slow readers? Prereading and other preparations help them improve their own reading abilities. Stories must be read accurately and with feeling to obtain accurate listener reactions. Then too, students are not embarrassed carrying juvenile literature for important research such as this.

796- I   (Restructure/Book Reports) "Hate Them Reports"

As an alternative to lengthy written book reports, students write brief descriptions and personal opinions on 3 X 5 index cards headed by title and author. These cards are then filed in a box according to title. Now students can read what others have to say about books they plan to read. If the descriptions are vivid and precise, curiosity may outweigh any negative comments about a book. The file box of book report cards can also be used by the teacher to monitor individual reading. Instead of a file box, cards could be placed in pockets inside file folders which, for the more popular books, have been decorated to resemble a book jacket. (See also ideas 600 and 671.)

797- G   (Restructure/Discussions) "No Danger of Copying"

Teachers who are not too concerned with individual scores can administer a group effort review test. Divide the class into small groups of about five students each. Group members work to-

gether discussing each question before answering. In this way
learning becomes cooperative and not competitive. Students
become less anxious and perform better. Since students do work
together, the questions can be more complex than might be
used for individual testing.

798- C   (Restructure/Book Reports) "New Roles for Book Reports"

Reporting on biographies and autobiographies presents an exciting
challenge to students when they
can role play the main characters in
the book. Let students who have
read the same book form a panel of
important visitors from the past who
will present the main ideas in the
book. This type of group activity
often breaks through the psychological barrier slow readers have for the
written book report.

SENTENCES

799- C   (Identify/Games) "Caught on Tape"

The class reviews voice inflection rules governing periods,
commas, and other marks of punctuation with this game. Play
a tape recording of a student reading. Ask the other students
to call out "stop" when they detect a vocalized mistake. They
must explain the violation they spotted. Points can be assigned
for each correct find.

800- C   (Restructure/Games) "Neat Card Trick"

A pack of fifty-two unlined, colored 3 × 5 index cards is made
up to contain thirteen each of adjectives, nouns, verbs, and adverbs. The object of this game, "Sentence Rummy," is to make
four-word sentences using an adjective, a noun, a verb, and an
adverb. Emulating Rummy terms, if desired, call each sentence
a "trick" worth one point. To play, five cards are dealt to each
of four players. When a sentence can be assembled—after his
draw and before he discards—a student plays the four cards face
up. At each turn, a player draws two cards, either from the

face-down pack or the face-up discard pile, and discards one
card, including the play on which he goes out. Two points are
scored for going out. A game is ten points, counting only tricks
and going out.

SPELLING

801- C   (Restructure/Chalkboards) "Moving Spelldown"

Two students go to opposite chalkboards. Choose a judge for
each student. The teacher stands in the middle of the room and
says a spelling word. The two students write the word quickly
on the chalkboard. Each judge checks for accuracy. The first
student to write the word correctly on the board wins this
round. The other student sits down and a challenger comes up.
All students get a chance to participate.

STUDY SKILLS

802- I   (Compare/Charts) "Two R's"

Periodic reading rate improvement exercises will help students
see the importance of reading rapidly while recalling the main
ideas. In one such approach, have the class read short stories of
250 to 300 words. Using complete sentences, each writes the
main idea of the entire selection. They may then write each
paragraph's main idea and finally answer some comprehension
questions. To keep it all in perspective, pupils keep individual
progress charts indicating speed and accuracy. Pairs can check
each other's rate and recall record.

803- G   (Identify/Games) "Auction Quiz"

To check ability to recall information, divide the class into
about five groups with a half dozen on a team. Each team is given
twenty points at the start. The object is for a team to retain as
many of these points as possible. Each team bids on an unknown
question (possibly in an envelope). The team bidding the highest
number of their twenty points gets the question. The more
points bid, the harder the question. If a team fails to answer a
question, they lose the number of points they bid. All members
can collaborate on the answer, but only one answer is acceptable.

804- C   (Identify/Problems) "Accidentally on Purpose"

This activity is designed to assess comprehending or recalling information and reading critically. After reading a story or article, each child writes a paragraph telling something about it, deliberately including at least one mistake (wrong word choice, incorrect fact, wrong name, or inaccurate time, for instance.) These paragraphs are read aloud so the class can find and correct the mistakes. Paragraphs may also be duplicated and distributed to the class. Of course, some mistakes will be natural. These should be found and corrected also.

805-C,G   (Restructure/Games) "Square Game"

"Categories" is a good game to build vocabulary and to practice recalling information. The words and categories can be tailored to suit many aspects of English (literature review, grammar drill, vocabulary building). Each student prepares a grid with an agreed-upon five-letter word written horizontally over the top squares. Five or six categories are listed vertically on the left side of the paper. For each category, each player must fill in a word which begins with the letter at the top of the column as in the partially completed grid below. Enough time should be allowed for players to feel they have completed as much as they can. Then the sheets are scored. For each correct word any player who has it gets as many points as there are other players who did not have it. For example, if only one out of ten players

	G	A	M	E	S
Authors	Nordhoff				
Books		Arrowsmith			
Characters			Madame Defarge		
Playwrights				Eliot	
Poems					Snowbound

wrote *Euripides* as a playwright beginning with E, it is worth 9 points. If nine out of ten players wrote Eliot they get one point each. The reward is for new and unusual names and, since the answers are read orally, all players profit.

806- C   (Restructure/Instructions) "Junior Cartographers"

Organization skills are best evaluated when students can apply them to new and interesting situations. Provide each student with one of possibly three sets of instruction for what is a simple process except for the fact that the instructions are out of sequence. Exercises can include such projects as brushing or feeding a dog, cutting the grass with a power mower, planting a terrarium, or antiquing some furniture. Those with the same set of instructions may share and compare order. Or the teacher can provide each with a key.

807- I   (Restructure/Paragraphs) "Order a Batch"

To assess comprehension and ability to organize material, paste the scrambled paragraphs of a short selection on tag board or in a folder. See if the students can rearrange the paragraphs in proper order. Selections can also be pasted on cards and the student simply lists the letters of the paragraph in a new order. Selections may be taken from comics, school newspaper articles, magazines, book passages, directions for assembling something, recipes, and other sources.

808- C   (Restructure/Paragraphs) "Sentence to Order"

On separate strips of paper, print sentences from short paragraphs. Place scrambled sentences into envelopes—a special, secret message for each student. They unscramble the sentences into smoothly reading paragraphs by arranging slips on their desks. Have keys available so that they can check their own ability to organize information. As a follow-up activity they can share their messages.

VOCABULARY

809- C   (Restructure/Games) "On Playing Vowel"

Play the decoding game. Write simple sentences or short paragraphs for the students, omitting vowels. Have the student complete the sentences.

Example: Th—y d—n—t l—v— th—t d—n—t sh—w th—r l—v—.

810- I,C   (Compare/Games) "Match a Batch"

The "Match Game" is a good vocabulary evaluator because students have to match word cards with their proper definitions. This can be a class game, dividing into two teams, or just for one person.

811- T   (Identify/Games) "Flash Recall"

Make flash cards for basic sight vocabulary. Form two piles with the words the student knows in one pile and those he has trouble recognizing in another. Have him study the troublesome word list. Decide on a reward when all the cards can be placed into the pile of words he knows. See how quickly he learns the words with this little extra motivation. Periodically review the words he already knows.

812- I   (Identify/Games) "Look Alikes"

Slow readers often have difficulty recognizing sight vocabulary words which look alike except for one or two letters. Perhaps this simple card game will provide needed but exciting practice. Using plain white 3 × 5 index cards, print two identical sets of cards containing troublesome vocabulary, troublesome because their configurations are so similar. One set is for the student and the other for a partner or the teacher. The partner begins by laying down one card at a time very quickly, word-side up. The student is to pick up a card only when it exactly matches the one on top of his stack. If he picks the wrong word, he loses his card. If he is right he takes both. The object at the end of any number of games is for him to collect all the cards, For slow readers who overuse configuration clues, words like these may give problems: *want, went,* and *won't; these* and *those; them, theme,* and *then; house, hose, horse,* and *hours;* and sometimes even *was* and *saw.*

813- G   (Identify Games) "Making Points with the Dictionary"

Divide the class into five or six groups. Using the dictionary, one group picks out an unfamiliar word such as "buckram," writes the word and its simplest definition on a piece of paper, and gives it to the teacher. The other groups, without a dictionary but using the same size paper, create their own definitions for the word and hand them to the teacher to be combined with the correct definition. Then each group, except the one which chose the word, listens to the definitions being read and tries to choose the correct one. If right, the group gets five points; wrong, two points. When a group's definition is chosen, even though it is incorrect, that group gets three points for being able to write a logical-sounding definition. If the right definition eluded everyone, the group which chose the word gets ten points. Then the dictionary is passed to the next group and the procedure is repeated until each group has had two turns. The group with the most points wins.

814- I,G   (Identify/Games) "Pass or Fumble"

The popular game of football can be brought into the classroom, modified, and used as a means of mental exercise in vocabulary enrichment. Draw a football field with proper yardline markings on a large sheet of green construction paper. Add some matchstick goal posts. The game begins on the fifty-yard line where a cardboard football is placed. The only other equipment needed is a stack of cards on which new vocabulary words are printed. In order to move the football a player must read the word on the card. If he pronounces it correctly, he moves the ball ten yards toward the opponents' goal. If he reads it incorrectly, it is considered a fumble and the ball is moved backwards ten yards. When a player crosses the goal line, he earns six points. If he reads the next word correctly, he gets the extra point. Then the ball is replaced on the fifty-yard line. This can also be a team game with the gameboard placed on an overhead transparency.

815- T   (Judge/Oral Reading) "Out with Doubt"

Listen to individuals read. Be alert to words which they ask to be defined or which they clearly puzzle over. Select some of these for vocabulary-building activities. These words are related to immediate needs and interests.

816- I   (Restructure/Transparencies) "Word Pictures"

Choose small pictures of objects which are familiar to a student

with a reading problem. Place them under a sheet of plastic. The
student or the teacher prints the name of each object either on
or near it. Each word should be pronounced aloud. Review each
word with the plastic still in place. Then remove the plastic,
place it on an overhead projector or just hold it up. See how
many words can be recalled without the aid of the pictures. If
the original pictures are clear line drawings in black and white
as in coloring books, make a transparency of them before proceeding as above. The latter is especially useful when working
with a class.

WORDS

817- C   (Compare/Sentences) "Blankety Blank Story"

The teacher chooses any illustration depicting a great deal of
activity and writes a short lively story to go with the illustration
but leaves out several key words. From the context students decide what the appropriate words should be. Compare the students'
choices with the original.

818- C,G (Restructure/Games) "Tic-Tac-Toe Know"

Play tic-tac-toe using three-letter words. To score, count each
horizontal, diagonal, and vertical word (forward or backward) as
one point. Two players take turns. Each has a grid. During each
turn, a player places a letter in a square. Whenever a word is built,
a point is scored. This continues until neither player can build
any more words. Teams can also be used.

Example:

m	u	m
u	u	u
g	a	s

mum (2)
mug (2)
gum (2)
gas (1)
sag (1)
sum (2)
_____
10 points

The same approach can be used for evaluating the ability to
make up short words which employ letter digraphs, blends, and
diphthongs and are built syllable by syllable rather than letter by

letter. (See Glossary for reading terms.) One player begins by putting the first syllable (or letter combination) of a known word in one box then the other player takes a turn. The first player to complete a three-part word wins the game. (Tic-tac-toe need not be limited to nine squares. Sixteen would be more useful at times.)

819- C,G,I (Restructure/Games) "Ai, Ai, Sir"

Here is a game that will reveal how well students understand vowel combinations in words. Begin by writing one or two vowel combinations like *ai* and *ea* on the board. Then five-student teams produce as many words as they can with each vowel combination. At the end of ten minutes, each team reads its list of words and receives one point for every real word correctly spelled. Vary the rules by scoring only for words no other team has.

820- C,G (Restructure/Lists) "Compound It"

Word building becomes a competitive game when the entire class uses the following or similar list of words to form compound words.

back	cook	milk	road
boat	drop	note	sail
book	mail	play	sand
box	man	rail	top
coat	mate	rain	wish

After writing these words on the chalkboard, give each student a sheet of lined paper. Tell them they have five minutes to write as many compound words as they can, using only the words on the board. Students with the greatest number of words read their lists, and the one with the most correctly spelled is the winner of the game.

821- C   (Restructure/Sentences) "Nice Idea"

This exercise checks on improvement in written expression. Students substitute weak words in model sentences with more interesting words. On the chalkboard write sentences which need improvement, e.g., "Joe got a good used car buy and fixed it up to look real good." The class offers substitute words for *got*, *good*, *fixed it up*, *real*, and *good*.

CHAPTER

16

APPLICATION

EXPOSITION

822- I,G,C (Write/Role Playing) "Explore This"

Reading and writing skills are best developed simultaneously. To motivate students, have them write stories about imaginary experiences in particularly appealing avocations or vocations, e.g., airline stewards and hostesses, television camera operators, archeologists, or police officers. Have them find basic information on the training and tools of the trade. Then ask them to make up a log of a typical day or to write a more formal piece. These papers can be shared with the entire class or read aloud in small groups.

JOURNALISM

823- C (Construct/Newspaper) "Small-time Publishers"

Empty writing assignments fail to interest many students, particularly the slow readers. The following idea works as well for them as for the bright students. If your school has a newspaper, students could submit jokes, crossword puzzles, games and riddles, and even some news articles. All these efforts involve writing and possibly some reading for research. This idea gives everyone a change to be responsible writers and readers with a purpose. It also proves to reluctant learners that speaking is not the only important form of communication. Some future jobs may very well depend on the ability to read and write.

LETTER WRITING

824- I   (Write/Forms) "Recall the Past"

For the noncollege bound students, useful, relevant instruction on how to complete job-oriented forms will result in better attitudes toward reading/writing assignments than the usual abstract composition assignments. Begin with simple forms—bank checks, W-2 forms, or applications for credit, and proceed to personal letters requesting job interviews or seeking information about a trade school.

825- I   (Write/Letters) "Count-to-Ten Words"

Help children release inner tensions by frequently allowing them time to write a letter to someone, including the teacher, about something which angered them. This helps teachers keep in touch with children's attitudes and helps prevent explosions by offering them a safety valve. One teacher used this approach as a substitute for assigned compositions. He found that student attitudes toward composition improved 100 percent.

826- I   (Write/Papers) "Take a Letter; Take Two"

Have students make up a letter to the editor expressing a definite opinion toward a subject in which they are particularly interested. Each student writes a second make-believe letter to the editor expressing an opposite opinion on the same subject. The assign-

ment can be carried a bit further if the student writes a short
paper or gives an oral report examining both arguments point by
point.

MEDIA

827- I   (Construct/Book Reports) "Artistic Book Reports"

As an alternative to the typical book report or book talk, allow
students to tell about their books in an artistic way. With specific
characters and events in mind, they can create a collage or montage, a bulletin board, a burlap wall hanging illustrated with felt
cutouts, or even miniature dolls and puppets. This activity might
be part of a language arts fair or a contest. Other possiblities are
mobiles, posters, book jackets, and even audio- or videotaped
episodes.

828- I   (Perform/Audiotapes) "Box or Tube"

To encourage motivated writing as well as to encourage reading
with understanding, place students in teams of four. A team prepares a ten-minute radio program to be tape recorded. Give them
rehearsal and planning time. Suggest linking the various group
projects together for variety: soap opera, sportscast, newscast,
commercials. With equipment available, the skits could also be
recorded on videotape.

829- I   (Write/Papers) "Classified Research"

Students read classified ads for autos. They cut out the ad for
the car they like best. Then they attach the ad to a sheet of
paper on which they write a brief statement on why they chose
this particular car. (A car is a good subject since both girls and
boys seem interested.)

830- C   (Write/Papers) "Spare That Cartoon"

To encourage recreational reading and a little writing, collect
cartoons from the local newspaper or from magazines. Group the
cartoons by theme or subject. Paste them on poster board or in
booklets. Students read these in their spare time or use them for
projects. For example, find a cartoon series which conveys the
idea that this is the "machine age." Prepare a short paper to tell
how the cartoons show this.

831-I   (Write/Papers) "This Idea Is Classified"

Students find a particularly interesting classified ad (lost and found, personal, miscellaneous for sale, help wanted) and write the story behind the ad—how the item came to be for sale or why someone is looking for a ride to Connecticut. A variation is to have students tie together—juxtapose—two ads to form a comic situation. A third possibility is to let students respond to a classified ad specially prepared by the teacher. Comparing results makes learning to write almost fun.

832-I   (Write/Sentences) "Watch Them Unfold"

One or several pictures are pasted on one half of the inside of a manila file folder. The other half contains words which might be used with the picture(s). The two sources should help even the least creative writers to write a series of sentences telling whatever the picture suggests.

NARRATION

833-C   (Write/Papers) "Clued-in"

Listening and writing skills are developed in this activity. Slips of paper are prepared bearing names of characters from a story which the teacher or an able volunteer reads. As they listen to the story, each student attends very carefully to clues which tell about a character he has randomly drawn on a slip. After the story is completed, students write a brief character description, or compositions may be presented orally with some attention to variety among characters.

834-I   (Write/Papers) "Live and in Full Color"

Character analysis becomes clearer for slower students when they consider a live model. After discussing character description, ask students to observe a television actor in a character role and to take notes while watching the program. Then have them write a description including all the features and habits they noticed and a summary of the character's personality. As an added attraction, let the rest of the class try to guess who is being described.

OVERVIEW

835- I   (Construct/Book Reports) "Book Sellers"

Students are motivated to read by hearing about good books their classmates have read and enjoyed. Reports need not be written. They can be different and creative. Students could paint or locate an appropriate picture and then explain how the picture relates to the story. Others could make a large poster advertisement to "sell" the books they read. Some could invent a very novel "sales pitch"—write a one-minute radio or television commercial advertising a book they have read. Be sure students include key points without giving away the plot. Suggest using props (objects) to improve the message. The teacher is also at liberty to make suggestions for appropriate books which lend themselves to good reporting.

836- I,G   (Construct/Demonstrations) "Research and Development"

This idea is for individuals or pairs. They must use at least three books and a few articles to research a free-choice topic. Each presents his research to the class in any fashion. Make sure all audio-visual aids are available to the students. Topics may run the gamut from ESP to famous clowns.

837- I   (Construct/Displays) "Collage Graduates"

"A picture is worth a thousand words" and may be effectively used to "tell" the plot or theme of a story. Depending upon the length and complexity of the plot, several pictures may be used to assemble a montage portraying action, theme, and characters more vividly. Conrad Richter's *Light in the Forest* is excellent for starters since pictures of Indians, forests, and pioneers are relatively easy to find or draw. Even so, the teacher should have a vast collection of magazines and catalogues (see idea 702).

838- C   (Construct/Models) "Swinging Bookmobile"

For an unusual approach to book reports have students make

swinging book mobiles. Each student will need a clothes hanger
and plenty of imagination. The first step is to cover the triangu-
lar base of the hanger with paper—plain, fancy, decorative, or
textured. Next make cutouts of characters in the book. Suspend
these cutouts from the bottom rung of the hanger with thread,
at different levels. Then write a synopsis of the book, mount it
on colored paper, and fasten on the back of the hanger. Hang
these mobiles around the room and watch how they inspire other
students to "look into" the books.

839- G   (Speak/Books) "Being Party to Reading"

Consider "reading parties" at crucial times during the year. Able
readers from the class choose several favorite stories or poems.
They practice until they can achieve a smooth, dynamic, oral
presentation. Another class and parents may be invited to the
event. Writing invitations can be an important facet of this activity. Students are motivated to do their very best reading and
writing when the audience extends beyond the teacher or the
class.

840- C   (Write/Book) "Junior Book Makers"

Does this teacher's case sound familiar? "A few years ago I was
assigned to teach an English class. The required anthology contained selections which were either irrelevant or outdated and
too difficult for my students to read. In response to my class's
complaints, I challenged them to write their own book. Working
in groups, they designed the cover and illustrated the stories,
poems, and plays they wrote."

Student-made materials like these could be collected over
the years and kept in the classroom library as models and motiva-
tors. Perhaps such a book could be donated to a children's
hospital or exchanged with other schools. Materials like these
meet both the interest and reading levels of the creators. Even
further, the pride of accomplishment is immeasurable.

POETRY

841- I   (Write/Poems) "Poetic Grammar"

Students can use parts of speech to write "near-poems" of five
lines each. Ask them to follow these simple directions: (1) On
the first line of your paper write a noun naming a person, place,

or thing (or use your favorite definition). (2) On the next line write two adjectives which give some additional information about the noun. Separate each adjective with a comma. (3) On the third line write three verbs, also separated with commas, which tell what the noun does. (4) On the fourth line write a short phrase about the noun—anything which seems to follow the verbs or relate to the noun. (5) For the last line repeat the word you wrote on the first line or write a related word. Result? "Near-poems" such as these:

leaves	snow
red, golden	white, soft
flutter, glisten, float	falls, floats, covers
nature's decorations	winter sports
autumn	skiing

This activity makes students more aware that each word in a poem must carry much meaning and emotion and, thus, must be chosen with great care. For the slower student, such attention helps build vocabulary.

SHORT STORIES

842- I   (Write/Forms) "Solve a Blank Problem"

Students who have difficulty reading and writing can become very discouraged by a blank piece of paper and a stiff composition assignment. Help them by providing a short story, complete with key words, punctuation, and paragraphs. Leave blanks to be filled in with their own words and ideas. Completed stories can also be used later as springboards for grammar lessons.

843- I   (Write/Papers) "Short Subjects"

The structure of a major writing assignment on a short story or novel is not a stumbling block to the student if he keeps in mind that he must answer the following questions in his paper:

1. Who is the main character?
2. Where does the story take place?
3. What does the main character set out to do?
4. What or who helps him?
5. What problems occur?
6. Does the main character succeed or fail?
7. How does everything turn out?
8. How does the reader feel about the book?

844- C,I   (Write/Papers) "What Happened Next?"

The first half of a story is mimeographed and distributed to members of the class. Students are asked to finish it any way they want. Minimysteries are good for this purpose. Completed stories will be imaginative, uninhibited, and surprisingly revealing.

STUDY SKILLS

845- C   (Construct/Models) "Model Lesson"

Accuracy in following directions is greatly increased when students are interested. The unusual motivates. Have each student bring to class a small cardboard box about shoe box size which can be cut with scissors. Then duplicate some written instructions (about three different forms) to be distributed on three colors of paper to assure better distribution of three projects. The student must build what he reads, e.g., a bird house or feeder with peculiar design, a psychedelic truck van, or an interesting store front. Scissors, felt pens, crayons, and construction paper are provided. No glue is needed if the directions instruct for making slots to hold roofs, wheels, awnings, and the like. The models need not consume much class time—about a half hour. The rest of the time can be used to compare each other's constructions and to view the three models the teacher built to help write the instruction sheets.

846- I   (Speak/Anecdotes) "Shares That Mature"

Once a week each student "discovers" something in the library and, during a Friday "know and tell" period, talks about it with at least one classmate. They could share information from a book, an article, or any reference. Each would try to explain his find in a well-organized, interesting way. Different partners could be chosen each week. This activity combines two desirable learnings in reading: locating and organizing information.

847- I   (Write/Instructions) "On Bows and Rugs and Things"

Students write instructions on how to perform some sort of activity connected with a hobby or a craft. How to shoot a bow and arrow or how to hook a rug are just two examples for an assignment which puts into practice skills on organizing information.

848- I   (Write/Papers) "New Designs on Composition"

Draw a simple design on the chalkboard such as a wavy or cren-elated line. Encourage students to complete the lines to make an object or a larger design. They then write a story or short essay which their sketch or design serves to illustrate. From this simple interesting approach the students apply knowledge of organizing information around one central idea. To cite an ex-ample, one student imagined gear-like crenel to be the tops of two castle towers. In one, a young man was incarcerated and in the other, naturally, a young girl. How the two communicate and finally meet became an interesting story.

VOCABULARY

849- T   (Solve/Puzzles) "Not So Crosswords"

Collect crossword puzzles from every possible source, and make them available to your class during free time. If you can create some crossword puzzle addicts, you give these students a relax-ing yet challenging recreation and also a lifetime source of vocabulary enrichment.

850- I   (Write/Paragraphs) "A Wordy Story"

Place four new words on a piece of paper. Select a willing stu-dent from the class to take the list and to write a very short paragraph or story using the same words in different contexts. That way the meanings are clarified in use rather than through unrelated dictionary definitions.

PART 5

room management

room management

Introduction

Chapter 17
Attitudes 269
Authorities 272
Books 273
Bulletin Boards 274
Chalkboards 275
Demonstrations 276
Discussions 276
Displays 277
Games 278
Handouts 278
Instructions 278
Lectures 279
Libraries 280
Mixed Media 280
Newspapers 281
Notes 282
Periodicals 282
Pictures 283
Plans 283
Projectors 286
Slides 287
Talk 287
Television 288
Transparencies 288
Tutors 289

Evaluation

Chapter 19
Attitudes 299
Charts 302
Conferences 302
Field Trips 303
Forms 303
Instructions 304
Inventories 304
Lectures 306
Notes 307
Questions 307
Talk 310
Tutors 311

Deliberation

Chapter 18
Bulletin Boards 291
Charts 291
Discussions 292
Field Trips 293
Games 293
Inventories 294
Lectures 294
Libraries 295
Mixed Media 295
Plans 296
Questions 296
Seating 297
Talk 297
Tutors 298

Application

Chapter 20
Attitudes 313
Book Reports 314
Bulletin Boards 314
Demonstrations 314
Displays 315
Games 315
Instructions 316
Letters 316
Magazines 317
Newspapers 317
Papers 317
Tip 1,001 318

CHAPTER
17

INTRODUCTION

For several reasons the ideas in the Room Management section break the established format. Since they are for the teacher, the symbols for "class," "groups," and "individuals" have been omitted. The process and vehicle descriptors have been dropped. Key words from the ideas themselves—words which seem to be appropriate enabling steps in the teaching-learning sequence—serve to group the ideas.

ATTITUDES

851   "Ceiling Zero"

Sometimes the best way to teach is to become inconspicuous in the classroom, allowing the students to do most of their own teaching and learning. In highly motivated groups of superior students, for example, the teacher's efforts to direct may actually curtail learning, extinguishing responses unintentionally by detracting from a learning challenge or by offering lower expectancies than students might demand of themselves. Teachers can practice being facilitators of information gathering rather than being distributors of information. It is an attitude which will foster better student attitudes.

852   "False Alarm"

Students soon begin to ignore teachers who call for class attention and quiet and who then continue their "housekeeping details" at the desk. "Quiet!" means "something is going to take place now, so please listen." If it doesn't mean that, soon "Quiet!" will mean nothing to the class.

853   "Creative Encounters"

For some reason, educators and authors seem to restrict truly creative lessons to elementary school children. Older students are destined to days of dull discussions and test reviews unless the instructor improvises. For ideas about class projects, motivational techniques, and culminating activities, middle and high school teachers can search the volumes written about elementary school approaches. Displays, puppet shows, games, skits, and other activities can be as stimulating in high school as they were in those early years.

854   "Feeling Ah-h-h!"

Comfort is an important aid to learning. If the teacher is relaxed and allows students to relax, the general attitude and learning process is heightened. Tend also to lighting, seating, temperature, extraneous noise, and other essentials which affect learning.

855   "Great Leveler"

A teacher must be honest and sincere with students. An open mind to their ideas and opinions is imperative to command their respect, stimulate their minds, and encourage their participation.

856   "Look to Yourself"

Discipline problems often stem from the teacher rather than from the class. Since no lesson plan, however perfect, will be successful in a class in which the teacher cannot be heard over the noise, here are some thoughts to keep in mind. Discipline breaks down when:

1. Demands, standards, and expectations of the teacher are too high,

2. Some students have too little work and not enough challenge,
3. Extreme authoritarianism or its opposite becomes the teacher's pattern,
4. The teacher is inconsistent,
5. Students can't keep up with the instruction,
6. Teacher overestimates the attention span of the class,
7. Timing of class activities is poor.

857 "Look Toward the 80's"

A successful junior high school teacher suggests this: "When English is taught at the middle and junior high levels, subject matter accounts for only 20 percent of the students' needs. Ideally, the other 80 percent concerns care, attention, and deepest empathy."

858 "Moderate Joiner"

A teacher's attitude toward the job and the desire to keep abreast in his field, are often reflected through active membership in professional groups. English teachers are fortunate to have one of the largest subject matter organizations in the world—the National Council of Teachers of English. Beside benefitting from its wide offerings of teacher resources and journals (elementary, secondary, college, and English Education), teachers can participate in conferences and hold office. Many states have English councils affiliated with NCTE. Membership in both state and national English groups should be a must for each English teacher.

859 "Sensitivity Activity"

Moderate sensitivity exercises help the student become more aware of himself and show how important he is to the group. Here are two which have been used effectively. Ask the class to join hands in a circle (outdoors if possible). Through much twisting and without letting go of anyone's hand, have the circle change so that everyone is facing outward. It's possible and fun. The second sensitivity exercise is valuable for studying persuasion, conformity, group effort, and so forth. One student volunteers to leave the room while the class decides on an act which they want him to perform. When the student returns, he must try to perform that act without any clues except the class's applause. When he begins to accomplish the act, applaud; when not, no applause. No matter how difficult or complex the problem is, the contestant, surprisingly, usually succeeds. A real class pleaser and ice breaker, this resembles the "hot-cold" game.

860   "The SAP on Which Every Student Thrives"

Successful classroom teachers need more than a good subject matter background. They need to know how to bring the "SAP of life" into the classroom, i.e., those three areas tied so closely with basic human needs. A student needs to feel the *security* of a class where an unthreatening learning climate prevails. He needs to feel and share *affection* (or appreciation)—the knowledge that he is a liked and needed class member. Finally he needs a chance to have successful learning experiences, to achieve his full potential, and to apply his particular talents—in short, he needs to gain *prestige* among his peers and with the teacher. Naturally, these three basic needs have many related aspects, but following the magic "three" will help solve many problems before they can occur.

861   "Write 1,000 Times: I Will Never . . . "

In establishing and maintaining order within a classroom, subject matter is never used as a threat. For example, to eliminate a disruptive element by requiring extra compositions or memorizing poems actually defeats the purpose of the English class.

AUTHORITIES

862   "Para Pros"

The paraprofessional school staff may be more "pro" than "para." Take an informal survey to find out how many talents exist that could be used in the English class to present new information. Some may be travellers, actors, poets, novelists, cinematographers, or painters who could enrich any experience in the fine arts. Representatives of various occupations (farmers, architects, plumbers, reporters, computer programmers) can make a valuable contribution in the areas of occupational and consumer education.

BOOKS

863   "Buying Library Stocks"

Students broaden their own reading backgrounds more readily
if good books are available. Start a classroom paperback library.
At the beginning of the year collect about fifty cents from each
student in all your classes and order a wide selection of paperbacks (probably 100–150) to be attractively stored and displayed. Students use the room library during free reading time
or after school. They may also sign out books overnight. Then at
the end of the school year and after the last class session, each
gets a chance for the "grab-book"—reaching into a box for a
book which he can keep, trade, or sell.

864   "Put Down That Book"

When teaching, avoid the common mistake of using irrelevant,
uninteresting textbooks. Old-fashioned WASPish illustrations
and inappropriate models can quickly cause kids to "turn off"
a text. Adjust teaching material to student needs and their social
situation. Realistic modern textbooks are being published. Learn
what those textbooks are and where to get them. If time permits,
write or assemble materials for your own text. This could well
be a departmental effort. You may find a publishing house which
will print small quantities (2,000), give advice on arranging for
releases of copyright materials, store and sell the books, and give
the teacher a small royalty if sales more than cover publishing
costs and a profit for the company.

865   "Spice Is Right"

Students are always ready for something different and unexpected to change their day. Bring in new material to read to the class.
There are many good short story collections. Among these are
A Subtreasury of American Humor (Capricorn Books, N.Y.),
Creative Choices (Scott, Foresman, Glenview, Ill.), or *Sunlight
and Shadows* (Thomas Nelson & Sons, Ontario, Canada). Some
modern poetry (Rod McKuen) if read well will also excite the
class. Time spent introducing new authors will be rewarded with
expanded reading lists. Sometimes this can be a pupil-led activity
with students reading things they have discovered.

BULLETIN BOARDS

866   "Dig That Display"

Copy good bulletin board ideas on 3 × 5 inch cards which are classified and filed in a recipe box. Both teacher and students will then have many ideas on which to base new installations. Solve the lettering problem by keeping envelopes containing several sizes and styles of cardboard letters. Whenever a new bulletin board title is needed, these templates can be traced on colored construction paper. Incidently, placing letters on banners is easier than trying to pin them up singly.

867   "Eye of the Beholder"

When designing a bulletin board, try to fit your themes, ideas, and illustrations into a pattern which will carry the eye across the board. Use connecting lines, diagonal lines, semicircles, wavy lines, and other devices.

868   "Leave It to Them"

Suitable space for storing bulletin board materials is difficult to find. A resourceful teacher, however, can devise a convenient filing system for illustrations and other materials by using folders or manila envelopes, each correctly labeled and filed in a brightly painted box. A volunteer-student bulletin board committee can keep up the file and install displays. The teacher need not be the only one to install bulletin boards when there are probably a dozen students more artistically inclined.

869   "Living Color"

The bulletin board is often the only source of classroom decor. Too often it is not used to good advantage. Take every opportunity to install bulletin boards coinciding with what is being discussed and investigated. Studying *Moby Dick*, for instance, provides the chance to display several vivid photographs of whaling and life at sea. Sources are weekly periodicals, travel magazines, and especially *National Geographic.* An empty or cluttered bulletin board speaks poorly of teacher planning.

870   "No Board 'Em"

Students need to relate to examples which teachers use. Good bulletin boards reflect student backgrounds and interests. Consider, then, more than just displays of colorful magazine illustrations and posters. Use small picture hooks for fastening many kinds of items to the bulletin board: record albums, framed or unframed art prints, miniature models from dolls to ducks. Anything in hardware should not be overlooked to enhance learning.

871   "Try Trivia"

Reserve a small corner of a bulletin board for a "Trivia Corner." Each week post a question which the students can answer by going to a dictionary or other reference book. Questions resemble this: What two presidents in the twentieth century did not seek re-election? At the end of the week post the answers along with a new question. This serves many purposes such as introducing students to subjects other than English and getting students to use reference materials.

CHALKBOARDS

872   "Chalk Talk"

Writing on the chalkboard doesn't seem to be a subject worthy of much attention. But many good lessons have gone down the drain because the teacher forgot some simple details:

>   Erase a dirty board with uniform up-and-down motions.
>   It makes new writing more legible and looks neater.
>   Write where windows do not cause a glare for some students.
>   Use draperies or shades if available.
>   Learn to write so that you are not in front of material as it
>   is being written. Stand to the side.
>   Keep the writing high enough so students don't need to
>   stand to see.
>   Allow students to help write on the board at times—especially
>   if you write poorly.

873   "Phrase-y Idea"

One way to spark interest in an otherwise unreceptive class is to use "asides." Each day write a one or two-line phrase to the side of the chalkboard. If the sayings are clever enough, student discussions on meaning and application often occur.

DEMONSTRATIONS

874   "Filling the File"

Teacher demonstrations are enhanced by resources from various media. Usually such materials must be collected by the teacher. But students can help and, in so doing, obtain a good review of concepts if not skills. One suggestion is to have a file folder for each chapter of the textbook or each part of a unit. Ideally, each folder contains a wealth of free materials and those clipped from magazines, newspapers, and government bulletins. Some teachers ask parents for contributions. Instead of throwing out those bundles of magazines, parents might pass appropriate materials on to the school.

Since all this material must be systematized, how does a teacher get time to do the searching, clipping, and proper filing? The best answer is to use an occasional class period for pupils to do this—with guidelines, of course. Near the end of the year, one teacher uses a group assembly line to update files, each group inspecting a folder for one phase of work. Some check on the currency of material, others check for gaps, some add, some throw away, some label and file. Obviously, if used in the right manner, this becomes a useful review of the year's work.

DISCUSSIONS

875   "Roll with the Punches"

On days that interest in the lesson begins to wane, abandon the plan and tell a story to the class or just talk about anything interesting. Don't drag a sluggish lesson plan to its conclusion. Start a discussion on archaeology, ghost stories, smoke signals, or any subject about which you are informed. The class will appreciate the switch. So will you.

876   "Warm Up"

Very often a class comes in chattering about something—last
night's football game, a new record, a TV show, or a serious
accident, for example. Start those days with a "rap session."
Not only will it open up discussion, it might be just the thing to
highlight a story or poem. It might also lead to a field trip or suggest a project. Tune in to the moods of your classes.

DISPLAYS

877   "Go Psychedelic"

A dull room environment can actually detract from good teaching and
learning. For students to feel excited
about English, science, or any subject, they should see exciting things
in their classrooms. Placing modern,
psychedelic posters or art prints
around may inspire a story or a poem.
Aquariums promote relaxing and
thinking. Mobiles, purchased or homemade, can swing intriguingly from
the ceiling, making even the dullest
room more interesting. Terrariums are easy to make and keep,
but perhaps the simplest and most effective decorations are flowers and plants. Students really appreciate a teacher with a green
thumb.

878   "Hall of Fame or Infamy"

Students discuss and then vote to elect local, regional, national,
or international candidates—all famous people—for their Hall of
Fame. They might also vote on a Rogue's Gallery of antiheroes.
After the candidates have been chosen, students can engage in
many related projects. Individuals or groups research a favorite
person and find pictures and biographies on each "honoree."
They write or report orally on their selection. Finally all cooper-
ate to construct a scrapbook containing all the gathered published and original information.

GAMES

879   "T.G.I.F."

Try to make Friday a better day for students and teacher. After four days of school, the class sometimes finds it difficult to settle down to serious work. Arrange an activity which does not bind them to their seats in silence. Group work, games, or free reading periods are some of the ways to go.

HANDOUTS

880   "Complete Returns"

If you have a habit of loaning pens to students and then forgetting to get them back, try one of these: Remove the cap of the borrowed pen and set it upright on the desk in front of you as a reminder. No one wants a capless pen in pocket or purse. Or write the name of the borrower on the corner of the board. This puts pressure on the student to return the pen, or whatever he borrowed.

881   "Pretty, Good Handouts"

Do your handouts look dull and listless? Are they always typed and run off on plain white paper? Give some of those important handouts a delightfully new look and new interest by applying a little artwork and an imaginative format. Hectograph masters are easy to draw on. Use attractive borders, cartoon figures, smiling faces, flowers. Copy may be hand-lettered or typed for emphasis. If you can't print, write legibly. Space out the copy without following conventional paragraph style. Place some copy in boxes or circles, some in comic strip balloons. If you can make your handouts look like circus handbills, your students will hardly be able to wait for the next "show."

INSTRUCTIONS

882   "No More Excuses"

When it comes to class assignments, prevent the usual "but I didn't know what I was supposed to read." Duplicate the assignments; include date they are due. One danger, of course, is that the frequent use of dull white sheets of paper will decrease the desire to read this outline. Avoid this by varying the color of the paper and the format.

LECTURES

883   "Coming Attractions"

When preparing an especially important lecture for presentation to the class, duplicate an outline of the more important points. This eliminates much unnecessary note taking, orients the class to the substance of the material, and, most important, frees them to think about what is being said. It is also a way to demonstrate the technique of note taking—a useful tool for the college bound.

884   "Common-sensical"

Some teachers still do most of the talking in the classroom. Lecturing—or whatever it may be called—for more than fifteen minutes at a time, unless the teacher is exceptionally interesting, will rarely hold student attention. During a class period, learning activities must be shifted several times. This does not mean shifting subject matter—just the approach.

885   "Delayed Action"

Irrelevant questions may sometimes prevent important discussion points from emerging. One way to handle such questions is to have the students or a class secretary jot them down in abbreviated form on the board. This way the teacher indicates to the student that he has been heard and can forget about the question since it will be answered later. Frequently the question is automatically answered by the end of the hour anyway.

886   "Maybe It's Not What You Say"

When speaking to a class, remember not to stand in front of a window. It is difficult for those opposite to look into the light. Listening is enhanced by being able to see the speaker's facial expressions and lips. Presentations of new material should be made with the teacher standing. Then, taking a hint from the drama coach, move purposefully and dramatically, particularly to emphasize a point or change the pace. These suggestions should help any speaker, even one without an announcer's voice.

887   "Punctuated Lectures"

When preparing a lecture try to anticipate unspoken questions the students might have, especially in the difficult areas. At these points make a comment such as "take notice" or "listen closely." A few simplified illustrations and a probing question or two will also assure getting the point across.

888   "Speaking Wisely"

In the classroom use a normal, literate vocabulary. Do not talk down to the students. Get into the habit of using appositives, synonyms, or explanatory phrases without breaking sentence flow. For instance, "When Siddhartha joined the ascetics—the self-sacrificing group—he learned things he couldn't have learned in his rich home." When using a word like "asceticism"—the philosophy of denying the body to improve the spirit—write it on the chalkboard while talking. Students will learn to improve their vocabularies if you pay close attention to your own.

LIBRARIES

889   "Research Me"

Library research for slower or undisciplined students may evoke negative responses. Circumvent this by including many research questions dealing directly with the popular culture. Students will already know many of the answers. They will realize that information can be found in many sources beside textbooks, even from their own life experiences. This will help improve attitude and self-image. Types of questions which might be used are: What is a sissy bar? Name three songs by the (current popular music group)? Which, if any, state capitols have the same names?

MIXED MEDIA

890   "All Work and No Fun"

Make full use of audio-visual aids to entertain as well as to teach. A child who has been having fun is more likely to accept a learning situation than one who is hopelessly bored.

891   "Machine Overdose"

Gimmicks and electronic equipment do not always make for live
and interesting classes. The number of days that projectors,
films, recordings and the like can be used are limited. Build plans
around what can be spoken, written, read, or duplicated on
paper, using the hardware as supplementary aids. As much variety
exists in ways students discuss, argue, respond, write, compete,
and learn as in passively watching films and listening to records.
Strive to create variety, enthusiasm, and novelty with traditional
materials.

892   "Pandora's Box"

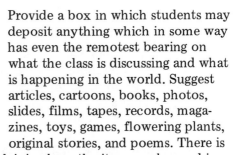

Provide a box in which students may
deposit anything which in some way
has even the remotest bearing on
what the class is discussing and what
is happening in the world. Suggest
articles, cartoons, books, photos,
slides, films, tapes, records, magazines, toys, games, flowering plants,
original stories, and poems. There is
one stipulation. A note explaining how the item can be used in
the class must be attached to the object. Select a student committee to empty the box periodically and to share with the teacher
the ideas they think can be worked in.

893   "Unconventional Thinking"

When teaching something which is difficult to simplify, find
common-ground subjects about which students can effectively
communicate. For example, one teacher used the "top forty"
songs of the week to teach spelling and reading. He used common
words in titles and lyrics instead of the typical lists. Unconventional, yes, but he captured the interest of his class and got the
learning across. The idea can be extended to include blurbs about
movies and television programs and to articles from periodicals
published just for teen-agers.

NEWSPAPERS

894   "Extra! Read All about It"

One of the most economical and exciting "textbooks" is the daily newspaper, and a large metropolitan newspaper is especially good. Make arrangements, if possible, to get a class supply for at least several weeks, until the students have caught the spirit and are actually reading their copies. If no class copies are available, ask individuals to bring them from home. Even if there aren't enough to go around, pull apart the copies and distribute sections to groups. All related work is based on the idea that good English is the key to good communication and that the newspaper reflects all the communication going on in the world.

NOTES

895   "Carry a Big Stick"

A problem for most teachers is keeping in touch with each student for make-up work, incompletes, arranging for and reminding about appointments, and the many other reasons a teacher has to prod a student. Solve this with a little carpentry. On the wall or a cabinet place a four-foot stick of wood with about 33 slots sawed partly through it. Identify each slot with a student number. (The same numbers may be repeated class to class.) Then using a small note pad for uniformity, write brief notes inserting them in the slots for whomever you with to contact. It is up to the student to check his mail slot each day.

896   "Smile"

Write happy notes to everybody. Get a few note pads printed up "From the desk of . . . . " Correspond widely with the staff and students. Tell a joke, quip, or draw a picture. It'll brighten their day as well as yours.

PERIODICALS

897   "Recycled Resources"

Everyone has experienced the frustration of having to look through stacks of old magazines for a picture or article once regarded as something worth saving. So as not to pass on a cut magazine to the next reader, examine periodicals with a pencil handy. After seeing something worth saving, write the page number of the item on the cover. This will make the treasure hunt a lot easier and will save much good material from the recycling machines.

PICTURES

898   "One for the Files"

Manila file folders need not be relegated to dusty file drawers. In folders (some available in colors) fasten interesting, individualized assignments created around colorful magazine illustrations. The main advantage is that folders can be labeled and filed in some order for reuse. These assignments can serve as strengthening exercises or extra challenge work. Once shown how, students can create their own sets of instructional materials or learning packets, an excellent resource for student tutoring.

PLANS

899   "Bridging the Gap"

Gimmicks may be employed as motivation for learning, but true motivation exists only when the students experience a gap—a curiosity gap, knowledge gap, generation gap, credibility gap, or whatever. This gap must be recognized directly at the start of the hour and with such force that everyone will want to "hang in there" until the gap has been bridged. The clever teacher doesn't lay the final plank until just before the hour is up.

900   "Good IDEA"

Lesson plans need not be elaborate. If overly detailed, they only discourage planning. Paradoxically some teacher education methods courses have forced a lengthy type of planning which will never be used even though all teachers need to plan. Use the acronym *IDEA* to sketch out the essentials of any daily plan with built-in variety (even useful when considering unit plans).

I means instruction (what should be taught), stated in several brief, student-oriented learning objectives.

D is demonstration (from simple models to feature films) to clarify instruction.

E is for evaluation (feedback to find out if the instruction got through), usually oral questioning but sometimes a written quiz.

A refers to application (putting the skills or concepts to use, outside the classroom as well as in, because unapplied ideas are soon forgotten).

A lesson plan, then, is a simple set of objectives and procedures—reminders—implementing the four phases of any lesson. Sound familiar? It should. This *idea*book is built around a similar format.

901   "Great Expectations"

When introducing any new unit of work to the class, make sure a brief outline is given to announce the topics and projects involved. This will enable the student to set objectives and plan his time more efficiently. Having a sense of direction will decrease anxieties about what the teacher expects.

902   "Listen and Learn"

Use students' ideas freely. Plan a unit now and then which is made up entirely of students' objectives and the procedures they suggest to achieve those objectives.

903   "Look, Listen, Stop"

Stop if you are getting clues that your class is becoming bored or that you are not getting across the information. Plan each lesson, but plan flexibly so that, if you are in trouble, you can change technique or even the entire plan. Lesson plans are guides not masters.

904   "On Being an Informer"

Since learning outside the classroom is so vital to a good education, promote outside reading and research by posting a day-by-day outline of classwork for a week or longer. When students know what is coming up, they will often try to prepare in advance. For each unit, prepare a list of research and reference books which, hopefully, can be set aside in the library. Give a copy of the outline to each student in addition to posting it on the bulletin board.

905   "Peer Group Disapproval"

Opening up a classroom for student-centered activities and assignments does not mean that the teacher becomes a teen-age peer to his students, nor that respect for the teacher gives way to anarchy. The open classroom is a way to achieve more comprehensive communication but without negating individual respondsibility or plain hard work.

906   "Positively Controlled"

The most effective way to maintain control in a classroom is to take a positive approach. If the teacher can get the students' attention and keep them interested, discipline problems generally disappear. Instead of emphasizing the negative, such as "Don't talk," get right at the most interesting part of the subject matter. Create some immediate curiosity gaps. Of course, this takes preplanning. The secret is to have a plan every day and to use a variety of approaches, many of which can be found in this book.

907   "Roll Role"

One way to avoid wasting teaching time with housekeeping duties and procedures is to assign room responsibilities to students. For example, one can take the daily roll call. Several can be responsible for the distribution and collection of materials. When tasks are performed consistently, students will soon feel responsibility for both discipline and learning.

908   "The NCTE's of Written Comp"

By using the abbreviation for the National Council of Teacher's of English (NCTE), a teacher can easily recall the four main aspects introducing any instruction. The illustration here is for composition.

"*N*" is for *needs*. This area can be divided two ways: between an individual's composition needs (from one paper to the next) and the need to write with a realistic purpose—not an empty exercise for a grade.

"*C*" is for *climate*. The atmosphere of the room must be conducive to relaxed, good writing. Providing unsurmountable hurdles is not the way to make eager writers.

"*T*" is for *topic* (or content). Each composition assignment must be broad enough to reach all interests and flexible enough to meet the ability levels of everyone.

"*E*" is for *evaluation.* No assignment should be overcorrected. Using a fair but challenging grading system which considers individual differences is a must. Eliminating fear of grades will help encourage more fluent writing.

909   "2 W's + 2 H's"

A well-written learning objective is meaningful as well as specific. A test for a good objective is to ask four journalistic-type questions: Who? What? How? and How Well? A meaningful objective tells or implies *who* it is for, *what* the learner is expected to be able to do if the objective is achieved, *how* this learning is to be facilitated (sources of helps, conditions), and *how well* the learner must perform to achieve the objective. Certainly not all objectives can or should contain each of the criteria, but the more information stated, the more specific and measurable the objective will be. (See also Appendix.) Here is an example of such a four-level objective:

Who? (Easily determined from wording—preferably student oriented)

What? To spell twenty words

How? To spell twenty words from the list of twenty-five in chapter one

How well? To spell twenty words from the list of twenty-five in chapter one and do so with 90 percent accuracy.

PROJECTORS

910   "Handwriting on the Wall"

All is not lost if the movie screen is missing. Project on a clear wall or even the ceiling. The back of a map or chart has been used effectively. If the room is dark enough, use the opaque projector to project student writing on a chalkboard where it can be corrected a few lines at a time. This method can be used when there is no time to obtain a transparency or when it is not convenient to write on the transparency itself.

SLIDES

911   "Everyone (yawn) Loves a Good Travelogue"

Although many teachers show slides to their classes, few use
their own. Now is the time to start collecting slides of your
travels. Sights around your hometown frequently add interest.
A personal touch is added when you can explain a slide and all
related circumstances. Your trip to Hannibal, Missouri, for example, could make a unit on Mark Twain come alive.

TALK

912   "Is Anybody Listening?"

While most schools include reading improvement at some level,
they neglect to show students they can improve language use in
its most common and basic form—listening. Include a unit focused
on listening techniques. Then stress listening throughout the
course. Often the simplest procedures can be used to explain the
need and to introduce the practice. Give oral directions or test
instructions, read brief selections while the class listens, encourage note taking while listening for main ideas. Thus, listening instruction need not be through formal programs. Common
everyday opportunities are the most natural and, in the end, the
most useful.

913   "Shy Guy"

To ease the quiet student into the mainstream of class activity,
divide the class into groups and select the quiet student to be
the leader of a group composed of cooperative students who
show signs of accepting such leadership. Each group makes a
presentation to the class of material or information being studied.
Perhaps the quiet student prefers to be a follower, but at least he
has been given an opportunity to express his ideas before a portion of the class. This may provide the needed confidence.

914   "Why Standard English?"

When only standard English is taught and recognized, students
from strong ethnic environments begin to feel uncomfortable
about their dialects. All students in a class should understand
there is nothing wrong with speaking in dialect. Standard

English, it should be pointed out, is emphasized only because it is considered an asset for upward mobility in most occupations.

TELEVISION

915   "Channeling Interests"

Take advantage of the educational resources available via television. Watch for announcements of stimulating programs and dramas. Assign classes to watch those which tie in with current units or are of special interest. This activity is useful for slower students who cannot read well. Networks and other agencies provide special program guides for schools. Try to get on their mailing lists.

TRANSPARENCIES

916   "Not Live but in Full Color"

Though machines which produce color transparencies are now on the market, their distribution is limited. A very suitable way to obtain a full-color transparency is through what some call the translift method. The process requires a magazine picture printed on clay-coated paper, press-on clear contact film, and some warm water. To determine if paper is clay finished, wet a finger and touch the sheet. If white material comes off or the spot becomes slightly sticky, this process should work. Any clear film with adhesive backing can be used. "Contac" brand works well. Then press the contact paper on the face of the picture, rubbing carefully to remove all the air bubbles. Finally dip the picture into the water, soaking the paper thoroughly, and gradually peel the paper from the plastic.

If done correctly, the colored inks will remain stuck to the plastic, forming a transparency amazingly close in quality to the original which is destroyed in the process. If the ink does not transfer, it may not be a common mixture, so you will have to abandon that particular picture. To prevent the ink from rubbing off after the transparency is dry, spray the surface with artist's charcoal fixative. A better product can be provided by heat laminating the photo to clear plastic before soaking off the paper. Then seal the ink side with another laminated sheet. Heat laminating machines are not that common in individual schools, but an up-to-date curriculum materials center in a city school system or the county should have such a resource. Either way the teacher will be able to collect an outstanding visuals file.

TUTORS

917   "Do-it-yourself Kid"

During any unit of work include a ten-minute teaching assignment which allows each student to present some instruction to the class, usually material on a subject under study. Student presentations should generally be followed by summations by the teacher. Students who teach in a given week may get together to devise a cooperative quiz based on their material.

918   "Peer Teachers"

 Students frequently complain that they get bored listening to the same teacher everyday. Occasionally allow a student to present the lesson on a relevant topic. This would involve some valuable research, since obviously the student cannot lecture on something he has not yet learned. One topic might be the history behind a novel, play, or poem. Besides the variety, students often get more information more quickly from their peers than from their teachers.

CHAPTER
18

DELIBERATION

BULLETIN BOARDS

919   "Big Bulletin Board Committee"

Rather than assigning several students to prepare a bulletin board
or doing it yourself, have each student bring in a drawing, photograph, or article which pertains to the unit. These items may be
combined into a bulletin board display. Since each student participates in the creation, the bulletin board will be more relevant
and interesting for each student.

CHARTS

920   "Blanket Security"

Learn students' names as soon as possible. It shows that the teacher is interested and, thus, helps establish rapport in class discussion and other follow-up work. The key is to keep a seating chart
for the first few weeks. Connect five faces with names each day.
Try the association technique, connecting the name with some
feature, action, or personality quirk. Sometimes associate a new
face and name with look-alikes from the past.

DISCUSSIONS

921   "No More Disgusting Discussing"

Some teachers fail when it comes to leading a good discussion. This may result from one factor in particular—a lack of open-mindedness. In leading a discussion, a teacher must be receptive to new ideas and must use these ideas in making objective comparisons with his own. The key word is *objective.* Children become easily bored with discussions in which the only acceptable ideas are the teacher's. Exciting and worthwhile discussion occurs when students and teacher share nearly equally in making contributions.

922   "Somethin' Brewin' "

Little is known about what creativity really is, but research has indicated that it can be fostered and developed. One way is to separate idea production from evaluation. During class discussions individuals should feel free to express any thought which comes to mind without fearing ridicule or the consequences of a lowered mark or adverse teacher opinion. Many good, creative ideas are sure to develop in a permissive atmosphere.

923   "Something Old, Something New"

Lead into a class discussion of new material with a few well-chosen questions prepared in advance. Questions should deal with something with which all the students are familiar: some relating past studies to a new material, others relating to world problems or student experiences. Questions should deal with comprehension of facts, vocabulary, and inference. Whatever the lead-in, it should pique student curiosity for the new material.

924   "Talking in Circles"

The "circular response" discussion is effective for involving every class member. Too often discussions are monopolized by a few but not necessarily by those who have the most to contribute. In this plan the class is seated in a circle. A question or topic is introduced and someone begins the discussion. The person sitting to the left of that speaker is next to speak (or can pass), and the discussion moves clockwise around the entire circle. No one person is allowed to speak out of turn. When a question has been thoroughly discussed, even though all students in the circle have

not spoken, the next question is introduced where the other
left off. While some students learn better by listening and others
by talking, there is no reason for not involving the quiet ones.

FIELD TRIPS

925   "Questionable Field Trip"

Before a field trip ask each student to write out and hand in
one question about the trip (the subject to be explored) that
he would like answered. After the field trip use these questions
for test reviewing the results of the experience. If desired, students can be graded not only on the questions answered but also
on those asked.

GAMES

926   "Altogether"

Whether you are teaching in a middle school, junior, or senior
high, competition can be used to build strong motivation. For
a unit project divide the class into teams to compete for the
best-project award in any one of several categories (best designed,
presented or written, most humorous). Or have one class compete with another.

927   "Are You Game?"

On days when class atmosphere is not suitable for serious discussions, e.g., the day before Thanksgiving or Christmas vacation,
allow the class to play a game. Games may be simple or sophisticated, brought from home or purchased, or patterned after TV
participation games where role playing and decision making are
the key elements. With a few changes in rules, such classics as
Monopoly and Easy Money can be used to practice recent learnings. Game boards can be drawn on plastic and, with the overhead projector, be projected for all to see. Player's markers can
be small stars, circles, square, or triangles which are silhouetted
on the screen to show moves. For further suggestions consult
the students and the Index in this book under "Games."

928   "Going on Record"

This game idea is good for review. It is also versatile enough for individual players, partners, or teams. All the instructions and moves are directed by an audiotape which has been planned and timed carefully in advance. Other equipment includes a game board, preferably an overhead transparency, and a beeper for the seconds and a bell to signal a minute. The process could go something like this: "Team One, the correct answer to the following question is good for a six-space move (on the board) and may be discussed by your group. You have one minute to answer this question: 'Judging from the action in the story, when would you say it took place, last half of the nineteenth century, early twentieth century, or the present?' " Then sixty beeps are followed by a "ding." If the team gets the answer before the bell, it moves its marker, and the tape then "cues up" the next team. This can get very exciting because there is no way to vary the speed of the action. Besides checking on knowledge, this approach tests ability to listen carefully.

INVENTORIES

929   "A Couple 'a Words"

Word relationships can be fun and are good practice for students who plan to apply to universities. Make up a series of multiple choice analogies that give the reader practice in analyzing a situation. For the educational value, include some words which are not familiar.

> Example: Gas : (is to) car : : (as) _____ : _____ .
> (a)   scepter : king
> (b)   food : man
> (c)   oil : engine
> (d)   scale : music

LECTURES

930   "Sensible Consensus"

Sometimes students will dispute the teacher's ideas or statements. Although such disagreements can be resolved by comparing evidence for both points of view, inevitably some teachers finally use their authority to settle the matter. To avoid this, write the objection(s) on the chalkboard. This gives time to think, and it indicates the students' point of view is worth considering. Matters reflecting differing cultural values or beliefs may be unresolvable but are worth discussing. Other, more factual, statements can be deliberated to attempt consensus.

LIBRARIES

931   "Cutting Class"

To help the class become more familiar with the school library and what it has to offer, send students to the library in small prearranged groups of five or six. This can be done on a daily basis after necessary instruction and information has been presented. This keeps the class size more manageable and tends to cut down the disturbance of sending an entire class.

MIXED MEDIA

932   "What Next?"

Discuss the various ways of communicating: oral or written methods, photography, painting, sculpture, music, body movement, and so on. Then class members think up one idea they want to share with others. They must find at least one way to present this idea other than formal conversation or writing.

PLANS

933   "On Being Unpredictable"

To avoid monotony in teaching, occasionally forget strict
schedules and inflexible lesson plans. Allow yourself freedom
for things students find exciting. Be unpredictable. Every once
in a while forget teaching English for a day and introduce a wide-
open discussion on current issues which affect students: changing boy-girl roles, educational innovation, and new ways to
feed world populations, to name a few. Often student remarks
during a discussion of the topic under study will be the catalyst
for opening an interesting, informative, not entirely unrelated
discussion. Look for those opportunities.

QUESTIONS

934   "Ask Me Anything"

After students have become familiar with whatever is being
studied, divide them into two groups. For fifteen minutes,
have each group make up questions to ask the other. They use
their books for this phase. Then have each side question the
other (without books), giving one point for each correct answer.
There are many different ways to design the questioning procedure, e.g., switch each time or go on until a side misses. This
is an excellent review procedure.

935   "Mutual Aid"

As a way to experiment with new learnings, each student writes
three to five or more questions he knows he can answer and an
equal number (on a separate piece of paper) he *cannot* answer.
Collect the questions the students cannot answer and review
these with the class. More often than not, some student will
have the same question on the list of questions he is able to
answer. Thus he can contribute to the discussion. If no one has
the answer, write the question (in abbreviated form) on the
chalkboard for further study. The questions turned in will also
make a good basis for a test.

SEATING

936   "Classy Arrangement"

Don't resist a pre-set seating arrangement. It helps in learning names, the first step toward rapport. If students can move around for group work, team work, and round-table discussion, they won't resent sitting in assigned seats for formal classroom activities.

937   "Seat of the Problem"

The basic horseshoe or circle seating arrangement is still a good idea to promote discussion and involvement since students feel more like participating. Just as the teacher wants to be able to see all the faces, each student wants to watch his class-mates react to what he says. In this seating arrangement, the teacher becomes more *a part* of the group, rather than *apart*.

TALK

938   "Breaking Up the Class"

To give each student a greater opportunity to speak and be heard, reorganize formal class sessions into group workshops. Try to place at least one energetic, cooperative leader in each group. Workshop projects are unlimited; anything from covering the textbook to assessing the human condition.

939   "Every Year Election Year"

Give practice in democratic living. Study parliamentary procedure. Students can obtain realistic prac-tice by forming a convention to nominate each other for classroom president, vice-president, secretary, treasurer, and a host of other positions. They run their meetings according to *Robert's Rules of Order.* Following these guide-lines, the class may want to prepare a "school improvement constitu-tion" or another worthwhile pro-ject. There are many possibilities, all accomplished efficiently and fairly using proper procedures.

940   "Party Line"

Demonstrate the need to communicate clearly. Give one child
a short sentence. He whispers the message to the next student
who, in turn, whispers what he heard to the next. This process
continues until all have participated. The last person then
announces what he heard. In an attempt to trace the message
breakdown, each student—beginning with the last—repeats
what he thought he heard. Generally the original message is
changed unintentionally at least once.

941   "Shoring Up the Shy One"

Offer alternatives to the students who find it difficult to speak
in front of the class. One approach is to conduct an interview.
The person interviewed may be another student, teacher, or
visiting dignitary. The fact that two subjects are sharing the
limelight may be just the thing to "crack the ice." Panel discussions serve a similar purpose.

TUTORS

942   "T-Day the Day"

For more student involvement in class, plan so that once every
week for fifteen or twenty minutes a student is responsible for
teaching or demonstrating something to the class. He could use
any subject matter from teaching a golf swing or a dance step
to discussing occupations which are disappearing and those for
which youth should be preparing. If T-Day is a Wednesday,
sometime on Tuesday, perhaps five or ten minutes at the end,
the student "specialist" should be able to confer with the
teacher about such things as timing, needed equipment, and
seating arrangements, just to make sure all is in readiness.

CHAPTER
19

EVALUATION

ATTITUDES

943   "Bang in the Eye"

Students are *looking* at the teacher
as well as listening. Instead of
sitting motionless behind the desk
while presenting information,
the teacher should move and use
meaningful gestures to maintain
interest. Annoying habits such as
rocking back and forth and playing
with the hair (women and some
men need to keep their bangs out of their eyes) only detract
from the oral demonstration. Most important of all, the voice
should be effective. If the presentation is weak or distracting,
the class won't listen long enough to find the message.

944   "Best Four-Letter Word"

Be K-I-N-D to students. Use positive reinforcement.

945   "Boxed Ears"

A box in which to collect class feedback and suggestions is still
a good way to encourage communications between students and
teacher. Too often teachers are evaluated at the end of the term
or year instead of regularly. Thus the current class cannot benefit
from needed changes. Teachers may read some comment

they'd rather not know, but the old maxim of learning from
our mistakes still holds. Student evaluation trends about
teaching quality, course content, and procedures are usually
quite reliable.

946   "Change of Angle"

Advising a school club or chaperoning a school activity is a
learning experience for you, the teacher! It helps to know your
students from different vantage points. Sometimes it will completely change the way you regard them in class.

947   "Duds for Duds"

Students evaluate their teachers daily—even if surreptitiously—
and sometimes see teachers appearing before their classes
looking dowdy and dull in face and figure. This seems to reflect
how they feel about school that day. Naturally, this attitude is
quickly transferred to the students and affects teaching and
learning. This may seem like a small point, but if a teacher has
had a "bad day," he might check on how it started—out of
school. The teacher sets the pace in the classroom. A sparkling
smile and tasteful, interesting clothes (even if put on to cover a
sour attitude) go a long way to engage a class fruitfully.

948   "Fifty-fifty Split"

Suppose the teacher finds two students who are cheating in an
examination. Further, suppose that a perfect score was 100
points, and the two wrote papers worth 90 points each. Divide
that score equally so that each receives 45 points—obviously
a failing grade, yet no points have been taken away. The punish-
ment is more positive than destroying the two tests and giving
the students zeros. Justify this action by saying that each
probably contributed an equal amount to the test and therefore
should receive half the credit. This matter is handled quietly
with only the two students involved, not in front of the entire
class in a fit of anger.

949   "How'm I Doin'?"

Periodically allow the students to grade themselves and comment on their progress. The teacher need not rely on this grade
as one to be recorded, but often it works out that way. From
this type of evaluation, the teacher can also assess his own
accomplishments.

950   "Let's Get Personal"

Show students that teachers are human too by telling some personal anecdotes about your school years. As a youth, you might confess, you were shy and awkward when participating in certain activities such as public speaking. Try to show that it is natural to feel socially uncomfortable at times. You might relate, if it is true, that you felt self-conscious about something physical which you built up in your mind as a "deformity," for example, skinny legs, small bust, boney shoulders, facial pimples, protruding ears, or even dissatisfaction about hair color.

As to school experiences, you might relate that you didn't much like to read poetry in school but you learned poetry can be lovely and personal and now you write your own sometimes. Student behavior and attitude can be directed positively through the judicious use of such personal glimpses.

951   "Shake, Pal"

Becoming friends with the school custodian will pay dividends when you need those extra services: a new bulletin board, some clay pots for flowers, a change in the seating arrangement, or a quicker response when someone parts with a too-hasty lunch.

952   "Switch Roles"

Each time you give a letter grade to a student, check the objectivity of your judgments. The following experiment may help you discover the value of this approach. When you grade a problem case, write down the reasons for giving that grade. Then imagine you are that student and ask yourself if you can accept the reasons the teacher gave to explain your grade. This self-test allows you to discover whether your basis for assigning grades is subjective or objective.

953   "Three Reasons for Promptness"

The teacher should see that homework and tests are returned to the students promptly for several reasons: (1) The more immediate the feedback from the teacher, the more valuable the assignment to the student. (2) It shows that the teacher recognizes the importance of the work in time and effort. (3) The teacher builds student rapport by showing consideration for their anxieties. When the teacher returns papers promptly, the class learns to expect it as a regular practice. If an emergency arises, however, and the teacher explains why the papers aren't done, the class will willingly accept.

954   "Will the Twain Ever Meet?"

John Gardner asks the inevitable question in the title of his book—*Excellence: Can We Be Equal and Excellent Too?* There is no single answer, of course, and it is a dilemma every teacher must face. Gardner feels that excellence and equality in education are inherently incompatible. Everyone must arrive at his own answer, but to refuse to consider the point Gardner has raised is a gross abdication of teacher responsibility.

CHARTS

955   "Spot Check"

An unusual and accurate evaluation technique is to check off on a seating chart the students who participate in class discussion each day. At the end of the week, by looking at the "scatter pattern," the teacher has concise knowledge of which students are and are not participating. The latter can then be brought into the discussions.

CONFERENCES

956   "Grading Put Down"

One way to avoid too much emphasis on letter grades is to use personal conferences and extensive written comments. These methods give the student a more accurate idea of how he is performing and show him exactly where he needs improvement. Also motivation is more likely to be intrinsic. What does the rest of the class do while conferences are being held? There are hundreds of ideas in this book to answer that question.

957   "More Than a Number"

Establish rapport by scheduling at least one conference a semester with each student. This can cover the particular problems the student is having in or out of class or can be for casual conversation. The important outcome is the personal contact.

Naturally, the earlier this can happen, the better for student and teacher. So provide some project or workshop days early in the term. If this is not possible, then resort to a "whenever possible" schedule.

FIELD TRIPS

958   "Be a Sport"

Attend the school's athletic and social events. Students are quick to notice who is really interested in what they do and who is not. Students like to know that someone enjoys the same things they do.

959   "Getting to Know All about You"

If you are new to a school system, get acquainted with the school and the community before the school year begins. Two things are gained by this evaluation. First, you become aware of the teaching resources available in the school and community. Second, you learn how this community differs from others you know. This may affect your entire teaching approach and will certainly reveal many unique opportunities for special assignments.

FORMS

960   "Color Me 'A'"

Prevent the grade book from becoming a mass of illegible letters, numbers, checks, and symbols. Arrange it so that it is clear at a glance what grade applies to what type of assignment (for both instructor and student). Use color in the vertical columns, keying each color to different areas of work. (See idea 961.) Each color could have a different weight in relation to the final grade. Another way to avoid confusion is to place cumulative points in the boxes, with the last entry always representing the total at a given time. This final figure can be easily translated into a letter grade without adding.

961   "Color-Vision"

Need a quick way to distinguish marks or scores for various assignments? To differentiate easily between small, medium-sized, and major projects and tests, record the marks in pencil, blue ink, and red ink respectively. When it is time to average marks, count the pencil marks once; the blue, twice; the red, three times, in a system of weighting by thirds. In fairness to them, tell students whether an assignment is to be worth one, two, or three points. As a double check, always identify each column of marks by a name, page, or exercise number.

INSTRUCTIONS

962   "Rules, Rules, Rules"

The first day of class is the time to introduce at least a few rules for the students to follow. You will be tested anyway as to your expectations, so speed the process by telling what you expect. Pages and pages of "do's" and "don'ts" may look impressive but will probably introduce more problems than they solve.

INVENTORIES

963   "Belief Relief"

A teacher is faced by two main problems when teaching adolescents: relating the past to the present or vice versa, and helping students to express themselves either orally or in writing. One method to accomplish both is to provide a duplicated questionnaire to solicit student beliefs about man, religion, government, and so on. Discuss these ideas in class, relating the past to the present. This method not only helps make the subject "real," but it also helps the student to evaluate his beliefs through peer reaction.

964   "If I Were the Teacher"

Students generally appreciate the opportunity to write one-page papers which describe what they would like to have you teach in the English class. Tell them that from these papers you will get ideas on which to base class assignments and longer units of work.

965   "Drawing Out a Class"

If you are concerned about your effectiveness as a teacher, try this different way to get feedback. Ask each student to draw a picture or design conceptualizing the class. Indicate you are more interested in an emotional rather than simply a physical response. Show a few samples from previous classes to awaken imaginations. Since the drawings need not be signed, some truthful responses should occur. Watch to see how large you appear in the drawings, perhaps an indication of you as an authority figure. Other traits to check are whether or not colors or shapes are dark and foreboding or light and cheery. A drawing cluttered with many objects might reflect on your neatness or on how your instruction is coming across. Generally, the more normal and beautiful the picture, the better the student views your class. By studying these impressions and selecting trends, you should be able to obtain a fairly good overall picture of yourself.

966   "No More Complaints"

A common student complaint is too much homework. On the second day of class the teacher can assess student feeling regarding homework and the pattern of their study habits. Tell them which units are to be covered, and how much they will be writing and reading. Explain the school and class requirements. Students and teacher can then work out a general outline which will suit both parties.

967   "Psych 'em Out"

To create a sense of group identity in the first few days of class, ask students to rearrange the seats to permit good eye contact among themselves. Do not give any directions. Do not appoint any leaders. The results will help answer these questions: Are the students auditory learners? Can they take oral directions? Who are the class leaders, the followers? Do the class members work well with each other? Who becomes involved and who does not? This information can be used to plan instruction.

968   "Self Check"

To discover the students' interests and to keep a check on yourself, devote an entire class session to such questions as "What
is English class to you?" "What would you like to see happen
in English class?" Answers to these questions are needed for
successful teaching.

969   "Teacher, Take Note"

The task of writing out final grade reports becomes easier
and more accurate if you select two or three students each
day, observe them carefully, and take brief notes. In four
weeks you can have an observation file on a class as large
as forty. This will help prevent blanks in your memory
when you have to write comments, when you must decide
between a C+ or a B-, or when a parent comes in to talk about
his child's performance in class.

970   "Who I Am and How I Change"

Make up a form containing twenty to thirty projective statements which the students can complete quickly. Ask them to
fill out this form at the start of the year and twice later. Consider their opinions to statements such as these:

(1) My mother (father) is _____ . (2) School is _____
(3) I would like _____ .

LECTURES

971   "It's a Vocal Thing"

A teacher who is not a particularly ardent scholar can still be
effective if he will master the art of communication, cultivating
a good speaking voice and using natural, meaningful gestures.
To improve voice quality, especially rate and inflection, he
employs the tape recorder, taping actual presentations. Hearing
how he sounds to his students may induce the teacher to work
on deficiencies so as to make lectures and readings of plays and
poetry much more effective.

NOTES

972   "Open Card Test"

If you have prepared a comprehensive objective-essay test high-lighting a unit, tell them that they may bring with them one 3 X 5 card of notes containing as many notes as they wish. This will help relax many who block when being tested. It is surprising how much writing can be written in such a small space.

QUESTIONS

973   "Checking the Traps"

Some teachers think of a test as an opportunity to trap students —to show them how much they cannot do or how much of the teacher's lectures they missed by not listening. Students resent this, and rightly so. Testing is as much an evaluation of teacher effectiveness as it is of student accomplishment. Thus, good tests are always prepared with the learning objectives in mind. Testing of this type is not likely to trap. It will be more valid and worthy of the time involved.

974   "Discriminating Tests"

The best indication of a good test is how each test item succeeds in discriminating, for example, between the top third and the bottom third in the final scores. Any question which is answered correctly or incorrectly by the same number of students in both the upper and lower thirds must be examined for its value. Unless such questions are included to achieve a motive other than to measure learning achievement, they should be eliminated. A simple tally of right and wrong answers for the two student groups will give the needed information on whether a question is "pulling its load."

975   "Everybody's Test"

When preparing tests, remember that the less academically inclined students need some incentive to at least try. If the test is too difficult, they may panic or, even worse, give up. Include some simple questions which they can answer. Naturally, enough of the difficult questions will be used so better students will also be challenged. Nothing is more defeating to student ego than not being able to answer a single question.

976   "Nothing but the Facts"

In an essay test, plan to include several "outline only" questions for which composition skills are not a major factor in answering. Thus, the student who must rush through essay questions to finish or the student whose poor grammatical skills are obstacles in presenting ideas is not penalized. In addition, you avoid much of the padding common to essay replies.

977   "One of Our Own"

Students learn more, prepare more effectively, and perform better on an examination which they have helped construct than on a teacher-made test. A few days before the scheduled exam time, ask each student (or groups) to compose questions for a short essay or objective exam on a particular unit. Collect all proposed questions, duplicate them, and distribute a day or so before the test as a "study guide." Students know that the test will include one or more of these questions but not which ones. Consequently they are motivated to study all the questions, thereby gaining knowledge of all the important parts of the unit. This process measures both student awareness of what should be stressed and, thus, the teacher's success in attaining objectives. And furthermore, even if editing is needed, a supply of questions will be available which is usually easier than starting from the beginning.

978   "Quiz Masters"

If you are tired of making up quizzes, turn this task over to the students. By giving the class a list of the various ways to phrase test questions, they can become at least semiskilled test makers and skilled test takers. Each class member is encouraged to compose a quiz. The one student whose quiz is judged by the teacher to be the best—fair, comprehensive, and well-worded— is given an automatic passing grade, because this is the test duplicated for use by the entire class. Quiz writers can also be selected by rotation or random choice. Students usually like this approach and yell "unfair" less often. Other fringe benefits include a painless review, an exercise in clear succinct writing and class leadership. Still other approaches can be used, for example, students taking each other's tests for review in smaller groups.

979   "Students Turned On"

For reasons must of us can supply from our own experiences, a student is frequently alienated by some of the questions on an essay exam. In such an event, what are the alternatives? One way is allowing the student to frame a question of equivalent worth and then write an essay answer to it. This alternate approach allows the student to take the initiative in deciding what information is important, gives an opportunity for self-motivation, and serves as a better learning experience by testing the student on what he knows instead of what he does not know.

980   "Testing the Test"

The first step in constructing a test is to write all questions on 3×5 file cards. This allows for easy rearrangement according to the types of questions. It also permits elimination and addition without disrupting the entire series. This technique has a number of other advantages. The same exam can be used year to year but with slight changes in questions to fit different content and emphasis. Notes can be kept on the back of the cards to show incorrect responses which can later be used to improve multiple choice items. (A student's incorrect answer is often a better alternative than one submitted by the teacher.) Finally, it permits tabulating the correct/incorrect responses. If too many A or B students get a question wrong, it is changed or eliminated. Enough easy questions must be included for incentive and enough difficult ones to separate the A and B students from the C and D students and failures.

981   "Test Plus One"

Teachers should add the following question to every test they write: "Has this been a fair test of the material we covered?" If the student can explain why a test has or has not been fair, he should receive extra credit. Students who hedge on that question are doing so because they fear retaliation. This should cause the teacher to reexamine his own attitudes as well as his teaching methods. Teaching is a mutual trust, and unless real communication is taking place, learning is not occurring. Such a question could also reveal special problems students may be having with the subject matter, indicating a conference is in order. Solid trends among answers to the question will provide more accurate feedback than through most other approaches.

TALK

982   "Cannot Tell a Lie"

After the procedural tasks are dealt with the first day of school, relax and get to know your students. One activity which will appeal to most of them is "To Tell a Lie." Students are to describe themselves accurately but to include one "white lie." The class tries to guess from the talk or the paper being read what portion is not true. Some students will telegraph clues when they reach the exaggeration. Others will handle it well. Start off with your own offering as an example.

983   "Get the Point"

This suggestion is designed to get the shy student to open up. The activity should, however, be introduced early in the year or semester because students often follow the roles and behaviors they establish during the first few weeks of class. Encourage participation by rewarding acceptable recitation with points. These point totals should be used several ways: to help raise a test grade, to excuse from a small assignment, or just to help raise the course grade. A lack of points would reflect on the student's final mark. If the volunteer method does not work, call on people to get the desired involvement from all.

984   "Shell Game"

A small effort which pays dividends is taking the time to find out what the special interests of a shy student are. A word after class about his stamp collection can create a bond and perhaps draw him out of his shell—even just crack it a bit.

985   "Triple Treats"

Early in the school year use this method to help your students get to know each other. Divide the class into groups of three students each. Have the group members tell each other about their happiest day. Then continue by sharing their saddest day, telling of a world leader they admire, discussing their favorite magazine, or revealing what they were like as a fifth grader. Do this for a half hour daily for the first week, switching groups so that every student has talked with everyone in the class.

TUTORS

986   "First Aid"

English teachers sometimes receive help in evaluating compositions from paid or volunteer lay readers. What should one do when this luxury is not available? First try to locate people in the community with enough education to serve in this capacity. Able students within the school or possibly in a future teachers' club can serve. If there is a university teacher education department nearby, English majors are frequently looking for experiences they will encounter in student teaching. Perhaps a complete teacher's aide program can be set up in all subject fields. Whatever solution is found, it will go a long way toward reducing the paper evaluation load of the typical English teacher. Perhaps more composition assignments will result, and the students will become better writers because they have had more frequent practice.

CHAPTER
20

APPLICATION

ATTITUDES

987   "Join 'em"

Many students do not participate in extracurricular activities because they are not interested in the offerings. Each class could offer suggestions for forming clubs and arranging other activities. The English teacher, for instance, might find how many students were interested in poetry, drama, or writing, and could sponsor such clubs. Extracurricular activities are useful because the participants are together in a social situation, in addition to the academic one, and get to know each other better. Through such involvement one teacher found that the most silent "loner" in class was quite a poet. His recognized success in writing poems gave him more confidence in the classroom, caused him to emerge from his shell, and improved his total outlook on school.

988   "Pat on the Back"

Platitude or not, praise is still the most effective way to involve students. Any student's work contains something which merits praise. If not, then the assignment or task was not designed flexibly enough so that everyone could succeed in some dimension of it.

989   "Replacing the Old Text"

Bring out student creativity by allowing them, as a class or in groups, to write and illustrate an English textbook. This activity, besides encouraging good grammar and knowledge of various literary forms and techniques, helps create an atmosphere of cooperation. Class members learn from each other and achieve that pride of accomplishment too often absent in the typical classroom.

BOOK REPORTS

990   "Three-day Borathon"

Are oral book reports or individual research reports really of that much value to students who have to listen to them for two or three consecutive days? If the purpose is to share information as well as provide speaking experiences, then one might answer Yes. But often these reports are done with such little imagination that listening becomes so boring that there is no sharing. This book contains many ideas for varying book reports (see the Index). Reporting can be done in so many ways that the teacher need not be locked into any single approach.

BULLETIN BOARDS

991   "Cut Ups"

Create more interest in bulletin boards by installing them as class projects. Divide the class into three or four groups, assigning a topic or letting them choose their own. Provide most of the materials (stapler, tacks, and tape, for example) and let them move ahead on their own. Everyone gets a job according to talent. Each group's chairman must write a report explaining various aspects of his group's display and read it aloud for discussion. Perhaps awards can be presented to the group preparing the best bulletin board. Competition encourages better work.

DEMONSTRATIONS

992   "Our Own Thing"

At the end of a semester, hold a student say-and-do day. Class members show they have assimilated subject matter by working alone or in groups to present readings, original poetry, parodies, essays, short stories, skits, or the like. The purpose, of course, is to see whether the instruction has been assimilated by the students and whether they are able to apply the knowledge constructively.

DISPLAYS

993   "Fair Idea"

If science students can have science fairs and art students art fairs, why not a language arts fair? All English teachers and their students can contribute something from simple haiku poetry booklets to feature length, student-made films. Prizes are always good for added incentive. The fair can involve a single school or an entire city.

994   "Marble Statues"

 Try not to assign home projects which require undue amounts of artistic talent or financial backing. What is desired is not a display of parental artistry or oversized piggy banks but rather a simple, honest demonstration of thought and understanding. Grades should be distributed on the latter, never the former. One way to insure this is to specify the medium and materials, making sure they are inexpensive and readily available to all.

GAMES

995   "All Lit Up"

Often this book mentions the use of teams, particularly in games, some of which are takeoffs on popular television quiz shows. These game shows often use elaborate systems of bells or buzzers and flashing lights. Why not have something similar in the classroom? Tuen over such a project to the less academic but manually skilled students. The first project could be a light signal system to show which person and which team has the answer. Two lighting panels with nothing more expensive than Christmas tree bulbs can be provided along with push buttons for each participant. They might even try some elaborate way to allow one team who answers first to cut out the push buttons for the other team. This construction project will give much prestige to those who need it most.

INSTRUCTIONS

996   "Crypotographic Assignment"

The next time you give an assignment, convert parts of it into some kind of code. Challenge the class to discover the assignment by breaking the code. Although some would just as soon not succeed, all students will appreciate the challenge and the different way of introducing an assignment. One easy approach is to use a code in which each letter is two letters left of the desired letter, for example, "ambc" spells "code."

LETTERS

997   "Club Amici"

For my pen pal.

Various communication skills are put into use by students enrolled in Club Amici. Pupils choose a foreign correspondent their own age. When specific countries have been selected, distribute names and addresses. Such lists are readily available from World Pen Pals, c/o Executive Secretary, World Affairs Center, Minneapolis, Minnesota 55414 or other groups. Students write letters to their pen pals as often as they wish. A bulletin board and large table can be set aside for displaying letters, pictures, and interesting objects from exchanges. Club meeting are held frequently so members can report on their correspondence.

MAGAZINES

998   "Topical Topics"

The English classroom needs to provide many speaking opportunities. Magazine articles, because of their availability, are a good
source of topics for extemporaneous speeches. Students can enjoy
relative freedom of choice in locating an interesting article, reading it, making notes, and then discussing the article before the
class. Unlike topics such as "a day in the country" or "my most
embarrassing moment," magazine articles provide the student
with significant material, chosen because of its interest to him
personally, and it leads naturally into many opportunities to
communicate.

NEWSPAPERS

999   "In the Know"

This competitive game focuses on current events and motivates
students to read a daily newspaper regularly. Divided the class
into two teams for the purpose of writing questions. Limit questions to top world news events. Groups quiz each other. Give one
point for each correct answer. A simple reward like free hours in
the library might be given to the winning group. The advantage of
this game over others is that it allows students to move away
from "English-y English" and to go into a related study. News
articles can be a jumping-off place for writing or language study.

PAPERS

1,000   "Trivia Hunt"

Research papers are usually assigned to help students learn how
to locate and use resource material. This same goal can be achieved
without requiring a lengthy and perhaps boring paper—boring to
write and boring to read. As an alternative, the teacher makes up
a list of fifty to a hundred "trivia" questions, all of which have
correct answers. The students must delve deeply into resource
materials for the answers and, thus, use the library quite exten-
sively. An example of one question is "For how long was the
Kittyhawk actually in the air?" or "What is the Statue of

Liberty's height and weight?'' With the right planning, questions can force use of most resource material in the library, a statement which can't often be made for the assigned research paper. The students are then evaluated on the number of questions answered correctly and on the quality and form of the bibliography they used in their search.

TIP 1,001 "The Beginning, Not the End"

1,001   There is no magic in the number 1,000. It just seemed to be a goal to shoot for and a point at which to halt this collection. Halting was a problem. The writer, completing the final draft, was constantly confronted with new ideas not included here. The temptation to include them was great but the task impossible. Since each reader will uncover new ideas which should be here, good ideas should not be allowed to slip away into oblivion. See inside the back cover and the facing flyleaf for suggestions to place ideas on cards similar to the ones used to compile this book.

APPENDIX

using ideas to frame cognitive objectives

Another way to use this book effectively is to employ specific nonbehaviorally stated activities as aids in writing performance objectives. Good daily lesson planning starts with some specific objectives founded upon one or more broad but significant goals.

In the description which follows, the author has chosen to use the term "learning objective" rather than the more broadly used psychological terms which emphasize behavior or performance. To many English teachers "performance objective" is even offensive, and "behavioral objective" reduces their enthusiasm completely for writing any objectives.

The learning objective is used to describe a learning task in terms which make its accomplishment observable if not measurable by quantity or quality. A simple test for a meaningful objective is to see if it answers four questions: Who? What? How? and How well? A well-worded objective tells or implies WHO it is for, WHAT the learner is expected to do, HOW the task is to be accomplished (the tools and activity), and HOW WELL the learner must perform to achieve the objective.

Certainly not all learning objectives can contain each of these criteria, but the more information an objective contains the more specific and measurable it will be. Since all learning objectives should be directed to the learner, it is not necessary to mention this fact in each objective. Thus, wordings like "the student will" are superfluous.

Obviously the ideas in this book are really activities used to carry out learning objectives and are, of course, not phrased as learning objectives. But with a little effort, each idea could be reduced to its essentials and become an objective. Then by changing content—specific titles, for example—the objective could apply to whatever a class is covering at the time.

Study this example from the Narration section of chapter 2.

88- I   (Experiment/Cartoons) "Balloon Talk"

Cut out entire sets of comic strips from Sunday papers. Remove the dialogue from the balloons. Give each student a comic for which he supplies his own dialogue which is both appropriate to the characters and to the situations and which tells the story succinctly. Print directly on the strip or on separate paper containing numbers corresponding to numbered balloons. This is an effective way to practice dialogue and conversational punctuation. Creativity should also be encouraged.

To locate needed information for objectives, we know that WHO is the class (more specifically, individuals in the class); WHAT is to experiment with dialogue; HOW is met by supplying new dialogue for that removed from comic strips (the vehicle is the cartoons); HOW WELL is not indicated in the idea but might be added to reflect the teacher's expectations. The resulting objective might look like this:

To experiment with dialogue by writing new and appropriate speeches for those removed from published comic strips (until the dialogue is punctuated correctly and until the story can be accurately and interestingly followed by a reader—the HOW WELL.)

Some may prefer this stimulus-response wording:

Given a published comic strip with balloon speeches removed, each learner will experiment with appropriate and imaginative dialogue by supplying his own which is punctuated with 100 percent accuracy and written succinctly and cleverly so a reader can follow a complete story.

With a little help from the ideas in this collection, teachers should be able to produce useful learning objectives. A list of verbs to help phrase statements of specific learning expectations can be found inside the back cover. Also with such help, teachers should be able to produce better, more pertinent learning objectives than subscribing to banks of objectives "cranked out" by others remote from the scene.

When using the Ideabook to formulate objectives, note that the WHO of a learning objective is usually understood if it is written for students; the WHAT is based on the process (or behavior) which appears as the first word in parentheses ahead of an idea; the HOW is the second word (vehicle) in parentheses and is drawn from key words in the activity; and the HOW WELL is added when known or needed. (See also Mager's *Preparing Instructional Objectives.*[1]

THE COGNITIVE AND AFFECTIVE DOMAINS

Now education has at least four kinds of objectives upon which to build learning experiences: cognitive, affective, psychomotor, and perceptual. Up to now, in the writer's opinion, none of these domains has been effectively translated into practical classroom operations to strongly affect the majority of America's classroom teachers. In focusing on just one domain—the cognitive—and acknowledging the importance of another—the affective—goals on which to base the former, perhaps this book will move English education just a little closer to the sensible utilization of learning objectives.

As educators learned from the second taxonomy produced by Krathwohl, Bloom, and Masia, educational objectives can be classified as either cognitive (dealing mainly with knowledge and recall of information) or affective (stressing "desirable interests, attitudes and character development").[2]

The affective domain, this writer is convinced, really represents the goals on which American education must focus. The cognitive objectives are the measurable steps along the way toward reaching the probably never fully achieved and certainly unmeasurable affective goals. Thus, a daily lesson plan (based on a unit plan founded on affective goals) begins with a statement of affective goals which will be attained, at least in part by achieving the cognitive objectives set forth in the plan.

The author, keeping in mind that objectives are used for attaining goals, has also drawn up affective parallels between his classification system and the affective domain described by Krathwohl et al.[3] The following chart draws this comparison. It will also help generate parallel affective goals for cognitive objectives. The processes listed inside the back cover will also help.

1. Robert F. Mager, *Preparing Instructional Objectives* (Palo Alto, Calif.: Fearon, 1962).
2. David R. Krathwohl, Benjamin S. Bloom, Bertram B. Masia, *Taxonomy of Educational Objectives, Handbook II: Affective Domain* (New York: McKay, 1965), p. 15.
3. *Ibid.*, pp. 176–185. (Used with special permission to paraphrase for the chart.)

Key Words for
Connecting Affective Goals to Cognitive Objectives

Affective Goals

**Ideabook Teaching-Learning
Sequences and Processes**

Receiving

Introduction

Appreciates

Discover (question)

Attends

Listen

Empathizes

Observe

Listens

Read

Research

Responding

Deliberation

Complies

Analyze

Enjoys

Consolidate

Is interested

Experiment

Participates

Interpret

Organize

Internalizing Values   ·

Accepts   ·

Becomes responsible   ·   (A link between first two

Reasons   ·   levels and last two)

Shows devotion   ·

Organizing Values

Evaluation

Selects

Compare

Systematizes

Extrapolate

Synthesizes

Identify

Judge

Restructure

Utilizing Values

Application

Behaves accordingly

Construct

Philosophizes beliefs,

Perform

  ideas, attitudes

Solve

Speak

Write

No claim is made that each of the above classifications is directly parallel. One can readily see, however, that many parallels do exist and that anyone interested in relating cognitive objectives to affective goals could be helped by the chart above. The scheme is at least a beginning for those who have had little or no experience in this area. Much educational research must yet be completed to refine methods for writing and using goals and objectives for all teaching but especially for teaching English.

The following serves to illustrate an affective goal which might be found under the classification, Receiving. The goal might read: "Empathize with the people who lived in the Dust Bowl in the early 1900's to help appreciate the value of conserving natural resources."[*]

A parallel cognitive objective for Introduction (receiving information) could be "To *read* (the process) the book (the vehicle) John Steinbeck's *Grapes of Wrath* and be able to tell the main idea orally or in writing and to trace at least one nonliteral symbol which reflects the era." The following hypothetical teacher-oriented idea which might appear in the Literature section (Introduction phase) of the Ideabook could have been the springboard for the affective goal and cognitive objective.

000-T   (Read/Book) "Ecological Sour Grapes"

Some of the reasons for today's ecological concerns are well demonstrated by several classic works of literature. A good case for concern can be found in John Steinbeck's *Grapes of Wrath*. Prepare a list of other such books to inform students of the need to conserve natural resources.

*Note: Affective goals here begin with a strong verb and learning objectives begin with the preposition "to" plus a process-type verb forming an infinitive. The wording helps to distinguish the two.

IDEABOOK ENTRY WORDS

Analyze—the first process under Deliberation in the teaching-learning sequence; distinguishing facts from hypotheses; determining relevance, idea relationships, persuasive technqiues, and other aspects. Analysis of literature may be used to recognize form and pattern to derive meaning.

Application—the fourth step in the teaching-learning sequence and fourth letter in the acronym I-D-E-A. This step includes ways a student can put into practice outside of class what he has learned in class. Most items in this phase may be regarded as "assignments," but hopefully, assignments will be ways to apply learning to life.

Argumentation—the classic form of rhetoric which comes closest to committing an oral debate to paper; usually included in the quartet of composition studies with narration, description, and exposition.

"C"—not a main classification term, this abbreviation stands for *class* and precedes activities which will involve the entire class.

Compare—the process of seeking similarities and differences among situations, ideas, and products and usually based on observable external qualities. It is a key entry word in the Evaluation phase of the teaching-learning sequence.

Composition—one of the five subject matter divisions used to designate a handbook section. As such it includes the entire area of written composition from friendly notes to best-selling novels.

Comprehension—as a reading term it typically describes three levels of taking in and processing information: literal, critical, and inferential. As a subject subdivision in this book it denotes being able to read words, understand their meanings, and make generalizations from words as they are combined in sentences.

Consolidate—a process in the Deliberation phase, it is gathering, selecting, and relating specific and useful new information to other previously learned but similar knowledge.

Construct—one of five processes in Application when the learner builds or assembles something having recently learned how. This could be a model of an Indian village, a work of art, a saleable product, or even a magazine.

Deliberation—one of the four steps in the teaching-learning sequence; the second letter in the acronym I-D-E-A. It is the phase when the learner attempts to work with the new information he has received in the Introduction phase and to practice with it by placing new generalizations into familiar frameworks, the key to reasoning.

Description—one of the four types of rhetoric typically studied in written composition; a rhetorical principle by which content takes on color, movement, and form.

Dialect—this Grammar/Language subdivision refers to the language spoken in particular regions of a country or among particular ethnic groups.

Discover—a process in the Introduction phase by which a learner receives information through a question-answer technique, through methods of inquiry, and even through class discussion.

Drama—used mainly to identify ideas in the Literature section for that genre so important to the study of English. The term may also be found in other sections since drama is not exclusive to literature. For example, drama can be written and be written about, and can stimulate language study to improve reading.

Experiment—this Deliberation process helps identify ideas which allow pupils to practice using new-found learnings in classroom situations such as completing drills and exercises or even playing simulation games.

Extrapolate—originally a mathematician's term which was popularized by Bloom and associates when they prepared their taxonomy of educational objectives—cognitive domain. (See page 321 for citation.) Complicated as it may seem, the term simply refers to an Evaluation process by which the learner tests his ability to extend given information and determine or predict implications, consequences, and effects when similar circumstances are applied in another context or situation.

Success in this step assures the learner he knows the material.

Evaluation—the third step in the teaching-learning sequence—the E in I-D-E-A. It applies to tips which help the learner to know if learning has taken place and helps the teacher discover if material was taught sufficiently. Evaluation also includes material assessment such as whether information is significant, useful, or worth retaining. Sometimes it takes the last step—Application—to prove utility.

Exposition—the area of written composition by which, as its root implies, a writer exposes his knowledge about a particular subject, usually how to do or make something or to tell why the author feels as he does about something. Its uniqueness is that it lends itself to organizing supporting details around a topic sentence or developing idea.

Film Making—this skill area has recently been recognized as a valuable subdivision of the English field; a dynamic communication instrument studied as a form of composition and as literature.

"G"—designates activities which lend themselves to *groups* within the classroom setting. The value of grouping for instruction has long been known, but too few teachers take advantage of the many possibilities.

Grammar/Language—one of the content area sections comprising about a fifth of the book and including both traditional and modern approaches. (Because the author supports an integrated study of grammar, many Grammar/Language ideas are scattered throughout the book.)

Humanities—a rapidly growing content area in English; often used to designate many multidisciplinary approaches to the field, sometimes becoming a field by itself with its own discipline. In this book, humanities designates ideas which cross the traditional English boundaries to take in the full range of fine arts. It's a catchword term which threatens to become a catchall.

"I"—this letter symbolizes ideas which are aimed mainly at individuals. Most frequently the ideas concern assignments such as written compositions and term papers for independent study. The term also identifies ideas involving projects designed to meet particular talents and skills.

Identify—a well-known term in the Evaluation phase of instruction, since learners are frequently asked to "identify" something for a test. Sometimes the task is to differentiate among various ideas and structures and to choose one or several which pertain to a particular situation. More typically, learners match meanings and definitions with parallel terms or sources.

Interpret—a process term, indicating activities in the Deliberation teaching-learning sequence. It concerns grasping the complete thought, for example, of a literary work to determine its purpose, theme, moral, or any other nonliteral device.

Introduction—step preceding Deliberation, Evaluation, and Application in the teaching-learning sequence. It names the operation which occurs when learners receive information through one or more senses. It represents a somewhat passive information input-intake operation, but it can become more active through processes of inquiry (questioning) and research.

Journalism—a content subdivision indicating tips which either enhance student knowledge of the field of journalism (includes both newspapers and magazines) or uses the field to help teach English.

Judge—in the Evaluation phase, this process represents what transpires when the learner tests an idea, product, or communication for usability, accuracy, logic, or other internal traits.

Letter Writing—simply that special content subdivision which is often the most practical learning for students working in a composition unit.

Linguistics—content subdivision dealing with the scientific approach to language study; causes English teachers to explain whether they are teaching "the old or the new grammar." The new grammar is scientifically based and entails transforming or generating sentences or treating them from a psychological view. Linguistics is descriptive; "old grammar" is prescriptive.

Listen—needs no definition; included as one of five processes in the Introduction or information-receiving phase of the teaching-learning sequence.

Literature—one of the five subject matter divisions containing ideas for teaching the novel, drama, poetry, and other forms.

Mechanics—Grammar/Language subdivision; includes helps for teaching capitalization and punctuation.

Media—print and nonprint ways for informing the general public. In this book film, generally included in media, is a subdivision by itself.

Narration—one of the content subdivisions primarily, though not exclusively, in the Composition section. It marks those activities concerned with story telling.

Novels—this subdivision entry word in Literature refers to activities devoted to reading and reacting to fiction.

Observe—method by which a learner receives information in the Introduction phase of the teaching-learning process.

Organize—this process under the Deliberation phase denotes what must take place occasionally to facilitate recall, particularly if incoming information is varied and unwieldy.

Overview—one of the twenty-five content area subdivisions, it designates approaches which serve to integrate the several skill areas in the field: composition, grammar/language, literature, and reading.

Perform—one of the five major processes under the Application phase and identifying activities in which the learner participates in some form of role playing such as in dramas, skits, simulation games, or in activities which require special skills—reading a poem effectively, singing a song, playing an instrument, and many other skills which must be acquired by practice.

Poetry—that content under Literature devoted to producing, reading, and studying various forms of verse.

Process—this is not one of the classifications or descriptors, but since it is used so frequently in the Introduction to the book and in the Glossary, it should be defined briefly. The term refers to the techniques or methods by which people learn and teachers teach; all the twenty ways which permit teaching and learning to transpire through the four generally accepted sequences of Introduction, Deliberation, Evaluation, and Application.

Read—one of the five information-receiving processes listed under the Introduction phase of the teaching-learning process.

Reading—the fourth main section in the book in which are found 250 Idea for teaching reading, most of them emphasizing reading and writing activities for slow learners.

Reading Rate—a subdivision found primarily in the content area of Reading. Ideas are given to increase words per minute and to vary that rate according to reading difficulty.

Research—a process among five in the Introduction section designating one way a learner takes in information. It usually involves out-of-class sources such as libraries and interviews with authorities.

Restructure—in the Evaluation phase of the teaching-learning sequence. This process designates activities which require sifting data and arranging it to fit a function similar to but not exactly like the original source.

Room Management—the last of the five main divisions; contains ideas to help the teacher handle anything from attitudes to tutoring.

Semantics—traditionally, a word referring to a branch of linguistics concerned with word meanings. Its use in this handbook is no exception.

Solve—a process in the Application phase of the teaching-learning sequence typifying the problem-solving and problem-clarifying activities made possible by having learned a body of material or information.

Speak—along with the four other Application processes—construct, perform, solve, and write—the word identifies activities which involve orally sharing knowledge of gathered information.

Spelling—the subject matter subdivisions referring to Grammar/Language ideas to improve this typical but sometimes neglected area of English.

Study Skills—one of the Reading subdivisions designating suggested activities to improve skills in locating, organizing, and recalling information, following directions, selecting and evaluating information. Thus, study skills help sharpen many processes in the first three teaching-learning sequences.

Syntax—this subdivision found mainly in the Grammar/Language section is used in its traditional sense to indicate activities for improving sentence structure, arranging words in normal message-carrying relationships.

"T"—this abbreviation found after many of the idea numbers, indicates tips directed to the *teacher*, mainly for carrying out some aspect of the content area in which they appear. It is not used with ideas for class or groups. The "T" abbreviation also designates tutoring approaches including all types of one-to-one instruction: peer, cross-age, cross-ability.

Usage—a subdivision of the Grammar/Language section; describes ways to use language in speaking or writing.

Vehicle—not a classification or descriptor, this term is the second word in the parentheses which precede each tip. As such it describes how the process is to be carried out. No standard list exists; instead the vehicle word is usually the main tool or teaching aid for facilitating learning.

Vocabulary—subdivision which classifies tips primarily in the Grammar/ Language and Reading sections. As usual, the term classifies activities for learning word definitions.

Words—one of the several subdivisions found in the content areas, this one usually in the Grammar/Language and Reading sections. The term signifies an activity dealing with word functions, or, in Reading, word calling. In the Reading area, word identification skills and sight word development are found under "Words."

Write—a process term under Application denoting activities based on written communication as opposed to oral and aural approaches.

READING TERMS

Blend—two or three consonants which when sounded keep their original, separate sounds, e.g., *st* in post, *str* in strong.

Comprehension—the act of reading with understanding; usually includes three levels: translating words and ideas, reacting to ideas, and making inferences (also known as literal, critical, and inferential levels).

Consonant—any letter sounded by momentarily obstructing the movement of air using the tongue, palate, or lips (b, c, d, t, etc.).

Context—the parts of a sentence or paragraph which occur just before and after a word and determine its exact meaning; sometimes the entire work or interrelated discourse is needed.

Critical Level—one aspect of comprehension which involves the reader in analyzing the material for author bias, objectivity, accuracy, feasibility, and so on, based on past experience with the same or similar material.

Decoding—translating letter symbols into oral (or thought) language.

Digraph—a combination of two consonants or vowels which give a single unique sound, e.g., *oa* in boat, *ph* in photo.

Diphthong—two vowels which when said together give their separate sounds, often retaining their individual nature, e.g., *oi* in oil, *ou* in out. (Similar to a consonant blend.)

Dolch Service Words—a list of 220 common words which every fourth grader should know by sight (not have to sound out). This list, containing no nouns and developed in the early 1900's by E. W. Dolch, is the widely accepted forerunner of more recent lists such as those offered by Fry, Kucera and Francis, Thorndike and Lorge, and others.

Experiential Level—(see "critical level.")

Inferential Level—that area of comprehension known as "reading between the lines." It involves extrapolating beyond the given or literal facts.

Literal Level—an area of comprehension which involves translating the words and giving them meaning.

Phonics—the area of reading which focuses on sounds made by individual letters and combinations.

Root—a main word or base to which prefixes, suffixes, and inflections may be added to alter the meaning.

Scanning—searching printed material rapidly to seek out specific information decided upon before the reading.

Skimming—a purposeful, quick reading of a particular piece of material to determine main ideas, subideas, and overall theme.

Speed—also known as rate, is the speed at which a reader can read so many words per minute. Rates vary with the purpose, the difficulty of the material, and the reader's knowledge of the material.

Structure—the analytical aspects of a word in its smallest parts (stems, roots, affixes).

Study Skills—a natural or acquired ability to obtain some information about a subject; usually locating, recalling, selecting, and organizing such information for a specific purpose.

Syllabication—separating words into units of pronunciation following certain accepted patterns and rules, i.e., each syllable contains a vowel sound; blends, digraphs, and diphthongs are not separated; words are always divided between twin consonants and between other consonants unless the first vowel has a long sound (se-cret).

Syntax—words arranged by grammatical pattern, usually in sentence formats.

Tachistoscope—any device used to flash a word or several at variable exposure times and is usually speeded up gradually.

Vowel—a letter voiced with the mouth open and unobstructed, such as the letter *a*.

Word Recognition—also known as word attack and word identification; relating symbol to sound by using such aids as context, word structure, phonics, or the dictionary.

resource bibliography

Composition   334
Grammar/Language   336
Literature   338
Media   341
Reading   345
Reference Shelf   347
  Booklists   347
  Curriculum   348
  Evaluation   350
  Ideas   350
  Learning Theory   352
  Methods   352
  Periodicals   353

This listing, of course, is just a fraction of what could or should have been included. But it is a beginning since many of the publications have their own bibliographies. Annotations are used when the title may not give sufficient clues about content. To save additional space, the abbreviation NCTE is used to cite the many publications of the National Council of Teachers of English, 1111 Kenyon Road, Urbana, Illinois 61801.

COMPOSITION

Bateman, Donald, and Zidonis, Frank. *The Effect of a Study of Transformational Grammar on the Writing of Ninth and Tenth Graders.* NCTE, 1966.

Bergman, Floyd L. *Manuscript Diagnosis: The Text-Ray.* Ann Arbor, Mich.: Campus Publishers, 1974. Describes a unique composition evaluation procedure. Relates grammar and composition functionally. Since students employ this objective technique themselves, the method saves teacher evaluation time.

Braddock, Richard; Lloyd-Jones, Richard; and Schoer, Lowell. *Research in Written Composition.* NCTE, 1963.

Brooks, Cleanth, and Warren, Robert Penn. *Modern Rhetoric.* 3rd ed. Harcourt Brace Jovanovich, 1972. Available in both a short and an unabridged version (the latter with models), the book is a very complete study of composition useful for teachers and students.

Carlson, Ruth Kearney. *Sparkling Words.* (Wagner Printing Co.) NCTE, 1973. Over 225 ideas to help young authors write creatively.

Christensen, Francis, et al. "The Sentence and the Paragraph." (*College English* and *College Composition and Communication.*) NCTE, 1966.

Articles on rhetoric of English prose including the generative paragraph and the tagmemic approach to paragraph analysis.

Corbin, Richard. *The Teaching of Writing in Our Schools.* New York: The Macmillan Company, 1966.

Ettner, Kenneth (chrm). "A Thousand Topics for Composition" (*Illinois English Bulletin.*) NCTE, 1971.

Farmer, Robert A. *1,000 Ideas for Term Papers.* New York: Arco Publishing Company, 1969.

Gerbrandt, Gary L. *An Idea Book for Acting Out and Writing Language K-8.* NCTE, 1974. Practical, proven ideas for individualizing the language arts. Also helpful ideas for teaching writing through completing unfinished sentences, writing fables and stories, and unscrambling sentences.

Glorfeld, Louis E.; Lauerman, David A.; and Stageberg, Norman C. *A Concise Guide for Writers.* 3rd ed. New York: Holt, Rinehart & Winston, 1974.

Holbrook, David. *Children's Writing.* Cambridge, England: Cambridge University Press, 1967.

Hook, J. N. *Guide to Good Writing: Grammar, Style, Usage.* New York: Ronald Press Co., 1962.

Ideaform Theme Paper. NCTE. Packaged (thirty sheets) ruled or unruled paper with an evaluation checklist on back to save teacher time. Free sample on request. (#31003 ruled; #31012 unruled.)

Katz, Marjorie P., and Arbeiter, Jean S. *Pegs to Hang Ideas On: A Book of Quotations.* New York: M. Evand and Company, 1973. Distributed by J. B. Lippincott Co. A collection of quotations from contemporary newspapers and magazines. Categories relate to personal development, environment, and major social and political issues.

Kunz, Linda Ann, and Viscount, Robert R. *Write Me a Ream: A Course in Controlled Composition for Job Training and Adult Education.* New York: Teachers College Press, 1973.

Macrorie, Ken. *Telling Writing.* New York: Hayden Book Company, 1970. Useful for the teacher or as a class text through its down-to-earth discussion about composition.

Moore, Walter J. "A Thousand Topics for Composition." (*Illinois English Bulletin.*) NCTE, 1971. One hundred teachers supply topics of interest to elementary children.

Murray, Donald M. *A Writer Teaches Writing: A Practical Method of Teaching High School Composition.* Boston: Houghton Mifflin Company, 1968.

National Writers Club, 1365 Logan St., Denver, CO 80203. Free information on writing careers.

O'Hare, Frank. *Sentence Combining: Improving Student Writing without*

Formal Grammar Instruction. NCTE, 1973.

Pandora's Box. Canadian Council of Teachers of English, c/o English Department, Glendon College, 2275 Bayview Ave., Toronto, Ontario M4N 3N6. 100 award-winning student poems in a kit with posters. Also contains children's illustrations and a recording.

Perrin, Porter G. *The Writer's Guide and Index to English.* 5th ed. Revised by Karl W. Dykema and Wilma R. Ebbitt. Glenview, IL: Scott, Foresman and Company, 1972.

Smith, Eugene. *Teacher Preparation in Composition.* NCTE, 1969.

Tate, Gary, and Corbett, Edward P. J., eds. *Teaching High School Composition.* New York: Oxford University Press, 1970. A substantially documented collection of articles on composition. An extensive bibliography is included, as well as a suggested minimal reference library.

The Whole Word Catalog. Staff of Teachers and Writers Collaborative. NCTE, 1972. A collection of open classroom assignments to stimulate student writing for both elementary and secondary.

Wilson, Grace E., ed. *Composition Situations.* NCTE, 1966. A collection of topics in forty-five categories under general sections: personal experiences, language study, mass media, and literature study.

The Writer. The Writer, Inc., 8 Arlington St., Boston, MA 02116. Student subscription rate available.

Writing Objectives for 1973–74 Assessment. National Assessment Office, Lincoln Tower, 1860 Lincoln Street, Denver, CO 80203.

GRAMMAR/LANGUAGE

Aarons, Alfred C., et al. "Linguistic-Cultural Differences and American Education." (*Florida FL Reporter.*) NCTE, 1969. Anthology of forty-three articles on problems of cultural pluralism.

Allen, Harold B., ed. *Readings in Applied English Linguistics.* 2nd ed. New York: Appleton-Century-Crofts, 1967.

Allen, Virginia F., and Forman, Sidney. *English as a Second Language.* New York: Teachers College Press, 1967. Catalog of 1,000 items: books, pamphlets, periodicals, films, filmstrips, records, tapes, charts, maps, games, and models. Categories are Linguistics, Language Culture, Language Learning, Texts, and References.

Benson, James D., and Greaves, William S. *The Language People Really Use.* Ontario, Canada MIS 3BC: The Book Society of Canada, Ltd. Suitable for high school, community colleges, and universities, it analyzes news bulletins, weather maps, ads, and literary selections.

Berbrich, John D. *101 Ways to Learn Vocabulary.* New York: Amsco School Publications, 1971.

Berger, Allen, and Smith, Blanche Hope, eds. *Classroom Practices in Teaching English, 1973-1974: Language Activities.* NCTE, 1973. Contains over fifty ideas and activities on language development at all educational levels.

Davis, A. L. *Culture, Class, and Language Variety.* NCTE, 1972. Ten articles to help teachers work more effectively with language problems of children who speak nonstandard dialects.

The Excluded Student. U.S. Commission on Civil Rights. Washington, D.C.: U.S. Government Printing Office, 1972. Insights into language problems of the Chicano student.

Fox, Robert P. ed. *Essays on Teaching English as a Second Language and as a Second Dialect.* NCTE, 1973. Gives ideas and examples for using English in a second language classroom.

Francis, W. Nelson. *The English Language: An Introduction.* New York: W. W. Norton & Co., 1965.

Grizzard, B. *Language Exercises.* Austin: Steck-Vaughn Co., 1965. A workbook which can be used as a resource book of language improvement exercises for high school students and adults.

Hayakawa, S. I. *Language in Thought and Action.* 2nd ed. New York: Harcourt, Brace and World, 1964.

Herndon, Jeanne H. *A Survey of Modern Grammars.* New York: Holt, Rinehart & Winston, 1970. Written for in-service and pre-service elementary and secondary teachers of language arts or English.

Hogan, Robert F. *The English Language in the School Program.* NCTE, 1966. Articles on theory, systems, dialects, usage, and curriculum.

Hunt, Kellog. *Grammatical Structures Written at Three Grade Levels.* NCTE, 1965.

Labov, William. *The Study of Nonstandard English.* NCTE, 1970. Suggests ways to develop insights on nonstandard English, thus making it an integral part of sociolinguistic structure.

Lefevre, Carl A. *Linguistics, English, and the Language Arts.* New York: Teachers College Press, 1973. An introduction to linguistics, it explains traditional, structural, transformational, and generative grammar and suggests what each contributes to language.

Linguistics and the Classroom Teacher. 1970 edition. Association for Supervision and Curriculum Development. Room 428, 1202 16th St., N.W., Washington, D.C. Introduction to linguistics and its use in developing communication skills.

"Linguistics and the New Textbooks." (*Kentucky English Bulletin.*) NCTE, 1968. Articles to help schools which have adopted linguistically oriented textbooks.

Malmstrom, Jean. *Language in Society.* New York: Hayden Book Company, 1973.

Marckwardt, Albert H., ed. *Language and Language Learning.* NCTE, 1968. Papers on language standards, attitudes, and linguistic components in teaching and teacher preparation.

———. *Linguistics and the Teaching of English.* Bloomington, Ind.: Indiana University Press, 1966.

McDavid, Raven I., et al. *Americans Speaking.* NCTE, 1967. Transcriptions of free discourse and readings by speakers in six dialect areas. Available with record and/or pamphlet.

Morse, J. Mitchell. "Fact and Metaphor in the Classroom." NCTE, 1973. (Cassette tapes, 65 min.) Cites the hazards of taking metaphors literally as he discusses methods for recognizing and confronting manipulated language.

Plumer, Davenport. *Language Problems of Disadvantaged Children.* Cambridge: Harvard Unviersity Press, 1968.

Pollock, Thomas C. "Misspelling in Grades 9–12," *English Record,* 22 (Fall 1971), pp. 46–53. Analysis of 388 of 50,000 misspelled words submitted by 1,706 teachers.

Pooley, Robert C. "The Teaching of English Usage." NCTE, 1974. A 1946 classic revised.

Publications of Interest to Teachers of English. Modern Language Association of America, Materials Center, 62 Fifth Ave., New York, NY 10011. (Free.)

Sapir, Edward. *Culture, Language and Personality.* Berkeley: University of California Press, 1961.

Selected List of Materials for Teachers of English to Speakers of Other Languages. Center for Applied Linguistics, 1611 N. Kent Rd., Arlington, VA 22209.

Smith, E. Brooks; Goodman, Kenneth S.; and Meredith, Robert. *Language and Thinking in the Elementary School.* New York: Holt, Rinehart & Winston, 1970.

LITERATURE

American Library Association. *A Basic Book Collection for High Schools* and *A Basic Book Collection for Junior High Schools.* Revised regularly.

Barnfield, Gabriel. *Creative Drama in Schools.* London: Macmillan Company, 1970.

Booklist. American Library Association, 50 E. Huron St., Chicago, IL 60611. A semimonthly with about 150 book reviews each issue.

Book Review Digest. H.W. Wilson Co., 950 University Ave., Bronx, NY 10452. A monthly and an annual accumulation of book reviews which had appeared when a book was first published.

Brooks, Cleanth, and Warren, Robert Penn. *Understanding Poetry.* 3rd ed. New York: Holt, Rinehart & Winston, 1960.

Burton, Dwight L. *Literature Study in the High Schools.* 3rd ed. New York: Holt, Rinehart & Winston, 1970. Discussion on constructive criticism of literature in the secondary classroom. Suggestions for setting up sample bibliographies.

Carlsen, G. Robert. *Books and the Teenage Reader.* New York: Bantam Books, 1972. An introduction to the reading interests of young adults.

Chicorel, Marietta, ed. *Index to Poetry in Collections: Poetry in Print.* Chicorel Library Publishing Corporation, 275 Central Park West, New York, NY 10024. Over 250,000 entries locating poetry by titles, first lines, authors, editors, translators, and collection titles.

The Children's Book Council, Inc., 175 Fifth Avenue, New York, NY 10010. Sponsors of National Children's Book Week, the organization will provide materials to stimulate reading. Free information on request in self-addressed, stamped envelope.

Ciardi, John, and Williams, Miller. *How Does a Poem Mean?* 2nd ed. Boston: Houghton Mifflin Company, 1975.

The Combined Paperback Exhibit. Combined Paperback Exhibit, Inc., Scarborough Park, Albany Post Road, Briarcliff Manor, NY 10510. A free catalog—elementary through senior high—of school exhibit information.

Dodds, Barbara. *Negro Literature for High School Students.* Urbana, IL: National Council of Teachers of English, 1968. Reviews 150 books by and about Negroes. Includes a curriculum guide for grade 9 and for a basic library collection.

Donelson, Kenneth, ed. "Adolescent Literature, Adolescent Reading in the English Class." *(Arizona English Bulletin).* Urbana, IL: National Council of Teachers of English, 1972. Brief articles about contemporary books young people enjoy, all based on interest surveys.

_____. *Censorship and the English Teacher. (Arizona English Bulletin).* NCTE, 1969.

Dunning, A. Stephen. *Teaching Literature to Adolescents: Poetry.* Glenview, IL: Scott, Foresman and Company, 1966.

_____. *Teaching Literature to Adolescents: Short Stories.* Glenview, IL: Scott, Foresman and Company, 1968.

Henderson, Harold G., for the Japan Society of New York. *Haiku in English.* (Charles E. Tuttle Co.) NCTE, 1965. Introduction to writing and teaching Japanese haiku, gives many examples.

Hiatt, Doris, and Klein, Celeste. *Kliatt Paperback Book Guide.* 6 Crocker

Circle, West Newton, Mass. 02165, A looseleaf quarterly service which reviews books for young adults.

Hodgson, John, and Richards, Ernest. *Improvisation: Discovery and Creativity in Drama.* London: Methuen, 1967.

Hogan, Robert F. "The Bible in the English Program." *(The English Journal.)* NCTE, 1965.

"Honor Listing of Young Adult Books." Books for Young Adults, University of Iowa, Iowa City, Iowa 52242. Reprints of 1972- 73 honored books for young adults. (Free.)

Howes, Alan B. *Teaching Literature to Adolescents: Plays.* Glenview, IL: Scott, Foresman and Company, 1968.

Improvisation Handbook. Glenview, IL: Scott, Foresman and Company, 1974. A collection of games and exercises to acquaint students with improvisation techniques. Also contains scenes for practice.

Kujoth, Jean Spealman. *Reading Interests of Children and Young Adults.* Methuen, N.J.: Scarecrow Press, 1970.

Moffett, James. *Drama: What is Happening—The Use of Dramatic Activities in the Teaching of English.* NCTE, 1967.

Nebraska Curriculum Development Center. *A Curriculum for English.* (University of Nebraska Press.) NCTE, 1966. Self-contained units for a literature program for grades 1- 6.

The New York Times Book Review. The New York Times Co., Times Square, NY 10036. A weekly general book review service of *The New York Times* Sunday edition. About twenty or thirty titles in each issue.

O'Neal, Robert, ed. *Teacher's Guide to World Literature for the High School.* NCTE, 1966. Reviews more than 200 world classics in translation and discusses importance and authors' lives. Suggests thematic study units.

Paperbound Books in Print and *Books in Print.* R. R. Bowker Co., 1180 Avenue of the Americas, New York, NY 10036. All the information needed for ordering books. Perhaps too expensive for teachers, but every library should have these.

Petitt, Dorothy, ed. *Poetry in the Classroom.* NCTE, 1966. Articles discussing twenty-two poems each of which can be handled in a single class period.

Pownall, David. *Articles on Twentieth Century Literature: An Annotated Bibliography 1954- 1970.* Kraus Thomson Organization Limited. Millwood, NY 10546. A seven-volume reference work providing access to more than 22,000 journal articles about contemporary literature throughout the world.

Purves, Alan C. ed. *How Porcupines Make Love.* Lexington, Mass.: Xerox College Publishing, 1972. Describes various fresh approaches to teaching literature.

Reid, Virginia M., ed. *Reading Ladders for Human Relations.* (American Council on Education.) NCTE, 1972. Annotated bibliography of more than 1,300 books arranged by maturity level. Focuses on expanding sensitivity toward people.

Root, Shelton L., ed. *Adventuring with Books: Twenty-four Hundred Titles for Preschool—Grade 8.* NCTE, 1973. Fourteen subject headings including picture books, fiction, biography, poets, social studies, general science, arts and crafts, and sports and hobbies.

School Library Journal. R. R. Bowker Co., 1180 Avenue of the Americas, New York, NY 10036. A monthly with book reviews including sections for junior high and young adults.

Simmons, Gloria M., and Hutchinson, Helene D. *Black Culture: Reading and Writing Black.* New York: Holt, Rinehart & Winston, 1972.

Smith, Dora V. "The Children's Literary Heritage." *Elementary English.* NCTE, 1964. Discusses children's literature—fables, folktales, gods, heroes, and favorite classics. Contains reading list.

Stensland, Anna Lee. *Literature by and about the American Indian.* NCTE, 1973.

The Supreme Court Obscenity Decisions. San Diego, CA: Greenleaf Classics, 1973. Complete texts of five opinions and the dissents of Justices Brennan and Douglas. Includes the "Miller" definition of "obscenity."

Turner, Darwin T., and Stanford, Barbara Dodds. *Theory and Practice in the Teaching of Literature by Afro-Americans.* NCTE, 1971.

Way, Brian. *Development Through Drama.* New York: Humanities Press, 1967.

Williams, Galen, dir. *A Directory of American Poets.* (Poets and Writers, Inc.) Urbana, IL: NCTE, 1973. Lists 1,300 published American writers (address by state, most recent work, and publisher).

Wilson, Jean A. *Books for You.* (Washington Square Press for NCTE.) NCTE, 1971. Describes over 2,000 fiction and nonfiction titles in forty-five subject categories.

MEDIA

Achenbaum, Alvin, et al. "Doublespeak: What is Deceptive Advertising?" NCTE, 1973. (Cassette tape, 87 min.) Focuses on current controversies over advertising aimed at children. Includes audience questions.

Anderson, Chuck. *The Electric Journalist: An Introduction to Video.* New York: Praeger Publications, 1973. How to videotape and edit, also production ideas and their influence on American life (cable TV and public access).

Andersen, Yvonne. *Make Your Own Animated Movies.* Boston: Little, Brown and Company, 1970. Easy-to-understand and step-by-step information for young filmmakers.

"The Arts—How to Become Involved." YWCA National Board. New York, NY 10022. (Color prints.) Shows how to stimulate student involvement through films, music, the dance, fine arts, graphic arts, multimedia events, and so on. (8½" × 11" color prints with supplementary text.)

"Audio-Visual Marketplace." Bowker Press, 131 Washington Ave.. Portland, Maine 04101. Extensive media bibliography.

Ayer Directory; Newspapers, Magazines, and Trade Publications. Ayer Press, West Washington Square, Philadelphia, PA 19106. Names and addresses in this annual publication which every library should have.

Berger, Arthur Asa. *Pop Culture.* Dayton: Pflaum/Standard, 1973. A book with a variety of subjects to discuss American culture and how our environment tends to shape the unaware.

Betancourt, Jeanne. *Women in Focus.* Dayton, Ohio: Pflaum/Standard, 38 West Fifth St. 45402. Catalog with reviews of over seventy nonsexist and feminist films for libraries, high schools, universities, and community groups.

Boutwell, William D., ed. *Using Mass Media in the Schools.* New York: Appleton-Century-Crofts, 1962.

Brown, Brian, ed. *Time English Program.* Chicago: Time, Inc. Requires at least five student subscriptions for weekly issues (9–12 grade).

COSMEP (Committee of Small Magazine Editors and Publishers), P.O. Box 703, San Francisco, CA 94101. Provides information on the nation's leading "little magazines."

The Creative Person—Richard Williams. National Education Television, 10 Columbus Circle, New York, NY 10019. (Film.) A close look at film animation. 16 mm, b&w, 30 min.

A Film about Filmmaking. International Film Bureau, 332 S. Michigan Ave., Chicago, IL 60604, 1972. (Film.) A group of college students produce a film from planning to editing. 16 mm. color, 18 min.

"Films and the English Class." *Arizona English Bulletin*, vol. 13, no. 2, (February 1971). NCTE, 1971.

Films in Review. National Board of Review of Motion Pictures, Inc., 210 E. 68th St., New York, NY 10021.

Film Library Quarterly. Film Library Information Council, Box 348, Radio City Station, New York, NY 10019.

For the Love of the Moon. Pyramid Films, Box 1048, Santa Monica, CA 90406. (Color film, 27 min.) An unusual presentation in which characters are hands with faces drawn on them. A study in illusion for high school students in any setting.

Four Ways to Drama. University of California Media Center, Berkeley, CA 94720. (Film.) A short dramatic incident is presented four ways: radio, television, stage and screen. 16 mm, b&w, 33 min.

Galvin, Kathleen, and Book, Cassandra. *Person-to-Person: An Introduction to Speech Communiction.* Skokie, IL: National Textbook Company. Describes communication to improve human relationships. Uses syndicated comic strips, photographs and posters.

Garrison, Cecil. *1001 Media Ideas for Teachers.* McCutchan Publishing Corp., Berkeley, CA, 1968.

Giblin, Thomas R. *Popular Media and the Teaching of English.* Pacific Palisades, CA: Goodyear Publishing Co., Inc., 1972. A collection of ideas dealing with the *why* and the *how* of popular media study in the secondary English classroom.

Heintz, Ann. *Exploring Television.* Chicago: Loyola Press, 1971. Introductory explanation on television for classroom use.

_____. *Mass Media.* Chicago: Loyola Press, 1972. Many activities, games, and discussion topics for the classroom.

Hornick, Joanne. *Creative Bulletin Boards for Junior High English.* New York: Citation Press, 1968.

Houk, Annelle, and Bogart, Carlotta. *Media Literacy.* Dayton: Pflaum/ Standard, 1974.

The Humanities and the Curriculum. Association for Supervision and Curriculum Development, Room 428, 1201 16th St., N.W., Washington, D.C., 1970.

Jackdaws: Collections of Historical Documents. New York: Grossman Publishers. Packets to enrich the study of history, biography, and classical literary characters.

Katz, John, ed. *Perspectives on the Study of Film.* Boston: Little, Brown & Co., 1971.

K-Eight (Instructional Management and Leadership). North American Publishing Company, 134 N. 13th St., Philadelphia, PA 19107. Ideas for educational innovation.

Littell, Joseph Fletcher. *Coping With Television.* Evanston, IL: McDougal, Littell & Company, 1973. A complete look at television: its workings, content, and influence.

Manchel, Frank. *Yesterday's Clowns: The Rise of Film Comedy.* New York: Franklin Watts, 1973. A visit with some of the screen's greatest comedians; over fifty black and white photographs with bibliography.

McLuhan, H. Marshall. *Understanding Media: The Extensions of Man.* New York: New American Library, 1973.

The Movies. Indiana University Audio-visual Center. Bloomington, Ind. 47405 (Film.) The motion pictures examined sociologically. 16 mm, b&w, 29 min.

Mitchell, Wanda. *Televising Your Message.* Skokie, IL: National Textbook Company. A practical, multi-purpose and very complete discussion of television from many points of view.

On Seeing Film and Literature. University of Southern California, Dept. of Cinema, Los Angeles, CA 90007. (Film.) Using footage from *The Bridge on the River Kwai,* demonstrates how literature is translated to the screen. 16 mm, b&w, 17 min.

Perkins, Flossie L. *Book and Non-Book Media: Annotated Guide to Selection Aids for Educational Materials.* NCTE, 1972. Guide to 250 selection aids covering books, pamphlets, films, and records for all ages.

Postman, Neil. *Television and the Teaching of English.* New York: Irvington Books, 1961.

Poteet, Howard, ed. *The Compleat Guide to Film Study.* NCTE, 1972. Ways to use film in the English curriculum.

Potter, Robert R. *English Everywhere: Meaning, Media and You.* New York: The Globe Book Company, Inc., 1971. Covers subjects of interest to students: advertising, movies, television, the newspaper, language of humor and politics.

Schrank, Jeffrey. *The Seed Catalog.* Boston: Beacon Press, 1974. Multimedia ideas for every classroom.

Schwarz, Ira P., and Karel, Leon C. *Teaching the Related Arts.* Kirksville, MO: Simpson Publishing Co., 1973. Approaches to interrelating the arts: music, painting, sculpture, architecture, crafts, literature, film, and dance.

Smallman, Kirk. *Creative Film-Making.* New York: The Macmillan Company, 1969. A beginner's book on film making, especially Super 8.

Sohn, David. *Film: The Creative Eye.* Dayton, O.: Pflaum/Standard. Features the aesthetic wonders of film.

Teachers Guides to Television, Box 564, Lenox Hill Station, New York, NY 10021. Guides to current TV programs. Write for subscription rates.

Teenage Movie Award Winners. Eastman Kodak Company, A-V Distribution, Dept. 396, 343 State St., Rochester, NY 14650. (Film.) Excerpts from award-winning student films. 16 mm, color, 27 min.

Television Highlights. Television Information Office, 745 Fifth Ave., New York, NY 10022. Ask to be placed on mailing list.

Ten Years in a Box. Ann Arbor, University Microfilms, 1969. Sixteen-pound, multimedia collection of records, slides, filmstrips, posters, booklets, newspapers, and so on, about the 1930's.

3M Loan-a-Library. Minnesota Mining and Manufacturing Co. One-week free loan of printed originals for making overhead transparencies. Contact local 3M dealer.

Valdes, Joan, and Crow, Jeanne. *The Media Works.* Dayton: George Pflaum, 1973.

Videoplayer. Videoplayer Publishing Co., Inc., 13273 Ventura Blvd., Studio City, CA 91604. A news magazine for the international video-tape player industry.

Young Filmmakers Foundation. *Young Animators and Their Discoveries.* New York: Praeger Publishers, Inc., 1973. Young filmmakers, age 14 and up, describe their animation experiments. General introduction to animated film production.

READING

Advanced Reading Skill Builder. Pleasantville, NY: Education Division, Reader's Digest Services, Inc. Booklets for 7, 8 and 9. Cassettes available. Write for information.

Bamman, H. A., et al. *Reading Instruction in the Secondary School.* New York: David McKay Co., 1961.

Burmeister, Lou. *Reading Strategies for Secondary School Teachers.* Reading, MA.: Addison-Wesley Publishing Company, 1974.

Cullinan, Bernice, ed. *Black Dialects and Reading.* NCTE, 1974. Information and practical suggestions regarding black dialect, oral language, and reading.

Cumulative Reading Record. NCTE. Folder 9 ½ × 11 ¾ to record reading and reactions. Special insert available. Free sample on request.

Donelson, Kenneth, ed. chrm., and the Committee on the Right to Read. *The Students' Right to Read.* NCTE, 1972. Updating of information on censorship. Lists sources of assistance.

Fallon, Berlie J., and Filgo, Dorothy, eds. *Forty States Innovate to Improve Reading Programs.* Bloomington, Ind.: Phi Delta Kappa, 1970. Describes seventy-five exemplary reading programs, elementary through high school.

Gephart, William J. *The Convergence Technique and Reading.* Bloomington, Ind.: Phi Delta Kappa, 1969. Interim report on the planning of a reading research program.

Goldman, Frederick, and Burnett, Linda R. *Need Johnny Read?* Dayton: Pflaum/Standard. Discusses the educational power of television and films and their use in schools.

Goltry, M. *Forms in Your Future.* New York: Globe Books Company. Presents twenty-four lessons built around various application blanks and forms which most students will eventually need to use in their lives. Tear-out, duplicated forms.

Goodman, Kenneth S., ed. *Miscue Analysis.* NCTE, 1973. Applications of miscue analysis in a full range of classroom situations such as teacher training, remedial reading, college programs, and in-service workshops.

Goodman, Kenneth S., and Niles, Olive S. *Reading: Process and Program.* NCTE, 1970. Discusses multiple behaviors in reading along with promising trends, teacher training, preparing reading materials.

Harris, Larry A., and Kimmel, E. Marcia. *Reading for the Reading Teacher: An Annotated Index to Elementary English, 1924–1970.* NCTE, 1972. All articles on reading listed by subject category, with cross references.

International Reading Association, Order Dept., 6 Tyre Ave., Newark, DE 19711. Write for publication list.

Journal of Reading. International Reading Association, Box 119, Newark, DE 19711. Official journal with articles of interest to elementary and secondary teachers of reading.

Karlin, Robert. *Teaching Reading in the High School.* 2nd ed. Indianapolis: Bobbs-Merrill Co., 1972.

Laubach, Frank C.; Kirk, Elizabeth; and Laubach, Robert S. *Everyday Reading and Writing.* Syracuse: New Readers Press, 1970. Interestingly presented skills workbook which stresses newspapers, instructions, recipes, maps, and business forms, among others.

Maberly, Norman. *Mastering Speed Reading.* Bergenfield, NJ: The New American Library, 1966. Useful for 8th grade and up. Includes charts, diagrams, and tests.

Massey, William T., and Moore, Virginia D. *Helping High School Students to Read Better.* New York: Holt, Rinehart, & Winston, 1965.

Right to Read Office, U.S. Office of Education, 400 Maryland Ave., S.W., Washington, D.C. 20202. For inquiries about reading programs and research.

Ruddell, Robert B., ed. *Accountability and Reading Instruction: Critical Issues.* NCTE, 1973. Contributors discuss behavioral objectives, tests, performance contracting as they relate to reading instruction.

Russell, David H., and Karp, Eta E. *Reading Aids through the Grades.* New York: Teachers College Press, 1951.

Spache, Evelyn B. *Reading Activities for Child Involvement.* Boston: Allyn and Bacon, 1972. Offers activities for any reading program in elementary or middle school.

Spache, George. *The Teaching of Reading.* Bloomington, Ind.: Phi Delta Kappa, 1972. Summarizes and analyzes the best known information on reading readiness, methods, and ways to reach the disadvantaged.

Strang, Ruth; McCullough, Constance M.; and Traxler, Arthur E. *Improvement of Reading,* 3rd ed. New York: McGraw-Hill Book Company, 1961.

Thomas, Ellen Lamar, and Robinson, H. Alan. *Improving Reading in Every Class.* Boston: Allyn and Bacon, 1972. Describes practical procedures for teaching reading in all high school subject areas. Reference to a variety of related publications.

Wardhaugh, Ronald. *Reading: A Linguistic Perspective.* New York: Harcourt Brace Jovanovich, 1969.

White, Marian E., ed. *High Interest-Easy Reading for Junior and Senior High School Students,* 2nd ed. NCTE, 1972.

Yellow Pages at every telephone. Everywhere: Bell Telephone Companies. More than phone numbers, these pages are really a course in Western civilization, its mores and ideals. Useful for improving reading skills (as in scanning) and providing topics to discuss.

REFERENCE SHELF

Booklists

Dieterich, Daniel J. "Bibliography of Research in the Teaching of English: July 1, 1972, to December 31, 1972." *Research in the Teaching of English* 7 (Spring 1973), pp. 114-140.

Frederick, Anthony, ed. chrm. *Annotated Index to the English Journal, 1944-1963.* NCTE, 1964. Includes article annotations grouped in 300 categories.

Harvey, Robert C., and Kirkton, Carole M. *Annotated Index to the English Journal, 1964-1970.* NCTE, 1972.

Interpreting Language Arts Research for the Teacher. Association for Supervision and Curriculum Development, Room 428, 1201 16th St. N.W., Washington, D.C. Comprehensive list of practical classroom aids; over 1,100 reference sources.

Moore, Walter J. *Annotated Index to Elementary English, 1924-1967.* NCTE, 1968. Brief descriptions arranged by thirty-five subject categories and cross-referenced.

National Council of Teachers of English. *NCTE Guide to Teaching Materials for English, Grades 7-12.* 1111 Kenyon Road, Urbana, IL 61801. 1974-75 Guide, #037575; 1975-76 Supplement, #03766J. Detailed, objective descriptions of commercially available instructional materials for students of English and language arts: anthologies, textbooks, workbooks, and other print-based materials.

_____. *Resources for English and the Language Arts* (current year). Free catalog. Lists publications from the Council, its affiliates, and other sources. Includes maps, filmstrips and recordings.

Salisbury, Gordon. *Catalog of Free Teaching Materials.* Riverside, CA: Ribidoux Printing Co., 1973.

Searles, John R. *Sources of Free and Inexpensive Material. (English Journal.)* NCTE, 1973. Listing of material from all sources.

Weisinger, Mort. *1001 Valuable Things You Can Get Free.* 6th ed. New York: Bantam Books #53892, 1968. A giveaway list of products, kits, maps, plans, films, Bible selections, manuals, and services. These are offered by American industries, profit and nonprofit organizations, and by local and national governments.

Curriculum

Association for Supervision and Curriculum Development. *Individualizing Instruction.* Room 428, 1201 16th St. N.W., Washington, D.C., 1970.

Bloom, Benjamin. *Individual Differences in School Achievement: A Vanishing Point?* Bloomington, Ind.: Phi Delta Kappa, 1971. Award winners, lectures which focus on mastery learning proposed as a basis for reorganizing learning.

———— , ed. *Taxonomy of Educational Objectives: The Classification of Educational Goals. Handbook I: Cognitive Domain.* New York: David McKay Company, Inc., 1956.

Burton, Dwight L., and Simmons, John S., eds. *Teaching English in Today's Schools.* 2nd ed. New York: Holt, Rinehart & Winston, 1970.

College Entrance Examination Board. *12,000 Students and Their English Teachers.* NCTE, 1968. Model teaching plans for units in language, literature, and composition, grades 9–12.

Curriculm Materials of (current year). Association for Supervision and Curriculum Development, Room 428, 1201 16th St. N.W., Washington, D.C. Catalogs the current Curriculum Materials Exhibit at ASCD annual conference, K-12 curriculum guides, and other instructional aids developed by school systems.

Daigon, Arthur, and LaConte, Ronald T. *Challenge and Change in the Teaching of English.* Boston: Allyn and Bacon, 1971. A collection of articles on promising directions for the English curriculum, language, literature, media, and writing.

Dale, Edgar. *Building a Learning Environment.* Bloomington, Ind.: Phi Delta Kappa, 1972. Clearly discusses the philosophical and the practical needed to create effective learning-teaching situations.

Dixon, John. *Growth Through English.* Oxford, England: Oxford University Press, 1969.

Elliott, Virginia A., and Josephs, Lois S. *English for the Academically Talented Student in the Secondary School.* NCTE, 1969.

The English Language Arts (NCTE Commission on the English Curriculum.) New York: Appleton-Century-Crofts, 1965. An always current discussion of the English curriculum. Also available from NCTE.

Evans, William H., and Walker, Jerry. *New Trends in the Teaching of English in Secondary Schools.* Chicago: Rand McNally and Company, 1966.

Fagan, Edward R., and Vandall, Jean, eds. *Classroom Practices in Teaching English, 1969–70. (Minorities: Communicating the Dream's Responsibility).* NCTE, 1973.

Farrell, Edmund J. *Deciding the Future: A Forecast of Responsibilities of Secondary Teachers of English, 1970–2000 A.D.* NCTE, 1971.

Summarizes responses from eighty experts writing on the future of English teaching.

Frazier, Alexander. *New Directions in Elementary English.* NCTE, 1967.

Gardner, John. *Excellence: Can We Be Equal and Excellent Too?* New York: Harper & Row, 1961.

Hoetker, James; Fichtenau, Robert; and Farr, Helen L. K. *Systems, Systems Approaches, and the Teacher.* NCTE, 1972. Discusses validity of educational objectives as well as uses of systems approaches. Also presents a model.

Houston, Robert W., and Howsam, Robert B., eds. *Competency-Based Teacher Education.* Chicago: Science Research Associates, 1972. Articles covering five areas: objectives, curriculum design, evaluation, certification, and consortia.

Jacobs, Paul H. *Criteria for Evaluating High School English Programs.* *(English Journal)* NCTE, 1968. A checklist covering curriculum, composition, language, literature, reading, speech, evaluation, and the environment. Includes teacher qualifications.

King, Martha L.; Emans, Robert; and Cianciolo, Patricia. *The Language Arts in the Elementary School.* NCTE, 1973.

Krathwohl, David R.; Bloom, Benjamin S.; and Masia, Bertram B., eds. *Taxonomy of Educational Objectives: The Classification of Educational Goals. Handbook II: Affective Domain.* New York: David McKay Company, 1965.

Mager, Robert F. *Preparing Instructional Objectives.* Belmont, CA: Fearon Publishers, 1962.

Maloney, Henry B., ed. *Goal Making for English Teaching.* NCTE, 1973.

Maxwell, John, and Tovatt, Anthony, eds. *On Writing Behavioral Objectives for English.* NCTE, 1970.

Moffett, James. *A Student-Centered Language Arts Curriculum: Grades K–13.* Boston: Houghton Mifflin Co., 1973.

Muller, Herbert J. *The Uses of English.* (Report of the Anglo–American Dartmouth Seminar.) New York: Holt, Rinehart & Winston, 1968.

Neff, Charles and Nancy. *Aids to Curriculum Planning: English Language Arts K–12.* NCTE, 1973.

O'Donnell, Bernard, ed. *Aids to Curriculum Planning: English Language Arts K–12.* NCTE; ERIC/RCS, 1973. Aids to committees developing curriculum guides: philosophy, objectives, evaluation, language, composition, media, reading, and literature.

Parker, J. Cecil, and Rubin, Louis J. *Process as Content: Curriculum Design and the Application of Knowledge.* Chicago: Rand McNally & Company, 1966.

Rice, Frank. *English and Its Teaching.* Professional Educators Publications. Lincoln, Nebraska: Cliff Notes, 1972. One of the first in a series of professional books, summaries to English teaching in its present state. Describes new developments and teaching methods.

Shuman, R. Baird, ed. *Creative Approaches to the Teaching of English: Secondary.* Itasca, IL: F. E. Peacock Publishers, 1974.

Taba, Hilda. *Curriculum Development: Theory and Practice.* New York: Harcourt Brace & World, 1962.

Whitehead, Frank. *The Disappearing Dais: A Study of the Principles and Practices of English Teaching.* NCTE, 1966. Suggests ways to get students talking and writing through poetry and drama by utilizing natural tastes in fiction.

Winkeljohann, Rosemary Sr. *Recommended English Language Arts Curriculum Guides, K–12.* NCTE. Educators will find this valuable when writing or revising their own guides.

Evaluation

Berger, Allen, and Smith, Blanche Hope, eds. *Classroom Practices in Teaching English, 1972–73: Measure for Measure.* NCTE, 1972. Focuses on measurement, testing, evaluation, and grading.

Carruthers, Robert B. *Building Better English Tests.* NCTE, 1963.

ETS Publications. Educational Testing Service, Princeton, NJ 08540. Free catalog including free or inexpensive items.

Stodola, Quentin, and Katz, Martin. *Making a Classroom Test: A Guide for Teachers.* Princeton, NJ: Educational Testing Service, 1961.

Uses, Abuses, and Misuses of Standardized Tests in English. NCTE, 1974. A special kit of materials to improve assessment programs in elementary and secondary schools.

Ideas

Brand, Stuart, ed. *The Last Whole Earth Catalog.* Menlo Park, CA: Portola Institute, Inc., 1971. Distributed by Random House. An unorthodox catalog of just about anything to stimulate thought, discussion, and even writing. Originally began as a bi-monthly periodical.

The Canadian Whole Earth Almanac. 341 Bloor Street West, Room 208, Toronto, Ontario, Canada. A collection of "tools for teachers."

Citation Press, 50 West 44th St., New York, NY 10036. Write for free catalog describing such aids as *Films Deliver, Teaching Creatively with Film, 100 Novel Ways with Book Reports, Learning Discussion Skills through Games, Creative Bulletin Boards for Junior High English.*

Daniels, Steven. *How 2 Gerbils, 20 Goldfish, 200 Games, 2,000 Books and I Taught Them How to Read.* Philadelphia: The Westminster Press, 1971.

"EJ Workshop," Kaufman, Betsy, ed. *The English Journal*, NCTE. Monthly feature in the journal reporting ideas submitted by readers. Each issue contains about four pages of a dozen or more ideas.

Graham, M. Robert, ed. *Alternative Strategy in English Classrooms.* (Michigan Council of Teachers of English.) NCTE, 1973. Teachers suggest activities which have worked for them.

Haskins, Mary Glen. *Half-Hour Notice, Fifty Mini-Lessons for High School Substitutes.* Citation Press, 50 West 44th St., New York, NY 10036. Fifty self-contained assignments with follow-up activities and suggested readings.

Hillocks, George. *Alternatives in English: A Critical Appraisal of Elective Programs.* ERIC/RCS, 1972. Appraises data from 100 schools in 37 states.

Judy, Stephen N. *Explorations in the Teaching of Secondary English: A Source Book for Experimental Teaching.* New York: Dodd, Mead & Co., 1974. Covers composition, dramatics, language arts, literature, media, oral English, semantics, and curriculum planning.

Judy, Stephen. *Lecture Alternatives in Teaching English* (Michigan Council of Teachers of English.) NCTE, 1971. Ten practical essays promoting the nonlecture classroom.

Michel, Lois A. *Another Way Out.* New York: Holt, Rinehart & Winston, 1974. A multiform, multilevel, multiethnic anthology to develop communication skills in essays, editorials, fables, letters, reviews, puzzles, short stories, and speeches.

Miller, Lynne, and Batten, Carol. *Short Span Activities: Ideas for Utilizing Spare Minutes in the Classroom.* Citation Press, 50 West 44th Street, New York, NY 10036. More than eighty games and activities for different subject areas and grade levels. Language arts activities include usage, spelling, memory, creative writing, and pantomime.

Poteet, G. Howard. *Tom Swift and His Electric English Teacher.* Dayton: Pflaum/Standard, 1974. A fun-and-games teacher resource book.

Reeves, Ruth, ed. *Ideas for Teaching English: Successful Practices in the Junior High School.* NCTE, 1966. A looseleaf binder containing more than 400 detachable pages detailing about 100 proven practices for composition, dictionary and language study, literature, listening, mass media, speech, spelling, and reading.

Schrank, Jeffrey. *Teaching Human Beings: 101 Subversive Activities for the Classroom.* Boston: Beacon Press, 1972.

Stanford, Gene, and Roark, Albert. *Human Interaction in Education.* Boston: Allyn and Bacon, 1974. Guide to activities which increase student interaction: group discussion, role playing, simulation games, and personal involvement with subject matter.

Wurman, Richard Saul. *Yellow Pages of Learning Resources.* Boston: The MIT Press, 1972.

Learning Theory

Bruner, Jerome. *Toward a Theory of Instruction.* New York: W. W. Norton, 1968.

Cry Help! NBC Educational Enterprises, 30 Rockefeller Plaza, New York, NY 10020. (Color film; 34, 30, 19 minutes.) A three-part color film which discusses mental disturbance among adolescents. Includes essays, poems, art work. For secondary school English and humanities classes.

Erikson, Erik. *Identity: Youth and Crisis.* New York: W. W. Norton, 1968.

Gagné, Robert M. *The Conditions of Learning,* 2nd ed. New York: Holt, Rinehart & Winston, 1970.

———. *Expectations for School Learning.* Bloomington, Ind.: Phi Delta Kappa, 1973. Award lecture dealing with questions and answers regarding educational goals.

Ghiselin, Brewster, ed. *The Creative Process.* New York: Mentor Books, 1955.

Gowen, John C., et al., eds. *Creativity: Its Educational Implications.* New York: John Wiley & Sons, 1967.

Kagan, Jerome, ed. *Creativity and Learning.* Boston: Beacon Press, 1967.

Langer, Susanne. *Mind: An Essay on Human Feeling.* Baltimore, Md.: Johns Hopkins Press, 1967.

Life Skills in School and Society. Association for Supervision and Curriculum Development, Room 428, 1201 16th St. N.W., Washington, D.C. 1970 edition. Views the cognitive and affective capabilities needed for truly functional education.

Long, Nicholas J.; Morse, William C.; and Newman, Ruth G. *Conflict in the Classroom: The Education of Children With Problems.* Belmont, CA: Wadsworth Publishing Co., 1971.

Schwebel, Milton, and Ralph, Jane, eds. *Piaget in the Classroom.* New York: Basic Books, 1973.

Simon, Sidney; Howe, Leland; and Kirschenbaum, Howard. *Values Clarification.* New York: Hart Publishing Co., 1972.

Summerfield, Geoffrey. *Creativity in English.* NCTE, 1968.

Thelen, Herbert. *Dynamics of Groups at Work.* Chicago: University of Chicago Press, 1967.

Methods

Fisk, Lori, and Lindgren, Henry Clay. *A Survival Guide for Teachers.* New York: John Wiley & Sons, 1973. Brisk, anecdotal, practical, no-nonsense book that's entertaining, instructive, and will help support you in your first few teaching years "on the other side of the desk."

Fowler, Mary Elizabeth. *Teaching Language, Composition, and Literature.* New York: McGraw-Hill Book Company, 1965.

Guth, Hans P. *English Today and Tomorrow.* New York: Prentice-Hall, 1964.

Hahn, Robert O. *Creative Teachers: Who Wants Them?* New York: John Wiley & Sons, 1973. Determines the climate needed in the public secondary school to keep teachers creative.

Hook, J. N. *The Teaching of High School English.* 4th ed. New York: The Ronald Press, 1972.

Kirkton, Carole M. *Teacher Training Films: A Guide.* NCTE, 1971. Annotates about 200 films, filmstrips, and videotapes for in-service education or English methods courses.

Loban, Walter; Ryan, Margaret; and Squire, James. *Teaching Language and Literature.* 2nd ed. New York: Harcourt Brace Jovanovich, 1969.

Morsey, Royal J. *Improving English Instruction.* Boston: Allyn and Bacon, 1969.

Sauer, Edwin H. *English in the Secondary School.* New York: Holt, Rinehart & Winston, 1961.

Periodicals

College English. NCTE, 1111 Kenyon Road, Urbana, IL 61801. Official monthly journal (September through May) especially for teachers in higher education.

College Composition and Communication. NCTE. Quarterly publication of the NCTE Conference on College Composition and Communication (CCCC). Includes articles for composition and communication teachers in two- and four-year colleges.

Elementary English. NCTE. Official monthly journal (September through May).

English Education. NCTE. Published four times annually: October, December, February, and May. Official journal of the Conference on English Education (CEE), mainly for those in teacher education programs.

English High Lights. Glenview, IL: Scott, Foresman & Co. Free service bulletin of classroom happenings, teaching ideas, plus a page for the bulletin board.

English Journal. NCTE. Official monthly journal; nine issues annually (September through May).

ERIC Clearinghouse on Reading and Communication Skills. ERIC/RCS, 1111 Kenyon Road, Urbana, IL 61801. Vast collection of unpublished research and abstracts. Send for information on ordering.

Exercise Exchange. Department of English, 315 Old Mill, University of Vermont, Burlington 05401. Subscription $2.00 individual, $3.50 institutions. Free teacher's desk copy with ten or more subscriptions.

Learning (the Magazine for Creative Teaching). Subscription Department, 1255 Portland Place, Boulder, CO 80302.

Media and Methods. Philadelphia: North American Publishing Co., 134 N. 13th St. A magazine (nine issues) devoted to general discussions and ads covering broad segments of the electronic and graphic media. Frequently contains tips for teaching language arts.

Media Mix. Clareton Publications, 221 W. Madison St., Chicago, Ill. A newsletter published eight times a year. Reviews and articles on films, filmstrips, TV programs, records, cassette tapes, books, teacher aids. Provides consumer reports and sources of "freebies."

Mersand, Joseph, Dept. of Teacher Preparation, York College of CUNY, 150-14 Jamaica Avenue, NYC 11432. Free reprints by enclosing postage and self-addressed clasp envelope. Write for list and specifications.

National Education Association, 1201 16th St. N.W., Washington, D.C. 20036. Send for English publications list.

National Park Service, Office of the Director, U.S. Department of the Interior, Washington, D.C. 20240. Write for information on environmental education programs.

Phi Delta Kappa Fastbacks, Box 789, Bloomington, Ind. 47401. Selections from the 50 available titles. Write for price list: *Performance Contracting: Who Profits Most?* (Blaschke); *Learning Systems for the Future* (Barnes); *Alternative Schools in Action* (Riordan); *How to Achieve Accountability in the Public Schools* (Dyer); *Needed: A New Kind of Teacher* (Wilson); *The Middle School: Whence? What? Whither?* (McGlasson); *How to Recognize a Good School* (Postman and Weingartner).

Research in the Teaching of English. NCTE. Issued three times annually.

School Bulletin. National Geographic Society, 17th and M Streets, N.W., Washington, D.C. 20036. Thirty issues for $2.75. Send payment with order. Write for publications list.

The Speech Teacher. Speech Association of America, Statler Hilton Hotel, New York, NY 10001. Official journal of interest to Speech/English teachers.

The Teacher Paper. 2221 N.W. 23rd, Portland, Oregon 97212. A quarterly journal written by teachers for teachers.

This Magazine Is about Schools, 56 Esplanade St. E., Suite 301, Toronto 1, Ontario, Canada. A straightforward alternative education magazine. Contains many useful ideas and discussions to make schools relevant.

biographical index

Specific activity numbers are in **boldface** type; page numbers are in Roman type. Capital C designates composition activities; G/L designates grammar and language; L designates literature; R designates reading; and RM designates room management.

Alcott, Louisa May, L: **465**
Allen Frederick, L: **463**

Baldwin, James, L: **492**
Beethoven, Ludwig van, C: **40**
Bierce, Ambrose, C: **224**
Blake, Robert, L: **507**
Bloom, Benjamin S., x, xi, xii, 321n
Bonham, Frank, L: **590**
Bradbury, Ray, R: **724**
Bruner, Jerome, xi

Carroll, Lewis (*pseud.*), G/L: **265**
Chaucer, Geoffrey, L: **537**
Churchill, Winston, C: **33**
Cleaver, Eldridge, L: **492**
Confucius, C: **33**
Conrad, Joseph, G/L: **356**
Cormier, Robert, L: **590**
Crane, Stephen, L: **463**
Cummings, E. E., G/L: **329**; L: **512**

Davis, Sammy, Jr., L: **492**
Day, Clarence, L: **465**
Dickinson, Emily, L: **523, 622**
Doyle, Arthur Conan, L: **465**
Dunbar, Paul Laurence, L: **492**
Dylan, Bob, C: **181**; L: **547**

Eliot, T. S., R: **805**
Ellison, Ralph, L: **492**
Euripides, R: **805**

Faulkner, William, C: **90**; G/L: **356, 383**
Fitzgerald, F. Scott, L: **463**
Franklin, Benjamin, C: **33**
Frost, Robert, C: **40**; L: **509, 524, 545, 688**

Gardner, John, RM: **954**
Gibran, Kahlil, C: **33**
Gregory, Dick, L: **492**

Hamill, Pete, C: **122**
Hansberry, Lorraine, L: **492**
Hemingway, Ernest, C: **90, 92**; L: **356, 533, 537, 667**
Herbart, Johann F., x
Hinton, S. E., L: **590**
Homer, L: **461**

Hughes, Langston, C: **181**; G/L: **383**; L: **492**
Huxley, Aldous, G/L: **383**

Jesus Christ, C: **33**
Johnson, Samuel, C: **184**; L: **504**
Jones, Leroy, L: **492**
Joyce, James, L: **461, 537**

Kerr, M. E., C: **122**
King, Martin Luther, Jr., L: **492**
Kipling, Rudyard, L: **562**
Krathwohl, David R., 321n

Lardner, Ring, G/L: **383**
Lee, Charles, L: **505**
Lewis, Wyndham, L: **505**
Locke, John, L: **460**

Mager, Robert F., 321n
Masia, Bertram B., 321n
McKuen, Rod, RM: **865**
Melville, Herman, L: **537**
Mitchell, George, C: **122**
Molière (*pseud.*), L: **455**
Moses, Grandma, C: **40**
Mozart, Wolfgang A., C: **40**

Neufeld, John, L: **590**
Newton, Huey P., C: **122**

O'Casey, Sean, L: **460**
O'Neill, Eugene, L: **595**

Parker, Cecil J., x, xi, xii
Peck, James, L: **492**
Perrine, Laurence, L: **505**
Piaget, Jean, xi
Poe, Edgar Allan, C: **223**; L: **562**
Pope, Alexander, L: **504**
Potok, Chaim, L: **590**
Prokofiev, Sergei, C: **39**

Ravel, Maurice, C: **40**
Richter, Conrad, R: **837**
Rockwell, Norman, C: **40**
Rostand, Edmond, C: **192**
Rubens, Peter Paul, C: **204**
Rubin, Louis J., x, xi, xii

Salinger, J.D., L: 592
Sandburg, Carl, L: 547
Service, Robert, L: 562
Seuss, Dr. (*pseud.*), C: 25
Shakespeare, William, C: 33, 63; L: 453–454,
    528, 632
Shelley, Percy Bysshe, L: 507
Sheridan, Richard B., L: 455
Sinclair, Upton, L: 463
Steinbeck, John, C: 90; G/L: 356, 383; L: 525,
    323

Stowe, Harriet Beecher, L: 463
Swift, Jonathan, L: 482, 504
Synge, John M., L: 460

Taba, Hilda, xi
Twain, Mark (*pseud.*), G/L: 383; L: 494;
    RM: 911
Tyler, Ralph W., xi

Whitman, Walt, C: 109
Williams, Ralph V., C: 40

title index

Alice in Wonderland, L: 484

"Barbara Allen," L: 517
Basic Principles of Curriculum and Instruction,
    xin
"Beowulf," L: 481
Bridge of San Luis Rey, The, L: 478

Canterbury Tales, L: 481
Catcher in the Rye, L: 567, 592
Chicago Sun-Times, C: 210
"Chickamauga" (film), C: 224
Chocolate War, The, L: 590
Chosen, The, L: 590
Creative Choices, RM: 865
Crucible, The, L: 631
Curriculum Development: Theory and Practice,
    xin
Cyrano de Bergerac, C: 192

David Copperfield, L: 497
Death of a Salesman, L: 452, 472, 643
Deerslayer, The, L: 477
"Design," L: 524
"Dover Beach," L: 497
"Drapier Papers, The," L: 482
"Dust of Snow," L: 524

*Excellence: Can We Be Equal and Excellent
    Too?* RM: 954

Faerie Queene, The, L: 481
Family of Man, C: 143
Farewell to Arms, A, L: 667
"Fetes" (Debussy), C: 30
"Flight," L: 525
"Frankie and Johnnie," L: 517
For Whom the Bell Tolls, L: 667
Freedom Ride, L: 492
*Funk and Wagnall Standard Hardbook of
    Synonyms, Antonyms, and Prepositions*
    (Fernald), G/L: 418

Giants in the Earth, L: 572
"Gift, The," L: 122
"Goldilocks and the Three Bears," C: 84
Go Tell It on the Mountain, L: 492
Grapes of Wrath, The, L: 485, 323
Great Gatsby, The, L: 463

Guiness Book of World Records, R: 757
Gulliver's Travels, L: 481

Hamlet, C: 63
Happy Journey to Camden and Trenton, L: 635
Henry IV, L: 453
"Highwayman, The," L: 515
"Hole, The" (film), C: 224
"Holy Thursday," L: 507
Hot Rod Magazine, G/L: 332
Huckleberry Finn, R: 703
"Human Abstract, The," L: 507

Iliad, The, L: 572
"I'll Tell You How the Sun Rose," L: 515
*I'm Somebody Important: Young Black Voices
    from Rural Georgia*, L: 122
In Our Time, C: 85
Invisible Man, The, L: 492
I Remember Mama, L: 635

"Jabberwocky," G/L: 265
"John Henry," L: 517
Julius Caesar, C: 115; L: 453, 632
Jungle, The, L: 463, 483

King Arthur: Tales of the Round Table, L: 579
King Lear, C: 184

Light in the Forest, R: 837
Lisa, Bright and Dark, L: 590
Literature: Structure, Sound, and Sense, L:
    505
"Little Red Riding Hood," C: 84
Lord of the Flies, L: 472

Macbeth, L: 453
Main Street, L: 483
Manchild in the Promised Land, L: 492
Man of Property, The, L: 543
Mayor of Casterbridge, The, L: 658
Member of the Wedding, L: 643
Midsummer Night's Dream, A, L: 481
Moby Dick, L: 572; RM: 869
"Mockingbird, The" (film), C: 224
"Moonbird" (film), C: 224
Mourning Becomes Electra, L: 595

National Geographic Magazine, RM: **869**
Native Son, L: **483, 590**
Nigger, L: **492**
"Noiseless Patient Spider," C: **109**
"Nothing Gold Can Stay," L: **524**
Not Without Laughing, L: **483**

"Occurrence at Owl Creek Bridge" (film), C: **224**
"Ode to Billie Joe," L: **517**
"Ode to West Wind," L: **507**
Odyssey, The, L: **461, 572**
Old Man and the Sea, The, L: **572**
Oliver Twist, L: **485**
Outsiders, The, L: **590**
"Ozymandias," L: **497**

"Paradise Lost," L: **481**
"Peanuts," L: **567**
"Peter and the Wolf" (Prokofiev), C: **39**
Pickpocket Run, R: **703**
"Pied Piper of Hamelin, The," L: **515**
"Playroom, The," R: **724**
Portrait of the Artist as a Young Man, A, L: **497**
Preparing Instructional Objectives, 321n
Process as Content: Curriculum Design and the Application of Knowledge, xn, xiin

Raisin in the Sun, A, L: **492, 530**
Reader's Guide to Periodical Literature, The, R: **726**
Red Badge of Courage, The, L: **463, 573**
Return of the Native, The, L: **472**
Revolutionary Suicide, L: **122**
Richard III, L: **453**
"Road Not Taken, The," L: **509, 688**
Robert's Rules of Order, RM: **939**
Roget's Thesaurus of the English Language, C: **313**; G/L: **418**
Romeo and Juliet, L: **456, 481**
"Runaway, The," C: **40**

Scarlet Letter, The, L: **530, 590**
"School Children" (Breughel), C: **121**
"Secret Life of Walter Mitty, The," L: **698**
Separate Peace, A, L: **573**
Seventeen (magazine), G/L: **332**
Silas Marner, C: **235**
Sixth ("Pastoral") Symphony (Beethoven), C: **4**
Son of Someone Famous, The, L: **122**
Soul on Ice, L: **492**
"Spring Pools," L: **524**
"Stopping by Woods on a Snowy Evening," C: **40**; L: **545**
Stride Toward Freedom, L: **492**
Stuffed Owl: An Anthology of Bad Verse, The, L: **505**
Subtreasury of American Humor, A, RM: **865**
Sunlight and Shadows, RM: **865**

Tale of Two Cities, A, L: **477**
Taxonomy of Educational Objectives, Handbook II: Affective Domain, 321n
Taxonomy of Educational Objectives, Handbook I: Cognitive Domain, xn, xiin
"Telemachos Remembered," L: **461**
Tempest, The, L: **481**
"Three Little Pigs, The," C: **84**
Tobacco Road, L: **483**
Tom Sawyer, R: **746**
Treasure Island, G/L: **321**
Two and the Town, R: **703**

Ulysses, L: **461**
Uncle Tom's Cabin, L: **463**

Viva Chicano, L: **590**

Webster's Dictionary of Synonyms, G/L: **418**
West Side Story, L: **456**
World Almanac, R: **757**
Wuthering Heights, L: **590**

topic index

Accountability, xi; G/L: **385**
Advertisements, C: **2–3, 9, 20, 44, 79, 137**; G/L: **277**; L: **631–632, 650, 687**; R: **704, 740, 828–829, 831, 835**; *see also* Magazines and Periodicals
Affective domain (*see* Goals)
Aides (*see also* Tutoring), C: **38**; R: **717**
Anecdotes, C: **24, 30**; L: **504, 670**; R: **846**; RM: **950**
Application, viii, x, xii, xiv, xvii; C: **60–78 (183–250)**; G/L: **137–140 (440–450)**; L: **195–212 (631–700)**; R: **257–265 (822–850)**; RM: **313–318 (987–1001)**
Argumentation, C: **1, 2, 3, 44, 45, 46, 47, 91, 114, 183, 184, 185**
Artwork, C: **40, 75, 121, 234**; G/L: **319, 440, 447**; L: **466, 531, 556, 564–565, 647, 671, 675, 691, 694**; R: **840, 848**; RM: **877, 881, 919, 932, 965**
Attitudes, teachers' and students', RM: **851–861, 943–954, 987–989**

Audiotapes, C: **18, 31, 36, 56, 74, 87, 101, 119, 145, 150–151, 161–162, 225, 234**; G/L: **252, 293, 349–350**; L: **516, 554, 560, 619, 637, 662, 681, 685, 694**; R: **715, 718, 724, 741, 780, 788, 799, 827–828**; RM: **892, 928**
Authorities, C: **12–13, 21, 36, 126, 163, 166, 235**; L: **460, 475, 482–483, 494**; R: **708, 757**; RM: **862**
Authors, G/L: **372**; *see also* Biographical Index
Autobiographies, C: **14, 200**; L: **670**; R: **798**

Biographies, C: **14, 57, 221**; L: **566, 605, 653, 670**; R: **798**; RM: **878**
Booklets, C: **147**; G/L: **276, 335**; R: **702, 830**; RM: **993**
Book reports, L: **503, 566, 598, 600, 606, 645, 647, 649, 652, 659, 666, 671–672, 674, 677–678**; R: **792, 796, 798, 827, 835, 838**; RM: **990**
Books, C: **14, 18, 25, 65, 122, 147, 219, 221,**

Books, C: *(continued)*
246; G/L: 257, 265, 275–279, 296, 335,
356, 372, 383, 413, 445; L: 463, 479,
486, 495, 497–502, 533, 544–545, 570,
607, 630, 654, 680, 686; R: 702, 709–
711, 722–723, 725, 727, 744, 750, 752,
795, 807, 839–840; RM: 863–865, 892,
989, 323
Brochures (*see* Circulars)
Bulletin boards, C: 3, 10, 33–34, 36, 56, 78,
80, 86, 92, 138, 236, 244; G/L: 284,
311, 339, 366, 377, 395; L: 466, 476,
484, 574, 594, 633, 670–671, 679, 694;
R: 715, 736, 748, 753, 827; RM: 866–
871, 904, 919, 991, 997

Capitalization, C: 164; G/L: 330, 384, 386;
see also Mechanics
Cards, C: 10, 29, 54, 105; G/L: 281, 304, 315,
422, 430; L: 503, 564, 568, 581, 600,
606, 630, 691; R: 728–729, 733, 756,
759, 768, 770, 773, 781, 796, 800, 811–
812; RM: 866, 972, 980
Careers, C: 8, 12, 13, 17, 18, 135, 142, 163,
191, 197, 207–208, 210, 212, 217; G/L:
254, 264, 285, 440; L: 494, 539, 642,
646, 658–659, 665; R: 764, 822, 824,
836, 862; RM: 932, 942, 970, 984, 987,
995
Cartoons, C: 23, 66, 81, 88–89, 139, 207, 234;
G/L: 266–267, 295, 336, 377, 412; L:
466, 538, 567, 571, 632, 647, 682; R:
721, 743, 745, 807, 830–831; RM: 881,
892, 320
Chalkboards, C: 26, 36, 41, 52, 228; G/L: 291,
307–308, 327–328, 331, 375–376, 388,
428–429; L: 527, 530; R: 748, 756, 762,
766, 773, 775, 801, 820–821; RM: 872,
880, 910, 930
Characterization, C: 5, 34, 51, 57, 62, 85–86,
91, 115, 118, 124, 141, 146, 192, 214, 232;
G/L: 264, 442; L: 452, 457, 467, 471,
476–477, 530, 534–536, 538, 540, 543,
563, 568, 574–575, 581, 584, 589, 592–
593, 597, 601–602, 604, 612–614, 617,
634, 640, 644, 648, 654, 657, 660, 666,
668, 674, 700; R: 744, 786, 798, 833–
834
Charts, C: 35, 148, 155, 157, 164, 175; G/L:
263; L: 499; R: 789–790, 802; RM: 910,
920, 955
Circulars, C: 15–16; G/L: 285; R: 702, 704;
RM: 874
Composition, topics for, C: 1, 4, 8, 11, 13, 16–
17, 21–23, 26–32, 35, 123, 132, 134,
136, 152, 190, 196, 198, 200, 209; G/L:
305, 405; RM: 908; *see also* Topics
Composition, viii, xiii, 1–250; *see also* Papers
Comprehension in reading, L: 624; R: 707,
712, 731, 750, 789, 791, 802, 804, 807
Conferences, C: 149, 152, 156, 166, 195; G/L:
391, 394; L: 587, 607; RM: 956–957
Contests, C: 236, 248; G/L: 393; R: 827; *see
also* Games
Context, G/L: 312, 352; *see also* Word recogni-
tion
Contracts, learning, G/L: 385; RM: 901, 902,
966, 983
Correction symbols, C: 148, 155, 157–158
Critical reading, R: 707, 744, 750–751, 786,
792, 804
Critiques, C: 7, 31, 127, 184, 214; L: 544, 588,
620, 647, 651, 669, 696

Dance, C: 107; G/L: 440; L: 556, 684
Debates (*see* Discussions)
Definitions, G/L: 255, 347; R: 705, 738
Deliberation, viii, x, xii, xiii, xvi; C: 17–36 (44–
113); G/L: 103–118 (323–382); L: 165–
174 (528–562); R: 229–242 (739–782);
RM: 291–298 (919–942)
Demonstrations, C: 11, 58, 66; G/L: 254, 340;
L: 451, 461, 565; R: 836; RM: 874, 992
Description, C: 4–5, 30–31, 48–62, 91, 115–
120, 186–190; G/L: 373, 449; L: 672
Diagnosis, G/L: 385, 386; *see also* Testing
Diagramming (*see* Sentences)
Dialect, G/L: 251–254, 323, 372, 443; RM:
914
Dialogue, C: 89, 99, 143–145, 161; G/L: 383,
412, 443; L: 586, 695–696; R: 724
Diaries (*see* Journals)
Dictionaries, C: 169; G/L: 299, 303, 309–310,
312, 314, 322, 364, 369, 445; R: 736–
737, 755, 771–772, 813, 850
Discipline, RM: 852, 854, 856, 860, 861, 905–
906
Discussions, C: 1, 14, 17, 27, 32, 45, 68, 108,
114, 165–166, 184; G/L: 272, 278, 286,
292, 295, 297, 308, 312, 324, 330, 359,
415; L: 452, 464, 470, 472, 487–488,
506–512, 528, 534, 536, 538, 547–548,
555, 576–578, 609–610, 618, 641, 652,
658, 662–664, 677, 681, 698; R: 706–
707, 716, 719, 797; RM: 875, 921–924,
941, 948, 963
Displays, C: 15, 53, 64; G/L: 267, 377, 395,
445, 448; L: 477, 489, 503, 521, 522,
579, 632, 655–656, 658, 672, 680, 687;
R: 827, 830, 835, 837–838; RM: 853,
870, 877–878, 993, 997
Doublespeak, C: 77, 79; G/L: 287
Drama, C: 6, 63, 107, 191–192; G/L: 363; L:
451–460, 528, 529, 530, 563, 631–644;
RM: 987
Drawings (*see* Artwork)

Essays, C: 31, 36, 43, 67, 115, 123–124, 196–
200, 238; G/L: 416; L: 552, 556, 639,
676, 688, 698; R: 848; RM: 992
Etymology, G/L: 303, 323, 352, 435
Evaluation, viii, x, xii, xiv, xvi; C: 37–59 (114–
182); G/L: 119–135 (383–439); L: 175–
194 (536–630); R: 243–255 (783–821);
RM: 299–311 (943–986)
Exposition, C: 6–17, 64–74, 122–134, 193–
206; R: 729, 783, 822

Fables (*see* Tales)
Field trips, C: 4–5, 36, 50, 77, 103, 135; L:
458, 513, 529, 565, 689; R: 767; RM:
876, 925, 958–959
File cards (*see* Cards)
File folders, C: 34, 36, 149; G/L: 371; L: 601,
716, 760, 763, 770, 772, 777; R: 796,
807, 832; RM: 874, 898
Film making, C: 18–19, 53; L: 467, 638
Films, C: 36, 107; G/L: 323, 440; L: 464, 651;
RM: 891, 892, 993; *see also* Movies
Filmstrips, C: 225; L: 565
Flash cards (*see* Cards)
Forms, C: 155, 157; R: 824, 842; RM: 960–
961
Free reading, C: 156

Games, C: 34, 37, 49, 54, 59, 71, 90, 102, 116,

118, 120, 125, 128, 166, 222, 248; G/L: 304, 309, 317–318, 370–371, 382, 388, 393, 396, 398, 400, 401–403, 405, 408, 410, 415, 418, 419–429, 434, 438, 534, 542–543, 564, 566, 568, 572, 580–583, 594, 596–597, 603–605, 611–616; R: 719, 727, 728, 732, 746, 749, 754, 756, 760, 762, 765–766, 769, 776, 780–781, 785, 787, 799–800, 803, 805, 809–814, 818–819, 823; RM: 879, 892, 926–928, 995

Goals, affective, vii, x, xii, 321–323

Graffiti, C: 36; G/L: 267; R: 748

Grammar, C: 73, 74, 87, 98, 104, 154–155, 158, 162–163, 167, 173–174, 178, 185; G/L: 282, 284, 286, 297; R: 805, 842

Grammar/language, viii, xiii, xvi, xvii, 251–450

Haiku, C: 42; L: 524; RM: 993

Handouts, C: 28, 35, 111, 114, 140, 147, 151, 166, 184, 207; G/L: 254, 260, 280, 282, 291, 293, 298, 309, 320, 332, 345, 384, 393, 436–437; L: 504; R: 844; RM: 880–883, 891, 904

Humanities, C: 75; L: 461–463, 531–532, 564–565

Inference in reading, C: 63, 81; L: 510; R: 707, 747, 750, 786, 792

Instructions, C: 129; G/L: 256, 532; R: 806, 847; RM: 882, 962, 996

Interviews, C: 21, 82, 200, 209, 220; G/L: 274, 302; RM: 941; *see also* Authorities

Introduction, viii, x, xii, xiii, xvi; C: 3–16 (1–43); G/L: 81–101 (251–322); L: 143–164 (451–527); R: 215–228 (701–738); RM: 269–289 (851–918)

Inventories, L: 453, 490; RM: 929, 963–970

Journalism, C: 20–23, 76–83, 207–212; R: 701, 784, 823

Journals, C: 23, 69, 76, 185, 239, 245; G/L: 417; L: 589–590, 599; R: 822

Lecture, C: 166; G/L: 308; L: 496, 694; RM: 883–888, 930, 943, 971

Letters, C: 12, 16, 63, 136, 152, 201, 213–214; L: 660; R: 825; RM: 997

Letter writing, C: 136–137, 213–215; R: 739, 824–826

Libraries, C: 17, 37–38, 195; L: 485, 501, 503, 526, 621, 653; R: 710, 726, 728, 754, 792, 840, 846; RM: 863, 889, 904, 931, 1000

Linguistics, G/L: 255–265, 275, 324–328, 354

Lists, C: 41, 43, 55, 111, 152, 158–159, 167; G/L: 251, 300, 309, 312–318, 322, 328, 341, 343, 353, 360, 367, 378, 395, 397, 414, 425, 427, 429, 437, 447, 449; L: 491, 514, 626, 630, 673; R: 730, 735, 737, 753, 764, 767, 771–772, 773, 782, 793, 820

Literal reading level, R: 707, 750

Literature, viii, xiii, 451–700

Magazines, C: 2, 15, 20, 60, 62, 70, 76, 84, 95, 138, 140, 207–209, 212, 216, 229, 246; G/L: 287, 302, 310, 332–333, 339, 348, 396, 425, 448, 469; L: 631, 656, 675, 680, 690–691; R: 702–703, 740, 767, 771–772, 774, 807, 837; RM: 869, 874, 892, 897–898, 998

Mechanics, C: 69, 154–155, 158, 162, 167, 178; G/L: 266–268, 329–330, 384; *see also* Capitalization; Punctuation; Spelling

Media, C: 138–142, 216; G/L: 277, 284, 323; L: 464–469, 645–651, 702–703; R: 740, 827–832

Media, mixed, C: 14, 107; G/L: 257, 285, 287, 301–302, 316, 333, 337, 379, 413, 440, 448, 451; L: 466, 484, 556, 631, 639–640, 645, 657, 694–695; R: 703, 721, 729, 740, 749, 759, 767; RM: 890–893, 932

Models, C: 42, 44, 64, 80, 85, 98–99, 100, 108–109, 112, 114, 116, 168, 180–181, 223; G/L: 263, 268, 281, 290–291, 294, 323, 338, 342, 344, 357, 359, 413, 432; L: 454–455, 505, 524, 549, 625, 627, 647; R: 742, 760, 834, 838, 845

Montage, C: 15; G/L: 306, 377, 448; L: 598, 601, 645, 672, 676; R: 702, 827

Movies, C: 18, 60, 93, 126–127, 131, 145, 202, 224–225; G/L: 380; L: 458, 467–468, 628, 656, 699; R: 721–722; RM: 893; *see also* Films

Music, C: 4, 30–31, 39–40, 101, 182; G/L: 440, 517, 551, 561; L: 550, 620, 685; RM: 932

Mysteries, C: 91, 226; R: 844

Narration, C: 24–26, 43, 84–97, 143–146, 217–233; R: 741–743, 785, 833–834, 320

National Council of Teachers of English, RM: 858, 908

Newspapers, C: 3, 15, 22, 44, 70, 76–80, 83, 88–89, 135, 137–138, 140, 210–211; G/L: 257, 287, 295, 310, 333–334, 357–358, 396, 441, 448; L: 482, 631–632, 680; R: 701, 703, 737, 740, 759, 767, 784, 807, 823, 826, 829, 831; RM: 874, 894, 999; *see also* Journalism

Nonfiction, L: 566, 652–653, 678; R: 704

Notebooks, C: 15, 23, 158; G/L: 315–316; L: 673, 774; *see also* Journals *or* Booklets

Notes, C: 12, 29, 50; L: 496, 535, 584, 589; RM: 895–896, 972

Novels, C: 85, 246; G/L: 296, 301; L: 470–485, 533–542, 567–593, 616, 654–669; R: 705–707, 744–747, 786–787; *see also* Structure, in literature

Objectives, cognitive, vii, x, xi, xii; RM: 900–903, 909, 921, 966, 319–323

Oral presentations (*see* Talks)

Oral reading, R: 815, 839, 971

Papers, C: 32, 47–48, 50–51, 74, 92, 100, 116, 120, 132, 139, 153–154, 159–160, 166, 169–178, 234–235, 240–242; G/L: 269, 271, 273, 361, 386, 389, 390–391, 404, 406, 415, 430, 433, 435, 442–443, 446, 449; L: 539–540, 573–574, 588, 595, 600, 643, 667–669, 679, 700; R: 715, 729, 739, 752, 783, 826, 829–831, 833–834, 843–844, 848; RM: 964, 982, 1000

Paragraphs, C: 10–11, 22, 72, 104–105, 117, 129–130, 167, 179, 187–188, 211, 216, 222, 227–228, 243, 245; G/L: 260, 282, 293, 298, 305, 320–321, 330, 350–351, 363, 373, 384, 386, 388, 393, 406, 411, 436, 444; L: 541, 585; R: 741, 761, 802, 804, 807–809, 842, 850

Parts of speech, G/L: **255-256, 346, 348, 375, 377-380, 382, 387, 392, 405-406, 408-409, 411-412, 417, 432-433, 436-438, 442, 444, 449;** *see also* Words

Periodicals, C: **3, 23, 37, 70, 138, 140;** G/L: **316, 425;** RM: **893, 897;** *see also* Magazines; Newspapers

Phonics, R: **738, 773-775, 779, 782**

Pictures, C: **11, 34, 54, 56, 60, 62, 86, 95, 107, 143, 212, 229, 234, 244;** G/L: **306, 339, 348, 366, 377, 445, 447-448;** L: **466, 473, 565, 598, 601, 633, 639, 645, 647, 654, 656-657, 672-673, 676, 681-683, 691;** R: **702, 722, 732, 734, 748, 753, 763, 767, 771-772, 777-778, 816-817, 832, 837;** RM: **864, 869-870, 892, 897-898, 919, 932, 997**

Plans, C: **70, 106, 149, 152, 154;** G/L: **270, 385;** L: **492;** RM: **856, 875, 891, 899-909, 933**

Plays, C: **126-127, 234, 246;** L: **458-459, 616, 634-636, 644, 646, 696;** R: **724;** *see also* Drama

Plots, C: **86-87, 89, 91, 219, 221;** G/L: **324;** L: **467, 471, 476, 485, 541-542, 569-570, 574, 588, 591, 612-614, 625-626, 628, 639, 648, 654, 668, 672, 700;** R: **705, 744-747, 750, 786-787, 835, 837**

Poems, C: **30, 31, 75, 99;** G/L: **283, 299, 329;** L: **459, 553, 556-557, 562, 587, 618, 624, 645-646, 682-683, 687, 689, 690-694;** R: **753, 839, 841, 892;** RM: **987**

Poetry, C: **25, 36, 39-43, 108-113, 180-182, 234, 246, 248;** G/L: **262;** L: **507-524, 547-562, 616, 618-624, 679, 680-693;** R: **753, 841;** RM: **950, 992-993**

Problems, C: **125, 183;** G/L: **386-387;** R: **712, 731, 776, 794, 804**

Processes:

analyze, xiii; C: **44, 48-49, 65, 76-80, 98-101, 108;** G/L: **323-325, 329, 331-334, 344-346, 357-359, 365, 372-374;** L: **528, 531, 533-535, 543, 547-549, 551, 628;** R: **739, 744-745, 762-763, 773-774**

compare, xiv; C: **109, 114-115, 136, 138, 147-149;** G/L: **397, 413, 418;** L: **564, 567-569, 594-595, 625;** R: **788-790, 802, 810, 817**

consolidate, xiv; C: **50-51, 64, 66-67, 85-86, 103, 110;** G/L: **335, 339-342, 347-348, 366-368, 375-376;** L: **532;** R: **741, 754, 764**

construct, xiv; C: **207-208;** G/L: **340, 440, 448, 450;** L: **631-633, 645, 654-658, 670-673, 675-676, 680-683, 694;** R: **823, 827, 835-838, 845**

discover, xiii; C: **1, 7, 18, 20, 27-29;** G/L: **251, 255-259, 269-271, 286, 288, 291-292, 296-298, 303-307, 317-318, 320;** L: **451-455, 461, 464-465, 470-474, 486-493, 507-515, 527, 536;** R: **702, 705-717, 730-732, 738**

experiment, xiv; C: **45-46, 52-56, 68-69, 73, 80-82, 87-92, 102, 104, 111-113;** G/L: **326-327, 330, 336, 343, 349-353, 360-362, 369-371, 377-381;** L: **529, 537, 550, 552-553, 629;** R: **742, 746, 748-749, 753, 755-756, 765-767, 775-779;** 320

extrapolate, xiv; C: **116-117, 121-125, 137, 143, 150-154, 156;** G/L: **383, 395, 404-405, 414, 419-420, 432-433, 565, 570-575, 596-602;** R: **785-786, 791-792**

identify, xiv; C: **155, 157-160;** G/L: **385-387, 415, 421-430, 434-437;** L: **566, 576-586, 603-605, 618, 630;** R: **784, 793-794, 799, 803-804, 811-814**

interpret, xiv; C: **57-61, 63, 70, 75, 83, 93-94, 107;** L: **530, 538-541, 544-545, 554-559;** R: **743, 747, 750-751, 757-758, 768-769, 780-781**

judge, xiv; C: **118, 126-134, 138-141, 144, 161-178, 180;** G/L: **388-391, 393, 396, 398-400, 406-407, 416-417;** L: **563, 587-588, 606-609, 619-623, 626;** R: **783, 795, 815**

listen, xiii; C: **9, 21, 24, 30-32, 39, 43, 112;** G/L: **252-253, 260-262, 272-273, 293, 391;** L: **456-457, 475, 494-496, 516-520, 525, 560-561;** R: **718-720, 724-725**

observe, ix, xiii; C: **2-3, 10-11, 19, 33-34, 40-42;** G/L: **254, 263-264, 266-267, 274, 319;** L: **458-459, 462, 466-468, 476-478, 521-523;** R: **721, 726, 734, 770**

organize, xiv; C: **47, 62, 71-72, 74, 87, 95-97, 101, 105-106;** G/L: **328, 354-355, 364, 382;** L: **542, 546;** R: **740, 752, 759-761, 771-772, 782, 806-807, 847-848**

perform, xv; C: **191, 217-218;** G/L: **450;** L: **634-638, 646, 659-661, 674, 684-685, 695-697;** R: **828**

read, xiii; C: **6, 22, 25-26, 35;** G/L: **265, 268, 275-283, 289, 294-295, 299, 308-310, 321, 337;** L: **469, 479-481, 497-505, 524, 562;** R: **701, 703-704, 722-723, 727, 733, 735, 323**

research, xiii; C: **4-5, 12-17, 23, 36-38;** G/L: **284-285, 287, 290, 300-302, 311-316, 322;** L: **460, 463, 482-485, 506, 526, 662;** R: **728-729, 736-737**

restructure, xiv; C: **119-120, 135, 142, 145-146, 179, 181-182;** G/L: **338, 356, 363, 384, 392, 394, 401-403, 408-412, 438-439, 589-593, 610-617, 624, 627;** R: **787, 796-798, 800-801, 805-809, 816, 818-821**

solve, xv; C: **183, 193, 234;** G/L: **450;** L: **639-640;** R: **849**

speak, xv; C: **184, 194-195, 220;** G/L: **450;** L: **641-642, 647-648, 652, 662-666, 677-678;** R: **839, 846**

write, xv; C: **184-192, 196-197, 199-206, 209-216, 219, 221-233, 235-250;** G/L: **441-447, 449-450;** L: **643-644, 649-651, 653, 666-669, 678-679, 683, 686-693, 698-700;** R: **802, 822, 824-826, 829-834, 839-844, 847-848, 850**

Projectors, C: **10, 19, 53, 56, 81, 166;** G/L: **332, 390;** R: **816, 891;** RM: **910, 927-928**

Proofreading, C: **163, 169;** G/L: **171, 174**

Punctuation, C: **88, 163;** G/L: **260-262, 266-268, 273, 282, 330, 384, 441;** R: **799, 842;** *see also* Mechanics

Puppets, L: **565;** R: **827;** RM: **853**

Puzzles, C: **230;** G/L: **368, 371, 392, 403;** L: **594, 616-617, 632;** R: **776, 823, 849;** *see also* Games

Questions, C: **8, 30-32, 139;** G/L: **286;** L: **468, 560, 578, 580, 583, 594, 596, 603, 608, 611-613, 615;** R: **727, 740, 745, 755, 784-787, 791, 797, 803, 843;** RM: **871, 885, 889, 923-925, 934-935, 963, 968, 973-981, 1000**

Quotations, C: **23, 26, 32-33, 44;** G/L: **360,**

368, 446; L: 520, 582, 594, 612, 649, 657, 668, 673, 679

Radio, C: 21, 32, 142; G/L: 253; L: 646; R: 835
Rate in reading, R: 706, 712, 731, 749, 789–790, 802
Reading, viii, xiii, 701–850
Reading, individualized, L: 499–500, 587; R: 713
Recordings, C: 94; L: 637; RM: 891–892; *see also* Audiotape; Records; Videotape
Records, phonograph, C: 31; G/L: 252, 301, 306; L: 456, 459, 518–519, 525, 558, 561, 565, 621; RM: 876
Reviews, C: 7, 20, 63, 127, 131; G/L: 440; L: 482, 641, 667, 675; R: 722; *see also* Critiques
Role playing, C: 46, 132–133, 183, 189, 192, 215, 217–218; G/L: 346, 362; L: 457, 459, 475, 526, 530, 563, 565, 586, 602, 629, 642, 646, 659–660, 665, 674; R: 822
Room management, viii, xiii, 851–1001

Scanning, R: 727, 759
Scrapbooks, C: 78; L: 631, 645, 654, 680; R: 774; RM: 878
Scripts, C: 18; G/L: 440; L: 639
Seating, RM: 936–937, 967
Self (selves), G/L: 258; L: 493; R: 713–715
Semantics, G/L: 286–287, 339–341, 395–396
Senses, C: 113, 117; R: 778
Sentences, C: 9, 44, 55, 65, 72–73, 87, 97, 104, 249–250; G/L: 259, 263, 274–277, 281, 285, 289, 291–292, 294, 298, 304–305, 307, 311, 315, 324–326, 328, 331, 333, 344–349, 351–356, 374–376, 381–382, 386, 394, 405–406, 408–410, 412, 430–432, 437, 439, 441–442; L: 545, 622; R: 730, 736, 761–762, 766, 779, 799–800, 802, 808–809, 817, 821, 832; RM: 940
Short stories, C: 22, 24, 75, 85–86, 93, 96, 219, 227, 230–232, 246; G/L: 324, 382, 443; L: 616, 639, 646, 655, 699; R: 724–725, 789, 817, 850; RM: 992; *see also* Structure in Literature
Short story, as a study, L: 525–526, 625–629, 694–700; R: 724–725, 842–844
Sight word vocabulary, in reading, R: 712, 731, 781, 811–812
Dolch list, 769
Skimming, R: 727, 759
Skits, C: 14, 61, 92, 191, 246; G/L: 254, 267, 274, 346; L: 569, 592–593, 661, 694, 697; R: 724, 726; RM: 992; *see also* Drama
Slang, G/L: 296, 301–302, 446–447
Slides, C: 36; L: 462, 468, 470, 522–523, 565, 656, 662, 681, 694; RM: 892, 911
Songs, G/L: 323, 407, 558; L: 621, 685; RM: 893; *see also* Music

Spelling, C: 155, 163, 169, 173, 178; G/L: 273, 282, 288–290, 342–343, 397–403, 441; R: 730, 771, 801; *see also* Mechanics
Structure, in composition, C: 85–90, 93, 141, 146, 167, 221; G/L: 324, 356; R: 752
Structure, in literature, G/L: 324, 333; L: 466, 471, 473, 478, 531, 540–541, 569, 574–575, 577, 588, 613–614, 618, 620, 621, 624, 629, 654, 668–669, 700; R: 705, 711, 744–745, 747, 786
Study skills, R: 712, 714, 726–729, 731, 754–761, 780, 802–808, 845–848
Style, C: 7, 67, 77; G/L: 333; L: 537, 668, 744
Syntax, C: 74, 249–250; G/L: 291–295, 344–356, 372, 404–412, 444

Tales, C: 146, 233; L: 480–481, 537; R: 742
Talks, C: 97, 102, 134, 144, 149, 156, 245; G/L: 253, 257, 261–262, 327, 333, 359, 365, 474; L: 515, 546, 559, 609, 623, 720; R: 741, 751, 758, 839, 846; RM: 912–914, 932, 938–941, 982–985
Television, C: 21, 32, 60, 141–142, 202–203; G/L: 253, 264; L: 464–465, 648; R: 721–722, 834–835; RM: 876, 893, 915, 927, 995
Tests, G/L: 288, 307, 311, 353, 428; L: 575; R: 784; RM: 917, 935, 948, 952–953, 973–981; *see also* Diagnosis
Theme, C: 12, 14, 20, 29, 36, 52, 75, 85–86, 99, 111, 176, 193; L: 461, 467, 488, 506, 530, 545, 587, 598, 612, 668, 676, 688; R: 705, 837
Thought units, G/L: 386, 405–406, 409, 411; R: 749, 752, 764, 768, 770, 776–778, 783, 789–790, 800, 802, 841
Topics, C: 27, 46–47, 190, 204–205, 235, 243, 246–247; G/L: 310; R: 702, 720; RM: 918; *see also* Composition
Transparencies, C: 166, 182; R: 816; RM: 910, 916, 927–928
Tutors, C: 153, 173, 219; G/L: 271, 306–307, 416; R: 717, 732; RM: 898, 917–918, 942, 986

Usage, C: 154–155, 178; G/L: 282, 293–302, 357–364, 413–417, 445–446

Videotapes, C: 186, 225; L: 569, 637–638, 662; R: 827–828
Vocabulary, xvi, xvii; G/L: 303–316, 365–371, 380, 403, 418–431, 441, 447; L: 527, 630; R: 730–737; R: 762–772, 789, 805, 809–816, 841, 849–850; RM: 888

Words, C: 43, 128, 249–250; G/L: 256, 308, 311, 317–322, 326, 352, 366, 372–382, 386, 420, 432–439, 448–450; L: 527; R: 738, 753, 773–782, 817–821; RM: 929
Word recognition, in reading, R: 712, 731, 765, 767, 773–775, 780, 782, 793, 817–820
Workshops, C: 166; RM: 938

This handbook contains 1001 activities for you to use to encourage creativity in the classroom. It is an excellent teaching aid and source of supplementary materials for units in Grammar/Language, Reading, Literature and Composition. Plus, there's a unit devoted to tips for improving Room Management. The book features:

- Group, individual and teacher-oriented activities
- 4-step learning process
- Activities for middle and secondary school students
- Glossary of terms and concepts

About the Author

Floyd Bergman is Associate Professor of Secondary Education at The University of Michigan (Ann Arbor). He has served on his Division's Executive Committee, on the School's Reading Committee, and for several years as Chairman of the Publication Committee. He has also served as English consultant for The University of Michigan Bureau of School Services. Before joining The University of Michigan staff, Dr. Bergman taught English, social studies, journalism, speech and dramatics on the junior and senior high levels.

Dr. Bergman received his B.S. and M.A. from the University of Minnesota and his Ed.D. from Wayne State University.

"This book contains many, many excellent practical ideas for improving the teaching of English . . . I emphasize practical because it seems to me that the audience for this book is quite diverse: everyone from the beginning teacher of English with or without an English major to the experienced teacher who needs some change-of-pace ideas to reaffirm his interest in teaching."

Model for Collecting and Filing New Ideas

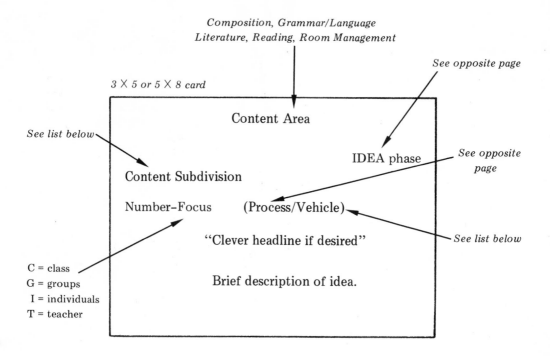

Content Subdivisions

Argumentation ○ *Description* ○ *Dialect* ○ *Drama* ○ *Exposition* ○
Film Making ○ *Humanities* ○ *Journalism* ○ *Letter Writing* ○ *Linguistics* ○
Mechanics ○ *Media* ○ *Narration* ○ *Nonfiction* ○ *Novels* ○ *Overview* ○
Poetry ○ *Semantics* ○ *Short Story* ○ *Spelling* ○ *Study Skills* ○ *Syntax* ○
Usage ○ *Vocabulary* ○ *Words*

Vehicles in the Sequence

Anecdotes ○ *Artwork* ○ *Attitudes* ○ *Audiotapes* ○ *Authorities* ○ *Biographies* ○
Books ○ *Book Reports* ○ *Bulletin Boards* ○ *Cards* ○ *Cartoons* ○ *Chalkboards* ○
Charts ○ *Circulars* ○ *Conferences* ○ *Critiques* ○ *Definitions* ○ *Demonstrations* ○
Dictionaries ○ *Discussions* ○ *Displays* ○ *Essays* ○ *Field Trips* ○ *Filmstrips* ○
Forms ○ *Games* ○ *Handouts* ○ *Instructions* ○ *Interviews* ○ *Inventories* ○
Journals ○ *Lectures* ○ *Letters* ○ *Libraries* ○ *Lists* ○ *Magazines* ○ *Mixed Media* ○
Models ○ *Music* ○ *Mysteries* ○ *Myths* ○ *Newspapers* ○ *Notes* ○ *Oral Readings* ○
Papers ○ *Paragraphs* ○ *Periodicals* ○ *Pictures* ○ *Plans* ○ *Plays* ○ *Plots* ○
Poems ○ *Problems* ○ *Projectors* ○ *Puzzles* ○ *Questionnaires* ○ *Questions* ○
Radio ○ *Recordings* ○ *Role Playing* ○ *Senses* ○ *Selves* ○ *Sentences* ○
Short Stories ○ *Skits* ○ *Slides* ○ *Songs* ○ *Tales* ○ *Talks* ○ *Television* ○
Term Papers ○ *Tests* ○ *Topics* ○ *Transparencies* ○ *Tutors* ○ *Videotapes*